Alaskan Eskimos

Chandler Publications in

ANTHROPOLOGY AND SOCIOLOGY

LEONARD BROOM, *Editor*

Alaskan Eskimos

Wendell H. Oswalt

University of California, Los Angeles

CHANDLER PUBLISHING COMPANY

124 Spear Street, San Francisco, California 94105

Science Research Associates, Inc., 259 East Erie Street, Chicago, Illinois 60611
Distributors   A Subsidiary of IBM   **S R A**

Contents

Illustrations

COLOR ILLUSTRATIONS

Wooden masks from Point Hope
Shaman's animal effigy, or kikituk, from Point Hope

MAPS

TABLES

Introduction

The word *Eskimo,* meaning "eaters of raw flesh," is from the language of the Algonkin Indians in eastern Canada, but the people to whom it referred did not use the term. They called themselves by a variety of words which usually meant "real people." Eskimos regarded themselves literally as real people, as a class apart from all other human beings. In a sense Americans, Canadians, and Europeans have come to agree with the Eskimos' self-image. About the Eskimo has been cast a romantic spell which finds eloquent expression in writings by travelers, novelists, and some anthropologists. The travel accounts and novels by Peter Freuchen present Eskimo life picturesquely, but probably the Greenlandic anthropologist Knud Rasmussen contributed more than any other writer to the propitious image of the Eskimo. Rasmussen wrote vivid descriptions of Eskimos, but more importantly, he allowed them to speak for themselves by recording their ideas and attitudes verbatim. From these texts the Eskimos emerge as sensitive poets, as mystics, and yet as practical men of the north. Those characteristics which are most admired are their ability to suffer adversity without complaint and to laugh at themselves or others on nearly any occasion.

The Eskimo of this romantic image was confined largely to the area near the polar seas. He lived along the northern fringes of continental Canada, on the adjacent islands or in northwestern Greenland, but not in subarctic Alaska, southern Greenland, or Labrador. Alaskan Eskimos in general have not received the attention paid to their linguistic relatives in Canada and northern

Greenland partially because of the nature of the Alaskan environment. Most Alaskan Eskimos have lived in a setting which was not a vast tundra wasteland but a land relatively rich in resources and not extremely different from the temperate regions familiar to Euro-Americans. Thus, the prevailing picture of Eskimo life has drawn heavily on the Canadian and Greenlandic forms; the present study seeks to offset this imbalance with the description of Eskimos as they have lived in Alaska.

Alaskan Eskimos, who dominated the western arctic subcultural area, formed a distinct isolate within an extensive American arctic cultural area. They ordinarily are classed under the general heading of Western Eskimos, giving recognition to their distinctive qualities. At the time of historic contact, there were some 26,000 Alaskan Eskimos in a total Eskimo population of nearly 48,000; in other words, there were more Eskimos in Alaska than in Canada, Greenland, and Siberia combined. Here existed more diversity in lifeways, greater overall complexity, and a more concentrated population than in any other region of Eskimo habitation. It is probable that Eskimo culture had greater temporal continuity in Alaska than elsewhere. Here the culture reached its most intensive development and climaxed.

In this volume Alaskan Eskimos are described as they lived when first encountered by Europeans. The Eskimos of St. Lawrence Island are not discussed since they represent an offshoot of the Siberian Eskimo population, and their cultural development has closely paralleled that of the Siberian group. The present is a particularly appropriate time to assemble and interpret Alaskan Eskimo ethnography for the period of early historic contact, since it is unlikely that any major block of information will be added by future field studies. In fact, some of the already published literature which purports to represent the aboriginal past is of the acculturative scene or is an idealized reconstruction. Extant manuscripts dating from the early historic period may be published at a future date, but it is doubtful that these will add greatly to the variations already recognized. The assumption is that most of the evidence has been collected and now may be examined systematically.

The opening chapters of this study provide background information about Alaskan Eskimos. The people are described in terms of the country they occupied and their numbers. Next their linguistic affinities, cultural origins, and prehistory are discussed. The third chapter deals with Eskimos as biological beings viewed by anthropologists, pathologists, and physiologists. These introductory topics are essential to the balanced view of Alaskan Eskimos which this book is designed to convey. The remainder of the text is devoted to ethnographic descriptions and their comparative analyses.

An overwhelming characteristic of many ethnographic descriptions is the breadth of the information assembled. The ethnographer is interested in literally everything, and he usually has at least some comments on any subject affecting the lives of the people he has studied. The dominant focus of interest established by different observers, however, rarely is as comparable as might be hoped. For the Alaskan Eskimos the tendency has been to present the same general types of information, and yet sometimes there are elaborate details on a topic for one tribe and little or no comparable data for other tribes. Thus, balancing the presentation in terms of regions and tribes has been the greatest organizational problem. In order to present the data as fully as possible, both comparable and unique information will be presented. Nonetheless, the descriptions tend to focus on four major sociocultural variants, linguistic divisions, and geographical areas. One base-line tribe is the arctic Nunamiut, who as mobile inland peoples lived mainly by hunting caribou. The second is the Tareumiut of the Arctic Ocean shore, where the emphasis was on sedentary coastal whale and seal hunting. The Bering Sea area is represented by the Nuniwagamiut and the Unaligmiut, who were diversified hunters of small sea mammals. Finally, the Pacific Ocean drainage area is represented by the Chugach, the most southeasterly of all Alaskan Eskimos, who depended on their land and sea hunting as well as on fishing skills to survive. In Alaska two languages, Inupik and Yupik, are spoken by Eskimos. The first two tribes cited above are Inupik speakers (Inuit), and the latter three are Yupik speakers (Yuit). The descriptions of these peoples are supplemented whenever pertinent information is available about tribes adjacent to them.

A major theme for most writers discussing Eskimos has been the relationship of the people to the environment. This is a well-established anthropological approach to the analysis of marginal peoples, since the limitations of the environment often are striking. The ecological dimension of Alaskan Eskimo life is not ignored in this study, but neither does it receive all the attention. Instead, the tendency has been to focus on the similarities and differences in the lifeways of Alaskan Eskimos who represent major linguistic groups and cultural variants.

It is important to point out the limitations of this book. First, the descriptions are not encyclopedic in their scope or detail. The major sources have been consulted, but there has been no effort to cite all relevant literature. Furthermore, the distribution of Eskimo characteristics beyond Alaska is not considered nor is there a distributional analysis by tribe. One final remark concerns the manner of presentation in the text. Whenever I have drawn data from another writer, I have included any qualifications he placed on his information. By contrast, my own general conclusions have been set forth with as few reservations as possible so that they may be readily subject to validation, modification, or rejection.

W. H. O.

Acknowledgments

It is a pleasure to acknowledge the aid which I received in writing this book. The foremost thanks go to Leonard Broom who read and criticized two drafts. Furthermore, James W. VanStone read most of an early draft and offered comments which were well worth receiving. Charles Lucier and Joan Townsend helped solve certain problems of Eskimo boundaries, and Clifford Fiscus provided information about the distribution of certain mammals and fishes. J. H. Rose was good enough to permit me access to unpublished information about concentrations of salmon. Harry Hoijer read and made worthwhile comments on the language section. The third chapter was read by Herman Bleibtreu, Joseph B. Birdsell, Charles J. Eagan, Frederick A. Milan, and George S. Tulloch. Each of these individuals made perceptive comments which enhanced the final presentation. The color photographs were taken by William Bradford, and it is with gratitude that I acknowledge his skill. The artifacts reproduced in color photographs are from the University of Alaska Museum collections, and I am grateful to L. J. Rowinski, Director, for permission to use these illustrations.

The three drafts of this manuscript were read and edited by my wife, Helen Louise Taylor Oswalt. To her my debt is greatest and my thanks most heartfelt.

Alaskan Eskimos

Chapter 1

The People and the Environment

Eskimos, according to popular literature, lived in a country of perennial ice and snow, built snowhouses, and subsisted mainly on raw seal meat and blubber. Such a way of life is exotic to dwellers of temperate regions and arouses their interest because it is both bizarre and romantic. The Eskimos first described in detail by European explorers lived in the arctic regions of Canada and Greenland, and here the stereotypic Eskimo characteristics do exist, at least during part of the year. A broader view of the Eskimo and his environment, however, reveals a somewhat different picture. No area of Eskimo occupancy is snow-covered perennially; in most regions snow is absent during at least two or three months of a typical year. Furthermore, most Eskimos never have seen a snowhouse, let alone lived in one. Snow dwellings were most typical of one sector of the central arctic, and in the rest of the Eskimo area houses were made of wood, turf, or stone.

1

The seal was indeed an important source of food throughout much of the Eskimo area, but it was not always eaten raw and was often supplemented or partially replaced by fish in the diet. Comparatively little of the Alaskan area of Eskimo occupancy has the severe environment of northern Canada or northern Greenland. In Alaska the resources are more abundant and the population is larger than in any other area of arctic or subarctic America occupied by Eskimos.

As a prelude to an extended description of Alaskan Eskimos, it is essential to replace the stereotypic view mentioned with a more realistic awareness of the environmental setting and its occupants. In this chapter Eskimo subcultural units and their local positioning are presented along with population numbers. The essential physical characteristics of the Eskimo environment are described in terms of biotic provinces or major zones of ecological associations, and these correlated with the population densities. From this correlation an overall perspective may be gained into the adaptive potential of the Eskimo way of life to the broad ecological zones in which it was found.

The Tribes

Each of the twenty-one tribes of Alaskan Eskimos has been located on Map 2. It is acknowledged that the term tribe is inexact when applied to these people, and yet there is no more satisfactory designation. The Eskimos so classified did not form distinct political units; in fact, political structure might scarcely exist even at the village level. However, animosities were exhibited more often outside rather than within a tribe, an indication of at least some in-group identification. Certain social and cultural ties, such as those pertaining to marriage and ceremonial gatherings, were stronger within a tribe. A tribe is designated as the people in certain villages, hamlets, or camps who were considered by outsiders, and by themselves, as being set off from other such units and having a sense of in-group identity. The Eskimos had names for the people of recognized areas which embraced more than a single settlement. For example, Zagoskin (1967, 103, 105, 209) makes it clear that the northern Yuit not only thought of themselves as "real people" living in particular settlements but also as members of what I would consider a tribe. The inland arctic Eskimos, according to Stoney (1900, 828–29), also conceived of themselves in similar terms, although Stoney confused their identifications by employing the Malemiut term in a generic sense. Likewise, the inland arctic Nunamiut of more recent times had a clear sense of their own unique identity (Gubser, 1965, 337; Larsen, 1958, 575).

In the following descriptions the names of most tribes conform to those which are well established in the literature. They are listed alphabetically, and whenever a change from a widely used tribal name is made, the alternative designation is added in parentheses. The tribal linguistic affinities are included; the Eskimos of Alaska spoke either Inupik or Yupik, with the latter including the Cux, Suk, and Yuk dialects. Alternative dialectic designations for Yupik, following Dumond (1965, 1235), are Mainland (Yuk), Nunivak (Cux), and Pacific (Suk). The population figures, which have been rounded, are the earliest and, hopefully, the most reliable counts or estimates for each group; the date or time period of the record is noted. My own estimates are based on projections from the numbers in a particular locality during the early twentieth century. When appropriate, comments are added to detail the tribe, and finally, the most important sources are cited.

The tribal boundaries on Map 2 are as precise as the published accounts permit, and in general I have lumped tribes rather than split them when there was a choice. The Eskimo boundaries have roughly comparable validity, but I have the least confidence in those for Kaialigamiut, Magemiut, and Peninsular Eskimos. The tribal map compiled by Petroff (1884) was my general guide, but for each boundary more specific sources were sought. The Indian boundaries I have drawn primarily from maps by McClellan (1964) and Hosley (ms.).

Aglegmiut: Yupik (language), Yuk (dialect); 500 [(1832) population]. The Aglegmiut have been the most perplexing of all Alaskan Eskimo tribes. They usually are represented as having occupied most of the Alaska Peninsula at the time of historic contact, and Hammerich classed them as Suk or Pacific Eskimos linguistically. However, their occupancy of the Alaska Peninsula occurred first in early historic times, and there is no compelling reason to regard them as Suk speakers. The position of the Aglegmiut can be clarified from information in the Russian-American Company records. A report of May, 1823, states that they had lived on Nunivak Island and were displaced by the Kuskowagamiut, Kiatagmiut, and other Eskimos. The Aglegmiut were pushed southward and settled in the vicinity of Alexandrov Redoubt (Nushagak), where they were under Russian protection. The implication is that they were in the process of moving into this area when the Russians arrived to build the redoubt in 1818. With Russian support they traded and hunted in adjacent areas. The same report suggests that the Aglegmiut might be removed to Kodiak Island if the hostilities then existing against them by the aforementioned tribes did not cease. Again in 1832, when the Russians had become more familiar with the peoples of the Bristol Bay region, there is an extended reference to the Aglegmiut. They were said to have lived originally in the Kuskokwim area and later resided at the Nushagak River mouth as well as along the adjacent southern coast. Their arrival pushed the existing south coast people onto the Alaska Peninsula. Here the latter people, not more precisely identifiable, were Russianized and subordinated to the Katmai station of the Russians. Around the time Alexandrov Redoubt was founded there were only sixty Aglegmiut men, but the total population had increased in 1832 to five hundred, of whom one hundred fifty were men. This marked increase in the adult male population over such a short period of time probably represents an ingathering of the previously dispersed Aglegmiut population. It seems that soon the Aglegmiut came to control most of the Alaska Peninsula under Russian sponsorship, and they may have assimilated the peninsular people as they had earlier pushed southward. By 1839 Veniaminov, as translated by Petroff, lists the people of the northern shore of the Alaska Peninsula, apart from the Aleuts, as Aglegmiut. Further substantiation of their origin is the fact that the distant Chugach associated the Aglegmiut with the Kuskokwim River. Hammerich apparently classed the Aglegmiut as Suk speakers on the basis of the dialect spoken at Perryville. The Eskimos of Perryville, however, represent a population recently displaced from Katmai rather than Aglegmiut. The Katmai people aboriginally were an enclave of mainland Koniag, who belonged to the Suk dialect group and were separate from the other Eskimo occupants of the Alaska Peninsula (Birket-Smith, 1953, 99; Hammerich, 1958a, 634; Petroff, 1884, 35–36; Russian-American Company, Communications Sent, v. 3, no. 164, folios 270–71, May 4, 1823, and Communications Sent, v. 9, no. 460, folios 345–51, October 31, 1832).

Chugach (Chugachigmiut): Yupik, Suk; 1,600 (1825). The Chugach were the most southeasterly Alaskan Eskimos, and of the nine subtribes the Tyitlkarmiut of Controller Bay were the easternmost. The "Ugalakmiut" or "Oughalakhmute" sometimes are reported as the most easterly Alaskan Eskimos, but they were in fact Eyak Indians. The Chugach were divided into nine subtribes with fluid membership, each subtribe centering about one or more villages (Birket-Smith, 1953, 18–22; de Laguna, 1934, 156; 1956, 10–35, 255–57; Petroff, 1884, 34).

Ikogmiut (Kwikpagmiut): Yupik, Yuk; 1,500 (1880). Zagoskin distinguished between the Yukon River delta Eskimos, his Kvikhlyuagmyut, and the lower Yukon River Eskimos, his Kvikhpagmyut. For the latter he recorded a population of 681 in 1842–1844 (Nelson, 1899, 26; Petroff, 1884, 11–12, 126; Zagoskin, 1967, 209, 306).

Kaialigamiut: Yupik, Yuk; 1,200 (1880). The 1880 count of nearly 900 is without much doubt lower than the actual population; thus a total of 1,200, based on more recent population densities in the area, has been entered. The separation of the Eskimos between the south bank of the Yukon River and the north bank of the Kuskokwim River into two tribes, the Magemiut and Kaialigamiut, is probably one of the least defensible boundary determinations. This division has been adopted largely on the grounds of published precedent. In the language of the local Eskimos they all may be termed Akulamiut or "tundra people," although the coastal segment also may be called Snakamiut or "coastal people." In more exact usage, Kaialigamiut refers to the people around Hazen Bay and a segment of the Nelson Island area people also called Kaluyuagamiut. The Magemiut were essentially an inland people centered about twenty miles southwest of Mountain Village (Lucier, letter, 12–18–65; Nelson, 1899, 26; Petroff, 1884, 11–12, 16, 126; Waskey, ms.; Zagoskin, 1967, 210).

Kauwerak (Kaviagmiut): Inupik; 900 (ca. 1880). From Solomon to Cape Douglas there were 320 persons, half of whom lived either on King or Sledge islands. The 1964 delineation of Eskimo boundaries for Seward Peninsula by Ray is the first important contribution to an understanding of Eskimo distributions in over fifty years (Ray, 1964, 61, 71–81).

Kiatagmiut (Nushagagmiut): Yupik, Yuk; 400 (1829). (VanStone, ms. 1; Zagoskin, 1967, 210).

Kingikmiut (Kaviagmiut): Inupik; 650 (ca. 1866). The settlement of Wales at Cape Prince of Wales, which had about 500 residents, probably was the largest Eskimo village in Alaska (Ray, 1964, 61, 78–82).

Koniag (Kaniagmiut): Yupik, Suk; 6,500 (1792). This number is from the Koniag census of 1792; a census in 1796 listed 6,200 persons. Although these figures make the Koniag twice the size of any other Alaskan Eskimo tribe, they were based on actual accounts (Hrdlička, 1944, 18–20; Petroff, 1884, 33).

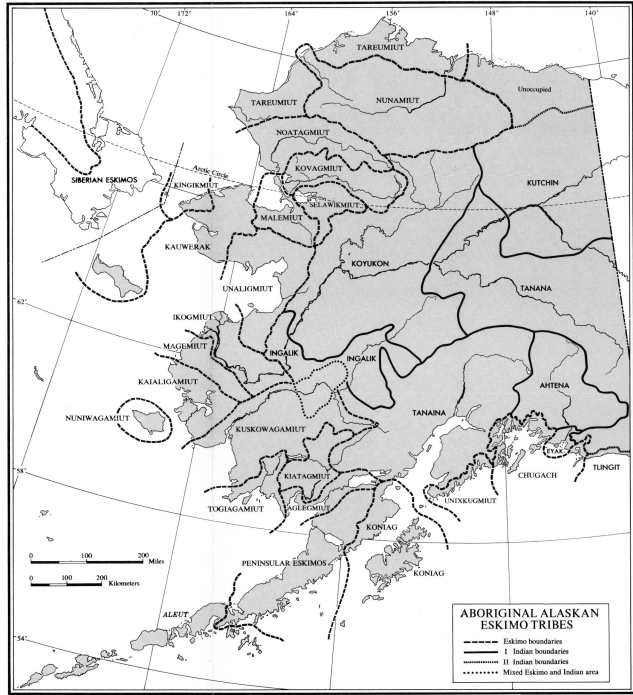

Map 2.

ABORIGINAL ALASKAN ESKIMO TRIBES

- – – Eskimo boundaries
- —— I Indian boundaries
- ········ II Indian boundaries
- •••••• Mixed Eskimo and Indian area

Vincent Kotschar

TAREUMIUT
TAREUMIUT
NUNAMIUT
Unoccupied
NOATAGMIUT
KOVAGMIUT
KUTCHIN
SIBERIAN ESKIMOS
Arctic Circle
KINGIKMIUT
SELAWIKMIUT
MALEMIUT
KAUWERAK
KOYUKON
UNALIGMIUT
TANANA
IKOGMIUT
MAGEMIUT
INGALIK
INGALIK
KAIALIGAMIUT
AHTENA
NUNIWAGAMIUT
TANAINA
KUSKOWAGAMIUT
EYAK
CHUGACH
TLINGIT
KIATAGMIUT
TOGIAGAMIUT
AGLEGMIUT
UNIXKUGMIUT
KONIAG
PENINSULAR ESKIMOS
KONIAG
ALEUT

0   100   200 Miles
0   100   200 Kilometers

70° 172° 164° 156° 148° 140°
62°
58°
54°

Map 1. Alaskan place names in the text.

Vincent Kotschar

Kovagmiut: Inupik; 500 (1880). The 1880 population estimate of 250 has been doubled to bring it more in line with Larsen and Rainey's estimate for the early historic period of 3,000 inland Eskimos in arctic Alaska (Larsen and Rainey, 1948, 31; Petroff, 1884, 4).

Kuskowagamiut: Yupik, Yuk; 3,100 (1880). The Kuskowagamiut jointly occupied at least one village, Kwigiumpainukamiut, with the Georgetown subtribe of the Ingalik. Elsewhere along the central Kuskokwim River the Eskimos and Ingalik appear to have lived in adjacent settlements. In the area of joint occupancy it is estimated that there were 200 Eskimos and the same number of Indians. The Kuskowagamiut occupied a village on Tikchik Lake, which feeds into the Nushagak River drainage, and it is likely that they also controlled the more northerly lakes between this settlement and the Kuskokwim River drainage (Oswalt, 1962, 1–4; Petroff, 1884, 16–17, 37; Russian-American Company, Communications Sent, v. 6, no. 244, folios 478–82, September 25, 1829; Zagoskin, 1967, 210).

Magemiut: Yupik, Yuk; 400 (1880). Petroff's total of 200 is without doubt below the actual population in 1880; thus, it has been entered as 400 (Nelson, 1899, 26; Petroff, 1884, 11, 126; Zagoskin, 1967, 210).

Malemiut: Inupik; 600 (1880). Counts and estimates of this Eskimo population would result in a total of 400, but since this is almost certainly too low, 200 were added (Petroff, 1884, 4, 125–26; Ray, 1964, 82–85).

Noatagmiut: Inupik; 400 (1880). Two distinct subtribes are recognized, the Noatagmiut who lived above Noatak village and were inland caribou hunters, and the Napaktumiut who were occupants both of the coniferous forest and the coastal area (Lucier, letter, 12–18–65; Petroff, 1884, 4).

Nunamiut (Nunatarmiut): Inupik; 1,500 (ca. 1890). This estimate is based largely on those of Larsen and Rainey and Gubser (Gubser, 1965, 317, 337–41; Larsen and Rainey, 1948, 31).

Nuniwagamiut: Yupik, Cux; 400 (1880). Nelson linked lin-

guistically the Nunivak Island Eskimos with those of the Cape
Vancouver area of Nelson Island, but since he is not followed by
any other writer in this classification, the Nunivak people have
been classed separately (Hammerich, 1958a; Nelson, 1899, 25;
Petroff, 1884, 16).

Peninsular Eskimos: Yupik, dialect unknown; 1,600 (1839).
As explained in the Aglegmiut descriptions, the Aglegmiut came
to the Alaska Peninsula in early historic times but previously had
been regarded as the aboriginal occupants of the area. This classification is invalid now that it is known that the Aglegmiut pushed
the former occupants of the peninsula southward in the early
contact period. Those displaced are probably the people listed by
Veniaminov, in Petroff, as "inhabitants" of the south side of the
peninsula in 1839. The assumption is that these aboriginal, peninsular Eskimos were partially absorbed by the Aglegmiut and both
were in turn rapidly Russianized. I have termed the aboriginal
occupants of the greater part of the Alaska Peninsula as Peninsular Eskimos since I know of no more fitting designation. Although they probably were Yupik speakers, their dialect is not
known (see Aglegmiut references).

Selawikmiut: Inupik; 300 (1880). The 1880 population estimate of 100 by Petroff seems unreasonably low; in fact, approximately 100 were reported in a single traveling group in 1884. The
1880 estimate has been tripled to bring it more in line with Larsen
and Rainey's total inland arctic Eskimo population of 3,000 (Larsen and Rainey, 1948, 31; Petroff, 1884, 4; Stoney, 1900, 546).

Tareumiut: Inupik; 1,500 (1850). These people were concentrated at or near a few points of land, with the major settlements
at Point Hope and Point Barrow. There was no permanent Tareumiut population east of Point Barrow (Simpson, 1875, 237–38;
Spencer, 1959, 17).

Togiagamiut: Yupik, Yuk; 1,000 (1880). Included with the
Togiagamiut are the Chingigumiut of the Cape Newenham area,
who numbered 180. The 1880 federal census report by Petroff
lists some 2,200 persons in the Togiagamiut area, but I regard this

figure as highly suspect. The villages along the Togiak River are listed by Petroff as ranging in size from 137 to 615 persons, with an average of 261 persons in each of the seven river villages. An 1879 census by Bailey lists four Togiak River villages with an average population of 80 persons each. Although the 1879 and 1880 census reports are not comparable, the 1880 figure seems disproportionately large in light of the figures for the previous year and when balanced against the populations in adjacent regions. Thus, I would reduce the 2,200 figure to 1,000 (Bailey, 1880, 27; Petroff, 1884, 17, 134–35).

Unaligmiut: Yupik, Yuk; 850 (ca. 1880). The population figure is an estimate based largely on the figures of Petroff and Ray. The northern Unaligmiut boundaries are satisfactorily presented only by Ray (Giddings, 1952b, 5; Nelson, 1899, 24; Petroff, 1884, 11, 126; Ray, 1964, 61, 66–71).

Unixkugmiut: Yupik, Suk; 600 (my estimate for 1800). The tribal name is the Chugach designation for these people, but hardly anything more than the name is known (de Laguna, 1956, 34–35).

Alaskan Eskimos occupied most of the coastal borders of the mainland from Controller Bay in the south to the northwestern Canadian border, an area which extends some eight hundred miles between the eastern and western extremes and over 1,000 miles from north to south. Their occupancy was broken in three places: at the Copper River mouth, where the Eyak Indians lived; at Cook Inlet, which was dominated largely by the Tanaina Indians; and on the western end of the Alaska Peninsula, which was occupied by the Aleuts. Eskimos controlled all of the islands adjacent to the mainland except the Shumagin Islands, held by the Aleuts; St. Lawrence Island was occupied by Asiatic rather than Alaskan Eskimos. The deepest inland penetrations were as much as two hundred miles in a direct line from the sea. The gap in tribal distributions near the northwestern Canadian boundary requires clarification. On Map 2 the northern coast east of the

Colville River mouth to the Canadian border and an adjacent sector of the interior are shown as unoccupied. The region in early historic times does not appear to have had a stable population. Occasionally families from the east or west wintered there, and the Nunamiut might sometimes range into the inland region, but no group of people identified the area as home (Gubser, 1965, 337–44; Murdoch, 1892, 43–45; Simpson, 1875, 265; Stefansson, 1914a, 9).

The Environment

The different ecological settings occupied by Alaskan Eskimos are described in terms of the biotic-province classification of Lee R. Dice (1943). The distributions of plants, animals, and fish are for the present, with comments entered concerning significant changes from the early historic period. Emphasis has been placed on those environmental characteristics of greatest importance to Eskimo exploitation.

SITKAN BIOTIC PROVINCE

Beginning in the southeast the Sitkan is the first biotic province encountered (Map 3). The Eskimos occupied only the small western portion of this province from Controller Bay to and including eastern Kodiak Island. Along Prince William Sound and the adjoining coastal areas a rather narrow band of land is backed by mountains and glaciers, usually in combination. Penetration to the interior here or on the Kenai Peninsula was impossible except at a few localities. The rugged mountains form an effective barrier against ready communication with inland peoples; they also, however, block the cold interior climate from reaching the coast. The area is marked by deep fjords, numerous large and small islands, sheltered bays, and sounds. The climate is relatively mild, owing to the mountain barrier and to the influence of the Japanese Current, and the amount of precipitation is heavy. At Latouche, for example, along the western edge of the sound, there are one hundred eighty-four inches of precipitation per year, with two hundred sixteen rainy days and a mean annual temperature of 42°F. Deep in the sound at Valdez the precipitation amounts to sixty inches, and the mean annual temperature is 36°F.

In general, the forests rise abruptly from the sea, the tides are extreme, and the dominant trees are the western hemlock (*Tsuga heterophylla*) and Sitka spruce (*Picea sitchensis*). Lesser numbers of red cedar (*Thuja plicata*) and Alaska cedar (*Chamaecyparis nootkatensis*) are present, and other species of trees include alder (*Alnus sitchensis*), cottonwood (*Populus trichocarpa*), willow (*Salix spp.*), and an occasional white spruce (*Picea glacua*) or paper birch (*Betula papyrifera*). Much of the area is at the fringe of a glacier or mountain, and barren rocks are common. Where adequate soil is present, diverse grasses, salmonberries (*Rubus spectabilis*), cloudberries (*R. chamaemorus*), highbush cranberries (*Viburnum pauciflorum*), and other plants form a dense ground cover. The most important land animal along the sound is the mountain goat (*Oreamnos americanus*). The moose (*Alces alces*) is found along the sound and on adjacent Kenai Peninsula, but Barren Ground caribou (*Rangifer arcticus*) live only on the Kenai Peninsula sector of this biotic province. Throughout most of the area bears, both black (*Ursus americanus*) and brown (*U. arctos*) are present. Also found are the hoary marmot (*Marmota caligata*), lynx (*Lynx canadensis*), mink (*Mustela vison*), pine marten (*Martes americana*), porcupine (*Erethizon dorsatum*), red fox (*Vulpes fulva*), river otter (*Lutra canadensis*), snowshoe hare (*Lepus americanus*), gray wolf (*Canis lupus*), and wolverine (*Gulo gulo*). The Dall sheep (*Ovis dalli*) occurs only on the Kenai Peninsula. On Kodiak Island the beaver (*Castor canadensis*), muskrat (*Ondatra zibethicus*), mountain goat, and snowshoe hare are recent imports. The mule or black-tailed deer (*Odocoileus hemionus*) is a recent import both on Kodiak Island and along Prince William Sound. The only notable land animals on the island at the time of historic contact were the river otter, red

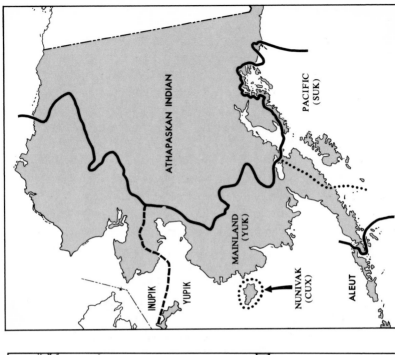

Map 4. Linguistic groupings.

Vincent Kotschar

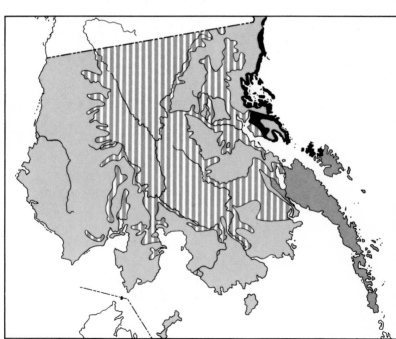

Map 3. Biotic provinces after Taylor

Vincent Kotschar

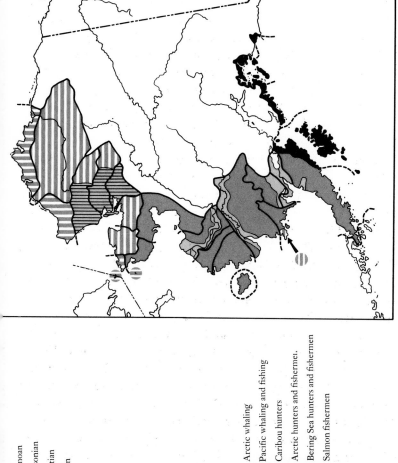

Map 5. Major subsistence patterns.

Vincent Kotschar

Map 4 — BOUNDARIES

	Aleut-Eskimo-Indian
	Inupik-Yupik
	Mainland-Pacific

Eskimoan
Hudsonian
Aleutian
Sitkan

Map 5.

Arctic whaling
Pacific whaling and fishing
Caribou hunters
Arctic hunters and fishermen.
Bering Sea hunters and fishermen
Salmon fishermen

fox, and the Kodiak form of brown bear. The geography of Kodiak Island will be considered further under the Aleutian biotic province since most of it falls within this ecological association.

The most important marine animals include the following whales: humpback whale (*Megaptera novaeangliae*), Pacific blackfish (*Globicephala scammoni*), and beluga or white whale (*Delphinapterus leucas*). Occurrence of the Pacific walrus (*Odobenus rosmarus*) was and is rare, whereas the Alaska fur seal (*Callorhinus ursinus*) formerly was common but is presently rare. Other sea mammals which frequent the area are the northern sea lion (*Eumetopias jubata*), harbor seal (*Phoca vitulina*), and sea otter (*Enhydra lutris*); the sea otter was abundant during the early Russian era. Alaska salmon, which always breed in fresh-water streams and descend to the sea to spend most of their adult lives, provided the richest and most reliable source of food. In the sequence of their appearance from spring to early fall, the king salmon or chinook (*Oncorhynchus tshawytscha*) arrive in May, to be followed by the red or sockeye salmon (*O. nerka*), then the humpback or pink salmon (*O. gorbuscha*), the dog or chum (*O. keta*), and finally the silver or coho (*O. kisutch*) in early August. Other important fish include halibut (*Hippoglossus vulgaris*), Pacific cod (*Gadus macrocephalus*), herring (*Clupea harengus pallasi*), and candlefish or eulachon (*Thaleichthys pacificus*). Along the beaches are found diverse invertebrates, including little-neck clams (*Paphia staminea*) and cockles (*Cardium corbis*). The most important birds found year-round are the Alexander's willow ptarmigan (*Lagopus lagopus alexandrae*) and Valdez spruce grouse (*Canachites canadensis atratus*). In the summer diverse migratory birds nest in the region; these include the northern pelagic cormorant (*Phalacrocorax pelagicus pelagicus*), Pacific kittiwake (*Rissa tridactyla pollicaris*), glaucous-winged gull (*Larus glaucescens*), the common pigeon guillemot (*Cepphus columba columba*), black oystercatcher (*Haematopus bachmani*), tufted puffin (*Lunda cirrhata*), and horned puffin

(*Fratercula corniculata*). Migratory ducks and geese also occur in the area during the summer. Probably the most important goose was the white-cheeked Canada goose (*Branta canadensis occidentalis*) which breeds mainly in the Prince William Sound region. Local ducks include the common mallard (*Anas platyrhynchos*) and American widgeon (*Mareca americana*). (see Birket-Smith, 1953, 16–18; Brooks, 1953, 10; Dice, 1943, 30–31; Fay, 1957, 431–32; Gabrielson and Lincoln, 1959; Manville and Young, 1965; Rhode and Barker, 1953; *Weather Summary*, 1944, 140, 154; Wilimovsky, 1954, 1958)

ALEUTIAN BIOTIC PROVINCE

The sector of the Aleutian province controlled by Eskimos included the major portion of Kodiak Island and most of the Alaska Peninsula. In general it is a treeless region with low but rugged mountains; in the southeastern sector some of the mountains have glaciers at their flanks. The crest of the peninsular drainages is near the Pacific shore; westward on the peninsula the mountains include scattered volcanic peaks. The south side of the peninsula is characterized by innumerable bays and coves along the mountainous coastline. On the north side the coastline is largely unbroken except by bays at river mouths, and the northern streams and rivers flow through relatively flat country into the Bering Sea. The northern portion of the peninsula has about twenty-five inches of precipitation per year, while along the south side the precipitation averages fifty inches per year. The mean annual temperature at the town of Kodiak is 41°F., and the mean annual precipitation is nearly sixty-two inches, with one hundred seventy-three rainy days. Apart from the timbered northeastern sector of Kodiak Island and the area at the base of the Alaska Peninsula which adjoins Iliamna Lake, the area has no trees larger than willows and alders (*Alnus fruticosa*). Associated with the willow thickets are reedgrass (*Calamagrostis canadensis*) and numerous species of ferns. The most abundant grass is strand wheat or wild rye (*Elymus arenarius mollis*), and diverse flowering plants are plentiful. Near the base of the peninsula a tundra vegetation emerges above 1,000 to 2,000 feet. Such vegetation increases in dominance to the southwest, where it is found at lower elevations, and is typical of the area draining into the Bering Sea.

The most typical land mammals of the Alaska Peninsula are the arctic fox (*Alopex lagopus*), arctic ground squirrel (*Citellus parryi*), Barren Ground caribou, gray wolf, hoary marmot, mink, moose, brown bear, porcupine, red fox, river otter, tundra hare (*Lepus othus*), and wolverine. Once again, however, it was not the resources of the land on which the people most depended but those of the sea. The most common sea mammals and fish are those found in the Sitkan biotic province. The only significant difference in the marine fauna is that the Pacific walrus is no longer common on the northern shore of the Alaska Peninsula.

A few of the more important birds are the emperor goose (*Philacte canagica*) which winters primarily on the Alaska Peninsula, Murie's willow ptarmigan (*Lagopus lagopus muriei*), and Nelson's rock ptarmigan (*L. mutus nelsoni*). Diverse cliff birds such as the Pacific fulmar (*Fulmarus glacialis rodgersi*), the northwestern double-crested cormorant (*Phalacrocorax auritus cincinatus*), and the northern pelagic cormorant also are present.

Kodiak Island and the smaller islands of the group are separated from the mainland by as little as twenty miles of open water. In relatively recent geological times the islands were connected to each other and to the mainland. A great deal of glacial erosion is indicated, with narrow channels, bays, and deep fjords characteristic of most coastal areas; some interior mountains rise more than 3,000 feet. None of the land is more than fifteen miles from salt water, and the drainages consistently are short. The two rivers feed into lakes, which are important breeding grounds for salmon. The northern section of Kodiak Island and the islands to the northeast are timbered with Sitka spruce, which grow at elevations up to about 1,000 feet. The tree line appears to be advancing at a rate of a mile per century. (see Brooks, 1953,

14–15, 36, 64–65; Capps, 1937, 112–23; Collins et al., 1945, 64–65; Dice, 1943, 29; Gabrielson and Lincoln, 1959; Manville and Young, 1965; *Weather Summary*, 1944, 81)

ESKIMOAN BIOTIC PROVINCE

The most extensive biotic province of Eskimo occupation was the Eskimoan, which extends along the coast from Bristol Bay to the northern Canadian border. It is a tundra setting, with grasses, lichens, and mosses the most common forms of ground cover. Along sheltered streams and rivers are growths of willows and, less often, stands of alders. The topography varies widely. Bluffs reach the sea in the vicinity of Bristol Bay, and low mountains approach the coast around Togiak Bay and on Norton Sound. Between the Kuskokwim and Yukon river mouths, as well as along the northern coasts facing the Arctic Ocean, the relief is low, the drainage poor, and innumerable lakes are to be found. In the entire region the climate is cold in the winter, and the summers are cool to cold, with little to moderate precipitation. On Bristol Bay at Naknek the mean annual temperature is 35°F., and 24.1 inches of precipitation fall during ninety-two days in an average year. Further north at Hooper Bay Village on the central Bering Sea coast the mean temperature is 30°F., and the precipitation 17.1 inches over one hundred forty-four days of the year. At Kotzebue at the head of Kotzebue Sound the comparable statistics are 20°F. and 6.1 inches during forty-five days, while at the top of the continent at Point Barrow the figures are 10°F. and 4.2 inches over fifty-four days. From this brief résumé it is apparent that the climatic conditions vary within the Eskimoan biotic province.

There is variability, too, in the land mammals which are present. The species which occur throughout most of the area include the following: arctic and red fox, arctic ground squirrel, Barren Ground caribou, brown or grizzly bear, gray wolf, tundra or arctic hare, and wolverine. On Nunivak Island the only land animals of importance are the tundra hare, the arctic and red fox, and mink, but there were caribou and wolves on the island late in the nineteenth century. Among the species with limited distributions the snowshoe or varying hare extends from the Yukon River mouth northward across the eastern end of Seward Peninsula and into the Kobuk River drainage. The hoary marmot is found around Bristol Bay and along the arctic slope of the Brooks Range except for the lower Colville and adjacent river drainages. The beaver is everywhere south of the Noatak River except in the low country between the Yukon and Kuskokwim river mouths and along Togiak Bay. The porcupine is widespread, and the black bear is found everywhere except on Seward Peninsula and in the extreme northern portions. Around Bristol and Togiak bays the pine marten is present; the mink is everywhere except on the northwestern sector of the arctic slopes of the Brooks Range. The river otter does not occur on Seward Peninsula or on the Colville and adjacent rivers which feed into the Arctic Ocean. The lynx is present along Norton Sound, across the eastern end of Seward Peninsula, and along the arctic slope except at the northwest.

Some significant changes in the distribution of land animals have occurred in this province. It would appear that at the period of historic contact moose rarely extended into the Eskimoan province, but today they are everywhere except along the lower Colville River and in the region which reaches from south of the Yukon River to the northern sector of the Bristol Bay area. The Barren Ground caribou was apparently everywhere, and its numbers were especially great in the Noatak River area and along the border of Norton Sound. Today the Norton Sound herds no longer exist, and those of other areas have greatly decreased in number. Dall sheep occur in the Brooks Range and in historic times musk-oxen (*Ovibos moschatus*) occupied the arctic slope of the Brooks Range; the musk-oxen on Nunivak Island, however, are recent transplants. Reindeer (*Rangifer tarandus*) were introduced into Alaska first in 1891, and by 1936 large herds were common in western and northern Alaska. Since that time, however, the number has decreased drastically.

The marine animals which occur along the coast include the Pacific walrus, harbor seal, and bearded seal (*Erignathus barbatus*). The ringed seal (*Pusa hispida*) is found from Cape Romanzof northward, and the ribbon seal (*Histriophoca fasciata*) from Kuskokwim Bay to Point Barrow. The fur seal is mainly in the Bristol Bay region. The northern sea lion ranges northward to the vicinity of Bering Strait, while polar bears (*Thalarctos maritimus*) are most often found on the pack ice in the vicinity of Bering Strait and northward. The two species of whales of greatest economic importance were the beluga, found both north and south of Bering Strait, and the bowhead whale (*Balaena mysticetus*) which was found most often north of Bering Strait.

In general, dog and humpback salmon range as far east as the Mackenzie River system, while from the Yukon River southward these species, as well as king, red, and silver salmon often occur in great numbers. Second to salmon in importance are the diverse species of whitefish which range widely and may frequent brackish or salt water as well as fresh water during their life cycles. The sheefish or inconnu (*Stenodus leucichthys nelma*) ranges from the Kuskokwim River northward; the broad-nosed whitefish (*Coregonus nasus*), in the Arctic Ocean drainages and southward to the Yukon River; the hump-backed whitefish (*C. lavaretus pidschian*), in the Bering Sea and Arctic Ocean drainages; and the round whitefish (*Prosopium cylindraceum*), from the Yukon River southward. The sailfin grayling (*Thymallus arcticus signifer*) is common in fresh waters feeding into the Arctic Ocean and Bering Sea. There are three species of smelt, with the pond smelt (*Hypomesus olidus*) and capelin (*Mallotus villosus*) in the shallow coastal waters of the Arctic Ocean and the rainbow smelt (*Osmerus eperlanus dentex*) there as well as in the Bering Sea. Other species of particular importance are the following: the blackfish (*Dallia pectoralis*), in lowland fresh waters from the Kuskokwim River drainage to the Arctic Ocean drainages; the arctic Alaskan cods, including the burbot (*Lota lota leptura*) of fresh and brackish water, the polar tomcod (*Boreogadus saida*) which frequents salt water but may enter fresh water, and the saffron (*Eleginus navaga navaga*), usually in coastal salt and brackish waters; and two varieties of sticklebacks (*Gasterosteus aculeatus aculeatus* and **G.** *aculeatus microcephalus*) which are found in the Bering Sea freshwater drainages.

Among the more important birds in this province are the diverse species of geese which breed here. These include the cackling Canada goose (*Branta canadensis minima*), the lesser Canada goose (*B. canadensis leucopareia*), black brant (*B. nigricans*), emperor goose, and the Pacific white-fronted goose (*Anser albifrons frontalis*). The most important ducks are the common mallard, American widgeon, pintail (*Anas acuta*), green-winged common teal (*A. crecca carolinensis*), greater scaup (*Aythya marila nearctica*), and old-squaw (*Clangula hyemalis*). The most important land birds present year-round are Nelson's rock ptarmigan and the Hudsonian spruce grouse (*Canachites canadensis canadensis*). The cliff birds which commonly nest here include the northern pelagic cormorant, north Pacific murre (*Uria aalge inornata*), Pallas's thick-billed murre (*U. lomvia arra*), commander pigeon guillemot (*Cepphus columba kaiurka*), as well as horned and tufted puffins. (see Gabrielson and Lincoln, 1959; Lantis, 1946, 173; Manville and Young, 1965; Walters, 1955; *Weather Summary*, 1944, 123, 134, 138, 142; Wilimovsky, 1954.)

HUDSONIAN BIOTIC PROVINCE

The Hudsonian province is dominated by spruce forests at lower elevations and a tundra vegetation above tree line. Found throughout interior Alaska, it reaches the coast only in scattered localities. The western and northern limits of the Hudsonian do not form quite as continuous a line as is indicated on Map 3 since there are isolated pockets of trees toward the coasts, especially along eastern Seward Peninsula. The Hudsonian areas of Eskimo habitat are either complete river systems, as in the cases of the Selawik and Kobuk rivers, or portions of rivers as along the Kuskokwim. The limit of the province is marked by the tree lines for white spruce (*Picea glauca*). Near the northern and western tree line black spruce (*P. mariana*) occur, and there are stands of paper birch, quaking aspen (*Populus tremuloides*), alder, and scattered tamarack (*Larix laricina*), as well as dwarf resin birch (*Betula glandulosa*) and willows. Above or beyond tree line a tundra vegetation like that of the Eskimoan province prevails. The climate of the sector of the Hudsonian biotic province being considered does not differ markedly from that of the adjacent coastal areas except that winds are likely to be less frequent and less strong and the temperature is somewhat milder. At Bethel, on the lower Kuskokwim River, the mean annual temperature is 30°F. and the precipitation 17.7 inches per year over one hundred thirty days, while at Noorvik along the lower Kobuk River near the Eskimoan-Hudsonian boundary the mean annual temperature is 21°F. with 15.8 inches of precipitation over ninety-nine days per year.

The land mammals commonly occurring include the arctic ground squirrel; Barren Ground caribou; bear of the black, brown, or grizzly forms; beaver; gray wolf; mink; moose; muskrat; porcupine; red fox; river otter; snowshoe hare; and wolverine. The migratory waterfowl which frequently nest in the Eskimoan biotic province are found often as transients in the Hudsonian biotic province. The most important year-round bird is the Alaska willow ptarmigan (*Lagopus lagopus alascensis*); the second is the Hudsonian spruce grouse. The species of salmon and whitefish mentioned for the other biotic provinces, with due allowance for their distributions, are found in the Hudsonian. The other fish of the Eskimoan biotic province, except those confined to salt water, are present in the Hudsonian. (See Gabrielson and Lincoln, 1959; Hustich, 1953; Manville and Young, 1965; Rhode and Barker, 1953; *Weather Summary*, 1944, 124, 144.)

Above all else Alaskan Eskimos were hunters and fishermen; thus the biotic-province descriptions have focused on animals which either were edible or had skins suitable for clothing. The

flora, while recognized as important, has been dealt with superfi-
cially. In a general evaluation of the Alaskan Eskimo setting it is
notable that important species of land mammals occurred in at
least some sectors of all the provinces. The arctic ground squirrel,
Barren Ground caribou, beaver, mink, muskrat, river otter, and
wolverine all were widespread. The breaks in distributions of
species did not follow the boundaries of biotic provinces although
most species clearly were more at home in one province than in
another. Thus, the numbers of animals belonging to a species
varied widely among provinces, although the sharpest breaks in
land-mammal populations occurred with reference to islands.

A different set of conditions existed regarding sea mammals.
The harbor seal and beluga whale were found along most of the
coast, but other sea mammals were much more limited in their
distributions. Furthermore, sea conditions differed greatly both
by season and locality, with the distribution of the winter ice
being extremely important. In areas where there were open seas
throughout the year the hunting conditions were more stable
than in areas where the ice formed, was present throughout the
winter, and then receded in the spring or summer. In general, ice
conditions were encountered everywhere except along portions
of the north Pacific Ocean. In the essentially inland Hudsonian
biotic province sea mammals were uncommon or unheard of.
Along the lower courses of large rivers harbor seals and beluga
whales were sometimes summer visitors, but they were not a
reliable source of food.

A study of fish distributions leads primarily to consideration
of the salmonini. Certain species of this subfamily played a dominant role in the subsistence activities of many Alaskan Eskimos,
but it is difficult to gauge their prevalence in any particular area.
The only approach is to view contemporary salmon concentrations as being essentially the same as those at the time of historic
contact. Admittedly, species were fished out of particular streams
in the Bristol Bay area and in other regions where intensive
commercial fishing operations have taken place. In limited areas,

such as localities on Seward Peninsula, mining operations have rendered streams unsuitable for salmon spawning. In addition, natural catastrophes in historic times have changed the spawning potential of streams and rivers. Because these factors have reduced the number of spawning areas, it may be assumed that salmon concentrations in aboriginal times were greater than at present but over the same general area as today. Insofar as areal distribution is concerned the dog or chum salmon was available over a larger area than any other salmon species. Rivers and streams between Prince William Sound and Norton Sound were particularly important. North of this region, only the Kobuk and Noatak rivers had heavy runs of dog salmon. The major runs of red or sockeye salmon were in the Bristol Bay region, but these fish were abundant also at certain localities on Kodiak Island, Prince William Sound, and along the Kuskokwim River. Pink or humpback salmon spawning grounds were concentrated particularly in Bristol Bay, Prince William Sound, and a sector of Kodiak Island, whereas silver or coho escapement probably was greatest along Bristol Bay. Finally, the king or chinook salmon were most plentiful in Bristol Bay and the Kuskokwim-Yukon region (Atkinson et al., ms.; Fiscus, correspondence; Mattson, 1962; Pennoyer et al., 1965). Salmon were abundant in at least some portion of all the biotic provinces and could have been a major source of food for many riverine or estuary populations from the Noatak River southward. The concentrated runs and at times astounding numbers of salmon in many localities would make them a seemingly obvious economic base.

Recognition also must be given to other species of fish which were key in the economy of certain localities. For example, blackfish, sticklebacks, and whitefish, often in combination, were critical in the subsistence activities of tundra-dwelling Eskimos of the Yukon-Kuskokwim region. Polar tomcod were important along the coasts of arctic Alaska, as were halibut along the Pacific shores.

In general, an economy based on land mammals, meaning the

Barren Ground caribou primarily, would lead to the most unstable base because of the numerical fluctuations of the species and the unpredictability of their exact patterns of seasonal movement. Sea-mammal hunting was more predictable, but fishing, particularly for salmon, was the subsistence activity likely to yield the most stable harvest.

Populations and Densities

Based on the population figures calculated for each tribe, the total for all Alaskan Eskimos at the period of relatively early historic contact was about 26,000. The tribal numbers are either the earliest figures for specific peoples or are conservative estimates if population records were not available. It is unlikely that there were fewer than 23,000 or more than 33,000 Eskimos in Alaska at early historic contact. One imponderable, for which I could make no reasonable allowance, was the effect of the smallpox epidemic which struck the Bering Sea coast south of Seward Peninsula in mid-1838. The population figures given for the people from northern Bristol Bay to Norton Sound date from 1880, some forty years after the epidemic. An account of the epidemic by Tikhmenev (1861, 365–69) states that many Eskimos around the redoubts at Nushagak and St. Michael as well as along the Kuskokwim River were vaccinated and that the number of deaths was small. Zagoskin (1967, 92, 100, 281), who was in contact with more isolated settlements a few years after the epidemic had passed, recorded the abandonment of settlements and the existence of remnant populations in others. Probably the Ikogmiut, Kaialigamiut, and Magemiut suffered most heavily since they were the most likely to have resisted any efforts which might have been made to vaccinate them. Thus it might be reasonable to double the number of persons entered for these tribes. Jonathan Jenness knows more than anyone else about the early historic settlement patterns in the Yukon-Kuskokwim tundra region. In conversations he stated that in his judgment my estimates for the peoples of this region were extremely low. In any event, I doubt that the Alaskan Eskimo population had reached 33,000 at the time of historic contact. A population estimate for 1740 by Mooney (1928, 31–32) is 40,000, but since he did not break his figures down by tribe, it is not possible to check the reasons for his greater number. The fact that Mooney's figure is larger than mine is not surprising, however, since many of his calculations are judged to be somewhat high (Kroeber, 1939, 132–34).

To relate the Alaskan Eskimo figures to the total Eskimo population: the Siberian and St. Lawrence Island Eskimo population probably totaled 2,000, and Canada, Greenland, and Labrador may have had 20,000, for a complete Eskimo population of about 48,000 or possibly somewhat less. Of all the Eskimos, therefore, slightly more than half lived in Alaska, and two-fifths were Yupik speakers from Alaska. In the major linguistic division within Alaska, approximately 6,350 Eskimos spoke Inupik and 19,650 spoke Yupik. Within Yupik, 400 spoke Cux (Nunivak); 8,700, Suk (Pacific); and 10,550, Yuk (Mainland).

A direct comparison of the biotic-province areas occupied by Alaskan Eskimos with the number of persons estimated for each area yields the following population densities per one hundred square kilometers: Sitkan, 18; Aleutian, 10; Hudsonian, 4; and Eskimoan, 2. These figures show that Bering Sea and arctic-tundra areas supported very few persons and that a setting in a riverine coniferous forest, while providing greater opportunities than the tundra, still had a very limited potential. Only on the grasslands of the Aleutian biotic province did the density increase drastically, and it reached a peak among Eskimos in a north Pacific forest environment. Thus, as a whole the populations of the Eskimoan and Hudsonian biotic provinces had low densities, whereas those of the Aleutian and Sitkan provinces stand apart with significantly higher densities.

When a corner of eastern Siberia and the expanse of North America occupied by Eskimos are regarded as one culture area, it is possible to consider the Eskimos and Aleuts of Alaska as inhabit-

ing the Western Eskimo-Aleut subarea. In the Western Eskimo
subarea there is more environmental diversity than in any other
Eskimo subarea. A description of the major ecological divisions or
biotic provinces and the size of their Eskimo populations makes
apparent the broad range of population densities and environmental settings. From this it might be assumed that Alaskan Eskimo
culture and society varied widely. One of the more interesting
problems is to determine whether the sociocultural variability is
correlated generally or specifically with different environments.

Chapter 2

Language and Prehistory

Eskimos are one of the few peoples who reflect racial, linguistic, and cultural homogeneity. They are a recognized segment of the Mongoloid population, their languages belong to a separate linguistic stock, and their cultural adaptations are distinctive. As a general introduction to the living peoples, the information about their languages and prehistory will be considered first, whereas the biological aspects of being an Alaskan Eskimo are described in the chapter to follow. The linguistic information in this chapter includes both classification and chronology to serve as a foreground for the analysis of Eskimo cultural emergence. A further introduction to the living people is provided by presenting briefly the major theories of their cultural origins. The next step is to summarize the key archaeological discoveries, and the chapter ends with some current opinions about the sources of Eskimo culture.

Linguistic Classifications

During the Russian era, the aborigines occupying the coastal mainland of Alaska from Prince William Sound to the west and northward were recognized as being one people. Regional differences in languages were acknowledged, but it was not until 1928, with the publication of materials collected by Diamond Jenness, that the major linguistic break became clearly apparent. Between 1913 and 1926 Jenness assembled Eskimo word lists from several settlements between Nunivak Island and Point Barrow and at East Cape in Siberia (Jenness, 1928a, 3). After making comparisons of these lists, he concluded that a major linguistic division occurred at Norton Sound. The language spoken by Siberian Eskimos and those Alaskan Eskimos south of Norton Sound was quite different from that spoken by northern Alaskan Eskimos. Between Greenland and northern Alaska, however, the linguistic differences were largely insignificant (Jenness, 1928b, 174). Studies by Swadesh, published in 1951–1952, further clarified the degree of variation. His word lists were drawn largely from the vocabularies of Jenness, the Kuskokwim data of Hinz (1944), and his own material collected from a St. Michael resident. His major conclusion supported Jenness's linguistic break at Norton Sound. Swadesh stated that the separation was between two major groups; he called the southern group "Yupik" and the northern one "Inupik." These two words mean "real person" or "Eskimo" among the Kuskokwim and Point Barrow residents respectively. The line dividing the two groups was considered to be near the settlement of Unalakleet, and the separation between the two was felt to approximate the difference between English and German (Swadesh, 1951a, 66–70). It should be noted that other terms comparable in part or full with the Inupik designation include Inuk and Inuit; for Yupik, terms used as alternatives have been Yuk and Yuit. The people of St. Michael, the Kuskokwim, and Nunivak were grouped together as Yupik, although the latter manifested some differences; in general, the Siberian Eskimos were linguistically closest to this group even though they had superficial characteristics of Inupik (Swadesh, 1951b, 28).

It is apparent that the greater internal differences were in Yupik, and a more refined classification of it was offered by Hammerich. He viewed the Eskimo spoken in Alaska from Norton Sound to the north and eastward as Eastern Eskimo (Inupik), while Western Eskimo (Yupik) he divided into Western Eskimo of Alaska and Asiatic Eskimo. The Alaskan portion of Western Eskimo he separated into three major dialects: Yuk, which included the coastal and adjacent riverine peoples from St. Michael to Bristol Bay and Iliamna Lake; Cux, on Nunivak Island alone; and Suk, represented on Kodiak Island, the adjacent mainland, and Prince William Sound. Speakers of Yuk and Cux can understand each other but possibly cannot understand Suk. A mutual intelligibility test, which consisted of reading a hunting story collected at Bethel to Eskimos in diverse localities, was administered by Hammerich. This Yuk story was understood everywhere in the area defined as Yuk, and understood "more or less willingly" among the Cux. It is stated, however, that the tale was "completely incomprehensible" to Eskimos of the Kodiak Island area. The experiment was not performed among the Prince William Sound Eskimos, but it was assumed that the latter would not be able to understand it. Thus Yuk and Cux seem more closely related to each other than to Suk. Stated in Dumond's dialectic terminology (1965, 1235), Mainland and Nunivak dialects were more closely related to each other than to the Pacific dialect. Asiatic Eskimos, within the Western Eskimo division, include the Eskimos of Siberia and St. Lawrence Island; those of the Diomede Islands are Eastern Eskimos or Inupik. The language and dialect boundaries as they have been reconstructed for aboriginal Western Eskimos appear on Map 4. The divisions are those proposed by Hammerich with two exceptions. The Alaska Peninsula population, apart from those people who were identified with the Koniag, have been classified but not with certainty for reasons presented in Chapter 1 in the Peninsular Eskimo discussion. Second, the northern Yuk boundary has been extended to conform with recent findings by Ray (1964). Asiatic Eskimo, because of its affinity to the southern Eskimo language, is considered as a separate dialect of Yupik which might be termed Yupǝk (Hammerich, 1958a, 638). On Map 4 it will be noted that the Yupik of Siberia and Alaska are separated by the Inupik by only a short distance on western Seward Peninsula. It is perhaps important that from a vocabulary he collected at Wales on the western tip of Seward Peninsula, Jenness (1927, 168) considered that there was a link between what have come to be called Inupik and Yupik at this settlement. In commenting on this observation, Swadesh (1951a, 70) suggests that the transitional forms recorded were likely due "to diffusional influences between Wales and its neighbors in relatively recent times, since we find nothing in this dialect which minimizes the depth of its separation from Yupik Eskimo."

The linguistic map shows that the three major coastal sectors were occupied by linguistically homogeneous tribes. The Inupik speakers dominated the coasts facing the Chukchi Sea and Arctic Ocean, the Yuk prevailed along the Bering Sea coast, and the Suk controlled the Pacific Ocean sector. Each of these large geographical areas apparently possessed qualities leading to the establishment of homogeneous linguistic zones. It would be too much to regard the boundary limits as resulting from historical chance alone. The only exceptions to the correlation are minor: the Inupik-speaking Kauwerak were present along southwestern Seward Peninsula, the Cux of Nunivak Island diverged somewhat from Yuk, and the linguistic status of the Peninsular Eskimos is uncertain.

A clear affinity between the Eskimo and Aleut stocks is well established; the only problem is to determine its dimensions. Eskimo and Aleut share structural characteristics, cognates, and some phonemic qualities, but nonetheless diverge so broadly that they must be considered separate stocks (Marsh and Swadesh,

1951; Swadesh, 1951a, 68; Bergsland, 1951). To classify Aleut and Eskimo within the general format of North American Indian language divisions by Trager and Harben (1958), the divisions shown below in tabulated form are reasonable. The linguistic affinities of the specific tribes were presented in the previous chapter.

phylum	Eskimoan			
	(or Eskaleutian)			
stocks	Aleut	Eskimo		
languages		Inupik	Yupik	
dialects			Cux	(Nunivak)
			Suk	(Pacific)
			Yuk	(Mainland)
			Yupǝk	(Siberian)

More distant generic relationships of the Eskimoan phylum have recently been established with the Chukchee, Koryak, and Kamchadal of northeastern Siberia (Swadesh, 1962); these connections were strongly suspected earlier by Boas (1933, 369). The time depth of the separation has been derived from glottochronological calculations and is cited in the section to follow. There is still another much more remote and tenuous possible relationship which should be mentioned. This one, between Eskimoan and Indo-European, is a hypothesis advanced by Uhlenbeck in 1935 and supported most recently in studies by Thalbitzer (1952) and Hammerich (1951). The reported affinities include not only etymologies for certain root words but also parallels in structural morphology. That there is a very distant relationship appears likely, but its dimensions are largely unknown.

Linguistic Chronology

To establish the degree of divergence between related languages by comparing vocabularies is an old and logical practice. However, to derive a formula which will produce an approximate date for the occurrence of a linguistic division is a much more complex operation. During the past fifteen years Swadesh has devoted great effort not only to establishing a workable formula but also to applying it to diverse languages. The premise for glottochronology, which is a form of lexicostatistics, is that a basic lexicon or vocabulary will remain relatively unchanged over a long period of time, and that the rate of word loss from such a basic list is relatively constant for all languages. By comparing lexicons of related languages for which the times of divergence are historically documented, an index to the degree of separation in a specific length of time may be derived. When this index is applied to related languages that have split at an unknown time, a date may be established for the time of the separation (see Lees, 1953; Swadesh, 1952d, 1955). However, the original calculation for the retention rate was slightly lower than the one proposed in 1955. In the table which follows are dates proposed for Eskimo

Units	Date	Source
Eskaleutian (Eskimo and Aleut)—Chuko-tan (Kamchadal and Chukchee-Koryak)	3000 B.C.	Swadesh, 1962, 1268–69
Aleut—Eskimoan	1000 B.C.	Swadesh, 1954, 362
Aleut—Inupik (s.w. Greenland)	2600 B.C.	Swadesh, 1958, 672
Inupik (Greenland)—Yupik (Yukon)	A.D. 1000	Swadesh, 1954, 362
Inupik (w. Greenland)—Yupik (Unaligmiut)	A.D. 820	Hirsch, 1954, 827
Inupik (s.w. Greenland)—Yupik (Unaligmiut)	A.D. 600	Swadesh, 1958, 672
Inupik (Tareumiut)—Yupik (Unaligmiut)	A.D. 1100	Hirsch, 1954, 827
Inupik (Tareumiut)—Inupik (w. Greenland)	A.D. 1700	Hirsch, 1954, 827
Aleut (Eastern)—proto-Eskimo (Inupik and Yupik)	2000 B.C.	Marsh and Swadesh, 1951, 210
Aleut—Eskimo	1000 B.C.	Swadesh, 1952d, 453
Inupik (Greenland and Labrador)—Yupik (Unaligmiut and Kuskowagamiut)	A.D. 1-500	Swadesh, 1951a, 67

relationships. It will be noted that the earliest published dates, listed at the bottom of the table, differ from some later dates for the same combinations of languages; this is due to different assessments of the retention rates and to the provisional nature of the early calculations. It should be made clear that the calculations are stated in terms of the most recent separation date possible. Thus, a date of A.D. 1000 most likely would indicate a split before this time, and a "date" may be so conceived only in a loose usage of the word.

Different and sometimes contradictory conclusions may be drawn from these glottochronological results. By emphasizing the more recently derived dates, searching for patterns, and making projections, the following interpretations are possible. Somewhere in northeastern Asia in the fourth millennium B.C. lived peoples whose descendants were ultimately to occupy the Bering Strait and adjacent regions. Before 3000 B.C. the Eskaleuts became separated from the segment of the original population which later became Chukotan. Before 2600 B.C. the predecessors of modern Eskimos and Aleuts remained unified, but around this time they began to drift apart. Following the Aleut division from Eskimo (later to become Inupik and Yupik) the ancestral Eskimos remained unified until A.D. 600–1000, when the people later to emerge as the Inupik of Greenland and Labrador separated from the Yupik. The Inupik-Yupik division did not occur at one place or at one time; the fragmentation went on throughout the latter part of the first millennium A.D. Soon after A.D. 1000 the Inupik and Yupik of Alaska were clearly distinct. Throughout the last nine hundred years the Inupik speakers have retained ties across arctic America, ties that were still intense just prior to historic contact. In contrast to the degree of contact among the Inupik tribes, the Yupik became comparatively more isolated from each other, and this separation led to the emergence of three or probably four Yupik dialects.

As presently applied, glottochronology is not a fully accepted method of linguistic analysis. One serious criticism is that the rate at which words are dropped from a basic vocabulary is not relatively constant for diverse languages. A second problem is translating words exactly from one language to another (Bergsland and Vogt, 1962; Hewes et al., 1960; Hymes, 1960). Even if the method is valid, some of the dates derived for Eskimo and Aleut are contradictory. For the Aleut-Eskimo separation the original and rough calculation was 2000 B.C., then 1000 B.C., and later 2600 B.C. Bergsland (1958b, 656) independently analyzed the data on which the 1000 B.C. date was based and arrived at 2000 B.C. However, if Aleut and modern Eskimo dialects are compared employing a refined methodology, the date of the division would be 4000 B.C. according to Bergsland. He states that the retention rate seems to vary so much that dating precision is not possible.

Attempts to correlate the linguistic and archaeological chronologies for Alaskan sites have been made by Collins (1954), Hirsch (1954), and Dumond (1965). Collins's analysis was based on early and provisional lexicostatistical dates. He accepted the 1000 B.C. split between Eskimo and Aleut but did not make a great deal of the point. Collins did, however, stress the significance of the A.D. 1000 date for the Inupik and Yupik separation, a date which more recently has been considered to range from A.D. 600 to 1000. In discussing the glottochronological results he cited evidence to suggest that the movement of the Thule culture eastward might have been around A.D. 1200 with the Inupik as the carriers. It should be noted that on the basis of an analysis of the pertinent artifacts in their context, Collins previously had placed the Thule movement from Alaska at around A.D. 900.

The glottochronological analysis of diverse Eskimo dialects and languages by Hirsch already has been cited, but he did more than refine the chronology. He also interpreted his results in light of Eskimo archaeology, particularly with reference to Alaska. He accepts a date of approximately A.D. 1000 for the Inupik separating from the Yupik and the 1000 B.C. split between Eskimo and Aleut postulated by Marsh and Swadesh. To explain the earlier split he tentatively suggests that the Na-Dene entrance into the

New World might have separated the Eskimos and Aleuts (Hirsch, 1954, 831). The assumption that an Indian population formed a wedge to separate these peoples is advanced also by Hammerich (1958b; 1960, 88), who would have the event occur in the Iliamna Lake area. A second important point by Hirsch (1954, 834) is the verification that no dialects have emerged between coastal and inland speakers of Inupik. When comparisons were made between the coastal Tareumiut and inland Nunamiut as well as between the coastal Iglulik of central Canada and the adjacent inland Caribou Eskimos, no significant differences were found in the speech of the various coastal groups or between coastal and inland groups. This observation is particularly important since the inland Eskimos often have been considered as survivors of an archaic inland population. Since their languages are the same as those of adjacent coastal Eskimos, an alternative explanation of inland Eskimo cultural origins is more reasonable. In both Canada and Alaska the inland Eskimos seem to represent a recent departure from a coastal way of life which became specialized to conditions on the inland tundras. We find, too, that according to the calculations of Hirsch (1954, 835), the Kuskowagamiut (Yuk) are removed from the Unaligmiut (Yuk) to about the same degree as the Siberian Eskimos (Yupǝk) and Nuniwagamiut (Cux) are removed from the Unaligmiut. This, however, does not fit with Hammerich's conclusions, nor with what is generally accepted to be the relationships among these dialects.

Dumond's evaluation of the lexicostatistical dates from an archaeological point of view is particularly revealing. According to him, the Eskimo-Aleut separation of 2600 B.C. should be about 4000 B.C., as it is by Bergsland's calculation. He thinks, too, that the Eskimoan and Chukotan split calculation of 3000 B.C. might more reasonably be doubled, based on archaeological and geological studies. Thus, two very critical glottochronological dates do not coincide with the other evidence. As Dumond has stressed, his interpretations of the linguistic chronology are concerned less with the absolute dating than with the network of relationships within Eskaleutian (Dumond, 1965).

In assessing the results of glottochronology for the Eskimos and Aleuts, the two provisional dates first issued were appealing since they stood in a logical relationship and they supported some existing interpretations. The release of later dates introduces more confusion than clarification. First, it is difficult to accept some of Hirsch's conclusions regarding Yupik dialectal divisions. Second, the Eskimo-Aleut split is more varied than ever if we accept Bergsland's calculations along with those of the others.

Cultural Origins

It would seem that Eskimo origins could be established rather easily since the people have a relatively uniform culture and occupy a broad but largely contiguous area. To make the matter even more straightforward, no peoples quite like the Eskimos exist anywhere else in the world, and there are comparatively few areas from which they could conceivably have arisen. Perhaps it is because of the conceptual simplicity of the problem that so many opinions have been ventured and hypotheses developed to explain how Eskimos came to be what they are, where they are. For two hundred years the subject has received attention, with study and speculation often intermingled. A brief review of the most plausible and lasting theories becomes the historical background for today's thoughts on the subject. For a recent and rather full discussion of the topic the reader is referred to Rudenko (1961, 7–19). The theories may be divided conveniently into three major groups, according to place of origin they support: somewhere deep within the Old World, somewhere in western Canada, or somewhere in the vicinity of Bering Strait.

One of the earliest supporters of an Old World origin was the Danish missionary Crantz, who in 1765 suggested that the Eskimos of Greenland were most similar to the Kalmuck, Yakut, Tungus, and Kamchadal of Asia. The ancestral Eskimos were visualized as having been driven northward by political upheavals in China. After wandering near Kamchatka, they entered the New World and arrived in Greenland during the fourteenth century A.D. (Crantz, 1767, v. 1, 258–60). The first theory based on substantive archaeological evidence was conceived by Dawkins and advanced in 1866. The theme, stated in contemporary terminology, was that an Upper Paleolithic European population with a culture adapted to arctic conditions, as represented by Magdalenian remains, moved out of Europe as the cold environment disappeared, spread eastward, and finally emerged in the New World as Eskimos. Supportive evidence was found in Magdalenian and Eskimo cultural similarities. Specifically, both peoples manufactured barbed harpoon heads, bird- and fish-spear side prongs, arrow-shaft straighteners, lance heads, and skin scrapers; their art was similar since both made engravings of hunting scenes and produced sculptured items; and finally, neither had a concern for the dead (Dawkins, 1874, 353–59). This line of reasoning was developed more fully by Sollas (1924, 577–78), who added the following traits to those cited by Dawkins: arrowpoints with ownership marks, pendant forms, snow scrapers, and smoothers. The discovery of the Chancelade skeleton in association with Magdalenian cultural remains in France seemed to validate the theory since the skull exhibited many characteristics of modern Eskimo skulls.

The first systematic archaeology in arctic America was undertaken in central Canada by Therkel Mathiassen, and as a result of his finds he developed another view of Eskimo origins. He considered the Thule culture which he discovered to be derived from the west, where its characteristic forms were present but less well developed. The theory of a western American arctic origin of Thule was based on a limited report of an excavation at Point Barrow and on the culture of the people living at Barrow at the time of historic contact. Mathiassen (1927, 182–84) concluded that Eskimo culture must have arisen somewhere north of Bering Strait in the western arctic of America or eastern arctic of Siberia.

The first orderly hypothesis based on ethnographic and linguistic data was proposed by Rink (1891, 3–23) in 1887, although
he had begun to formulate his theory earlier (Rink, 1875a,
230–32; 1875b, 70–72). Rink supported a New World center for
the coalescence of Eskimo culture. He suggested that an inland
hunting people followed interior Alaskan rivers to the sea and
here gradually developed a maritime economy. For those who
favored origins in interior North America, however, the specific
sector most often singled out as the Eskimo cultural cradle was
the area to the west of Hudson Bay. The reason cited most often
for selecting the central subarctic was that here Eskimo culture
existed in its least complex form. Such a homeland was advanced
by Murdoch (1888, 129–30), who for ethnographic reasons favored the area to the south of Hudson Bay. He concluded that
one segment pushed to Labrador and another to the west of
Hudson Bay, eventually to populate the Canadian arctic and
reach Greenland. From the same homeland came another Eskimo
population stream that moved north and west into the Yukon
River drainage, from which one segment crossed to the Mackenzie drainage to reach the sea, spread west to Bering Strait and
Siberia, and eastward to Cape Bathurst. Some of those that remained in the Yukon River system crossed to the Kuskokwim
River to spread along the southwest coast of Alaska. Boas (1888,
39) singled out the lake region to the west of Hudson Bay as the
area of dispersal but for a different reason. His judgment was
based on an analysis of myths, including origin myths, of the
surrounding tribes, and their mythology seemed to point to this
area as their homeland. The theory that Eskimo origins were east
of Alaska found additional support from Boas after the results of
the Jesup North Pacific Expedition had been evaluated. Bogoras
(1902, 670–71) already had pointed out rather striking similarities
between the folklore of the Kamchadal, Koryak, Yukaghir, and
Chukchee and that of the Indians of the Northwest Coast of
America. The same theme was developed by Jochelson (1908,
355). The Eskimos, whose folklore was said not to fit into the

pattern, formed a wedge separating these two groups. Boas (1905, 97–99) deduced that the Eskimos caused the separation when they moved into Alaska from the east. However, these general conclusions based on folklore analysis have been challenged by Chowning (1962, 1–5).

A central Canadian origin, this time in the Coronation Gulf area, was favored by Steensby. His reconstruction of Eskimo beginnings was based on an elaborate analysis of ethnographic traits and complexes, with particular reference to hunting methods and associated technology, viewed as strata or layers. The Coronation Gulf region Eskimos, who represented the oldest or Paleo-Eskimo level, had specialized arctic developments, such as hunting on the sea ice and the construction of snowhouses, which were not found in the eastern or western subarctic because of the difference in geographical factors and contacts with other peoples. This Eskimo subculture, Steensby felt, had originated from a northern Indian culture whose winter subsistence methods became adapted to hunting on sea ice as they moved into the northern ocean area. The Paleo-Eskimos, after they had reached Alaska, developed into Neo-Eskimos as a result of influences from Paleo-Siberians and other peoples in eastern Asia (Steensby, 1917, 169–71, 186, 206, 211). Hatt (1916a, 288) accepted the essence of Steensby's distributional analysis but evaluated it in terms of an age-area concept. Traits such as the throwing board, seal nets, umiaks, urine skin processing, and others which were found in the eastern and western but not the central region were old because of their widespread distribution. To explain the specialized central arctic developments, he postulated that between Hudson Bay and the Mackenzie River an inland people pushed to the coast, absorbed and partly changed the earlier peoples, and spread the Eskimo language across northern North America. A more comprehensive hypothesis, including the development of all circumpolar cultures, was later advanced by Hatt (1916b, 248–50), based largely on the analysis of clothing styles. The earlier arctic developments were oriented toward the exploitation of coastal settings, while later developments were essentially inland in character and both were of ultimate Old World origin. A key to inland survival was the snowshoe, which made it possible to hunt large land mammals during the winter. The earlier of the circumpolar cultures were found in Asia, but the inland orientation in some aspects reached its greatest complexity in the New World.

The most recent and most complex projection of Eskimo beginnings has been by Birket-Smith, and his is the last broad hypothesis based mainly on trait distributions. In a refinement of the thesis by Steensby, the Mackenzie region was considered the homeland of Proto-Eskimos, who possessed a lake-ice hunting stage of culture. The modern representatives of the Proto-Eskimos are the Caribou Eskimos who, at the time of historic contact, had combined the essential features of the lake-ice hunting stage with recent borrowings from coastal peoples to become the Eschato-Eskimos. The Proto-Eskimos migrated to the coasts north of the Barrens, and by adapting their interior hunting techniques to hunting on the frozen polar seas, they gave rise to the Paleo-Eskimos. After Paleo-Eskimo culture had expanded both east and west, the Neo-Eskimo culture developed from it, and this culture has survived in modern Alaska and Greenland (Birket-Smith, 1929, 219–33).

A thorough comparison of Eskimo and Upper Paleolithic European art was published in 1932–1933 by de Laguna. This study was designed to establish the extent of those parallels which had been assumed to exist, and was the first thorough test of an archaeologically derived hypothesis. The analysis established that similarities in motif were so few and so general that they could not be cited to favor any clear relationship (de Laguna, 1933, 98–103).

On the basis of linguistic studies, Bogoras (1924, 228) regarded the Siberian dialects of Eskimo as the most archaic, whereas Sapir (1916, 82–83) considered the center of Eskimo dispersion to be Alaska. Furthermore, both Thalbitzer (1904, 266) and Jenness (1933, 380–81), on the basis of language comparisons, favored a spread of Eskimo out of the Bering Strait area. The more recent studies by Swadesh and Hirsch, cited earlier, document the deep Alaskan roots of the Eskimo language with far greater precision than had been attempted previously.

The preceding summary of theories about Eskimo cultural origins has been introduced for historical perspective, and the examples cited are sufficient to exemplify certain points. It is notable that most linguists have considered the Bering Strait area to be the region with the deepest roots of the language. The archaeologically derived hypotheses which sought Eskimo origins deep within the Old World were based on trait similarities between peoples isolated from each other in both time and space. The work of Mathiassen, on the other hand, had a much more modest aim, to find the base from which Canadian Thule emerged, and his conclusions, which still stand, shed a narrow light on the broader problem. The only comprehensive, archaeologically based analysis was de Laguna's point-by-point comparison of Eskimo and Paleolithic art. The most complex theories were those based on ethnographic data. The wide diversity of known traits and the problem of weighing each made elaborate interpretations expectable. By and large, the later theories were refinements of earlier ones without any drastic shift in stance. It is now revealing to describe briefly the prehistory as it is seen today on the basis of archaeological discoveries and then return to more recent statements about Eskimo cultural origins.

Prehistory

So long as artifacts of Eskimo manufacture were the only types found, the problem of Eskimo emergence was separate from other northern American developments, but this is no longer the case. The time has come when finding pre-Eskimo and non-Eskimo sites in northern North America is rather commonplace, and the typological parallels reach deep into both the Old and New World. The affinities among these lithic assemblages still are vague, the areal gaps large, and temporal continuities little known. Artifact forms with the clearest and most direct bearing on Eskimo cultural origins are from the Arctic Small Tool tradition, best known from the Denbigh Flint complex levels at Iyatayet on Norton Bay (Giddings, 1964). The Arctic Small Tool tradition finds are from coastal sites or those near tree line with a geographical range from Alaska to Greenland. The manufactures are distinctive, and yet no form is restricted to this tradition alone. This assemblage may represent a flexible coalescence which became distinctive in the Bering Strait area, for in this area of Alaska the tradition seems to have been best established and is most homogeneous. There is no evidence that it is a direct transplant from the Lake Baikal area of Siberia or any other Old World stem. Typical of the finds are extremely well-made flint forms, including burins (tabular pieces of flint from which blades or spalls were struck) and retouched spalls, microblades from conical or prepared cores, small crescentic inset side blades, and small or medium-sized end points (Irving, 1962, 56–57). The Arctic Small Tool level at Iyatayet dates around 3000 B.C., but the tradition, according to William Irving, may have extended elsewhere from 4000 B.C. to 1000 B.C. The question is whether or not this tradition is in a direct line of Eskimo developments. The Arctic Small Tool tradition should logically have an economy based on sea-mammal hunting if it is to qualify as a source for Eskimo developments. Since organic preservation at this time period is exceedingly rare, judgment must be made primarily on the basis of lithic materials and site locations. The best evidence to link the Arctic Small Tool tradition with a sea-mammal-hunting economy is the coastal setting of many of the sites. These include Iyatayet on Cape Denbigh and sites near Cape Prince of Wales, Cape Espenberg, and Cape Krusenstern (Giddings, 1964, 251–57). In the Denbigh Flint complex level at Iyatayet two bone portions identified as being from small seals were recovered. Flint points for toggle harpoons of varying sizes were also found. The identification of harpoon blades is based on similar forms from the more recent Ipiutak collections (Giddings, 1964, 233).

Giddings (1964, 239–43), in a summary of the Denbigh Flint complex at Iyatayet, concluded that since there were no cache pits or house remains the site was a summer sealing and possibly caribou hunting camp. For their marine hunting the people are assumed to have had boats and perhaps to have taken walrus as well as seals. However, caribou are regarded as their primary source of food during most of the year. In the winter they are considered to have lived in a forest setting and may have had snowshoes. Giddings (1964, 242–43) was unwilling to term the remains as Eskimo, but stated: "Regardless of how we designate them, these Denbigh people appear to be in a direct line of cultural continuity with Eskimos." An inland occupancy for the makers of Denbigh Flint complex tools is clearest at sites in the Brooks Range (Campbell, 1962, 44; W. Irving, 1953, 65). The most appealing interpretation is that the Denbigh Flint complex people were both sea-mammal hunters along the coast and caribou hunters either inland or along the coasts.

By 1800 B.C. an Eskimo way of life clearly was present on the Alaskan shore of the Arctic Ocean at Cape Krusenstern. Evidence of one form of dwelling, with round or oval floor plan and a central fireplace, was found at ground level; this probably had been some type of summer tent or log structure. The second dwelling form was semisubterranean with rounded corners, a short, shallow tunnel, and several rooms, with the main room at times supported by four posts. The main room had a large central fireplace, but the one to three smaller adjoining rooms had no fireplaces. The residents hunted small seals and great whales, but they rarely took bearded seals or caribou. It has been suggested by Giddings (1961b, 164–66; 1962, 46–48) that the occupants hunted whales in an organized manner from umiaks. Furthermore they possessed the dog. Although these manifestations, called Old Whaling, are known from only one site, it is clear that this technology was separate from the Arctic Small Tool tradition and was based on sea-mammal hunting.

Just as the Old Whaling culture is ill defined, so is the succeeding phase, the Choris culture. The latter finds date about 700 B.C. and are known from the Choris Peninsula on Kotzebue Sound. At the type site one of three large oval houses, with the largest pit measuring about forty feet long and twenty-five feet wide, was excavated and interpreted as a large dwelling. The excavated structure had been heated and lighted with lamps, and the people had made thin, feather-tempered pots which they decorated with a linear stamp. The lithic technology in some of its characteristics was obviously derived from the Arctic Small Tool tradition, but in general the manufactures in flint were distinctive. One innovation was the occasional use of slate, which was not polished as would be expected but was scraped into knife-blade forms. The inventory of artifacts included sea-hunting equipment, but remains of caribou were prevalent in the bone counts. These remains again have a distinctiveness which may without doubt be termed as emergent Alaskan Eskimo. The typological similarities are nearer the succeeding Norton culture than the earlier Denbigh Flint complex remains (Giddings, 1957, 121–35; 1962, 37–38).

The Norton culture, best known at Iyatayet, began slightly later than Choris and may with even more clarity be identified as Eskimo. The Norton people were firmly committed to coastal living. The one excavated house was occupied throughout most of the year, and seal hunting was seemingly more important than any other subsistence activity. The seventeen-foot-wide house was basically rectangular, but an extension at the front of the dwelling made this section as long as the house was wide. A short tunnel, with a floor lower than the house floor, led off the extension. There was a central fireplace, but stone lamps also had been used. The people cooked in clay vessels, usually with rounded or conical bases; some vessels had small suspension holes. The pots were most often fiber-tempered, and surface treatment was most often made with check or linear stamps. Seal hunting probably was accomplished largely during the spring at the edge of the ice, whereas salmon fishing with gill nets possibly was most intensive at the mouths of nearby rivers. In technological terms the people still worked stone by the chipping process and favored basalt as a raw material. Slate scraping was rare as at Choris, and heavy woodworking adzes were not present. Flake knives and beaver-tooth tools were the primary woodworking tools, and other manufactures included labrets and stone saws. Since organic preservation was poor, the picture of the nonlithic technology is inadequate (Giddings, 1964, 135–37, 184–90, 271–74).

The Norton culture is approximated with the Near Ipiutak finds at Point Hope, and they share such distinctive features as pottery, an emerging slate industry, and stone lamps. Near Ipiutak developed into Ipiutak, which on the basis of radiocarbon dates is more recent than either Norton or Near Ipiutak and dates around A.D. 300. Seventy-two of the six hundred or more houses at the type site were excavated along with about one hundred burials identified as Ipiutak. The square, semisubterranean houses were built of driftwood, but it is unlikely that all the houses were occupied simultaneously. The roofs, when their construction form was discernible, were supported by four posts, and the floors of short entrance passages, when they were found, were either at the level of the house floor or above it. Inside the house was a fireplace, and low wooden platforms usually had extended along three sides for sleeping and lounging. It was reasoned on the basis of the thin debris layer on the floors and the animal bone counts that the houses were occupied during spring and summer when seals and walrus were hunted by a population that spent the remainder of the year elsewhere hunting caribou. Furthermore, 22 percent of the total number of artifacts were associated with the bow-and-arrow complex, whereas only 3 percent were associated directly with sea-mammal hunting. About half of the nearly 10,000 artifacts recovered were of flint, and diverse forms were knapped, including end points and side blades for arrows;

knife, lance, and harpoon blades; diverse scrapers; and less common forms. The stoneworking approached the Denbigh Flint
complex in its refinement, and a few of the characteristic forms
from the Arctic Small Tool tradition are present. It must be
noted, too, that one small piece of wrought iron found at Point
Hope Ipiutak is a clear Old World tie. The most remarkable of all
Ipiutak manufactures were the grave goods. Among the finds
were skulls in which artificial ivory eyeballs with jet pupils replaced the actual eyes, while in other cases ivory covers were
placed over the eyes of the dead. Nostril plugs and mouth covers
of ivory were found, and in one instance an ivory rod had been
inserted into the spinal canal of a skeleton. Associated with burials, too, were swivels which appear to have been nonfunctional,
chains carved from a single piece of ivory, and fantastically
shaped nonfunctional arrowheads. These and other finds suggest a
complex cult of the dead and well-developed shamanism (Larsen
and Rainey, 1948).

The Birnirk site at Point Barrow, which dates around A.D.
700, has many more typological similarities with the St. Lawrence
Island periods of Okvik and Old Bering Sea than with nearby
Point Hope Ipiutak. Okvik, Old Bering Sea I, and Birnirk shared
such characteristics as the umiak, kayak, and baleen toboggan;
snow goggles of one piece; knife-blade and knife-handle forms;
the fire drill; and pottery which was usually crudely made and
thick (Ford, 1959, 240). By Old Bering Sea and Birnirk times the
organic preservation of artifacts is excellent in most Eskimo sites,
and the equipment for sea-mammal hunting is quite complex. The
toggle harpoon head fit into a foreshaft which in turn was seated
in a socketpiece (Fig. 1). The socketpiece was attached to a
wooden shaft, which might have a finger rest for greater control
in propelling the weapon. An ice pick was hafted to the base of a
shaft, but if an ice pick and finger rest were not used, then the
weapon was propelled with the aid of a throwing board. A line
from the harpoon head was tied to a float with a distinctive type
of plug. After an animal had been wounded, a detachable lance

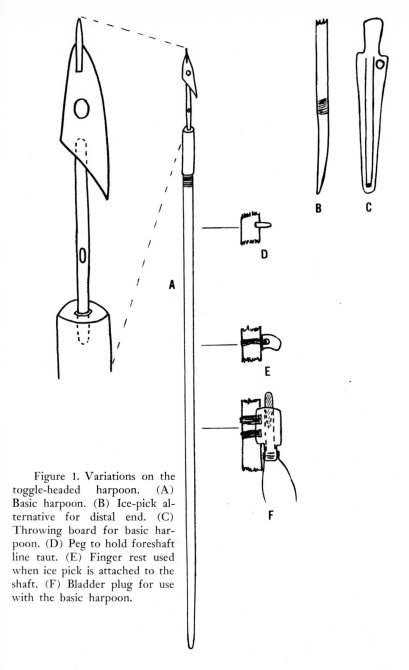

Figure 1. Variations on the toggle-headed harpoon. (A) Basic harpoon. (B) Ice-pick alternative for distal end. (C) Throwing board for basic harpoon. (D) Peg to hold foreshaft line taut. (E) Finger rest used when ice pick is attached to the shaft. (F) Bladder plug for use with the basic harpoon.

might be fastened to the retrieved harpoon shaft and the animal killed. Wooden plugs were inserted into the wounds of dead animals in order to save the blood. The harpoon complex remained much the same down to the time of historic contact, and except for some stylistic variations and decorative motifs, the oldest forms often are like the most recent ones (Ford, 1959, 75–116; Rainey, 1941, 544).

It was out of a late Birnirk or a closely associated phase that Western Thule stemmed around A.D. 1300. Forty-six traits connect early Thule of central Canada with Birnirk of Alaska. A few of the more distinctive ones include the sinew-backed bow and associated sinew twisters; the whaling lance and whaling harpoon heads; large, crude bola balls; and the bow and fire drills, as well as adz, knife, and scraper forms (Ford, 1959, 241). By about A.D. 1400 modern Eskimo culture in the American arctic had taken form. Although there were subsequent changes before historic contact, none were as great as those which had given rise to Thule. Accepting Old Whaling as the first unquestioned Eskimo adaptation to an arctic maritime economy and Thule as the culmination of Eskimo adaptability, almost 3,000 years elapsed before the final emergence.

In the archaeological summary thus far, the geographical focus has been in the vicinity of Seward Peninsula. In this region the sequence is most complete, although lengthy gaps exist between cultures and the dimensions of such critical phases as Old Whaling and Choris barely are known. The conservatism of Alaskan Eskimos tends, however, to make the line of development relatively smooth even without closely successive local sequences. The names for the various archaeological cultures suggest a discreteness of the units, but they are better regarded as convenient markers of general time periods.

The longest and most reliable sequence of Eskimo prehistory south of Norton Bay is for the Naknek River drainage adjoining Bristol Bay. The earliest remains identified in the Naknek River drainage are termed Brooks River Gravels phase and date about

2000 B.C. The stone tools recall those of the Arctic Small Tool tradition except that burins are absent. Just before 1000 B.C., during the Brooks River Hilltop phase, the affinities in lithic technology again point to northern Alaskan sources, although the ground-stone adzes suggest ties with the Northwest Coast. There are no finds for the first millennium B.C., but by the time of the Smelt Creek phase, early in the Christian era, the influence of the Norton culture is well attested. Some types suggestively parallel Choris forms; on the other hand, they might have been derived from the north Pacific coast. A clear northern source for new ideas ranged through the first millennium A.D., whereas the Brooks River Falls phase, at the end of this time period, witnessed a shift in the lithic technology which might have been caused by influences from interior Alaska. Two hundred years later in the Brooks River Camp phase we have changes from the north which ultimately were of the same nature as those which gave rise to the Thule expansion eastward from northern Alaska. This phase carried across the Alaska Peninsula to the Pacific Ocean drainages. For the first and only time in the sequence, at around A.D. 1200, the southern Bering Sea coast cultural forms were paralleled by those on the Pacific drainages in important details. After this time ties between the Naknek River area sequence and the Pacific area were far less striking (Dumond, 1962).

A deep kitchen midden along the northern edge of Bristol Bay at the head of Togiak Bay was sampled by Markoto Kowta. The excavated area of the midden was judged to date from A.D. 1000 to 1700. It is particularly worthy of note that artifact forms and bone counts indicate a fluctuation of economic pursuits in the upper levels of the site. The Togiak Eskimos throughout the time of the excavated midden deposits had always hunted sea mammals, but from the proportions of bones and forms of weapons it appears that winter and spring sealing increased in the latter period, but without marked success. Accompanying this shift was an increase in land hunting, possibly in the winter, and summer shellfish gathering became more important. Another change was toward a decrease in summer netting of fish and an increase in ice fishing in the winter. The decrease in seal takes, as indicated in bone counts, perhaps resulted from a combination of over-hunting and a gradual silting up of the bay. These factors to-gether would tend to lead to a search for the partial replacement of seals in the diet. The result seems to have been that the people left the village during the summer and fished along the Togiak River (Kowta, ms.). What seems most important in the recent but prehistoric Togiak developments is the flexibility of the economy, a characteristic which conforms to our expectations of Eskimos. They could turn either to the sea, the rivers, or inland as environ-mental and social conditions changed.

In this résumé of Alaskan Eskimo archaeology it has been assumed that the Arctic Small Tool tradition is the most likely source out of which Eskimo culture could have arisen. The tradition has a number of characteristics which make it an appeal-ing base. Seemingly it was functioning at about the right time period, it has been identified both with coastal and inland settings, and the original forms fade gradually from the inventory which reflects later Eskimo developments. Furthermore, from the Chukchi Sea to Bristol Bay the succession of changes during the last three thousand years has been much the same, with the general spread of ideas from north to south. Thus far attention has focused on the Western Eskimo heartland from the Arctic Ocean to Bristol Bay, and only those developments leading in a clear line to modern Eskimo emergence have been considered. It is now necessary to turn to more tangentially pertinent develop-ments, those finds which are earlier than the Arctic Small Tool tradition and those characteristic of the historic Pacific Eskimo area.

At Cape Krusenstern two lithic complexes which emerged before the Arctic Small Tool tradition have been identified. The earlier, dating prior to 4000 B.C., is termed Palisades I, and most numerous among the finds were bifacially flaked tools which had been percussion chipped. Some bear a broad resemblance to Asian chopping tools, while others invoke comparison with the Levalloi-sian flaking technique. Any Old World parallels seem both vague and very generalized according to Giddings (1961b, 157–59). The Palisades II complex from the same area is judged to date around 4000 B.C. The most striking form from this period is the side-notched end point, which is accompanied by scrapers and broad end blades. The side-notched points find widespread paral-lels in forms, suggestively early, in interior Alaska and at other localities in the American arctic (Giddings, 1961b, 159–61). Men-tion must also be made of the Anangula Island finds. This small island is five miles off the northern coast of Umnak Island near the base of the Aleutian chain. The manufactures include mainly large stone blades struck from polyhedral cores, plus retouched blades formed into scrapers, knives, and gravers; the finds date prior to 6000 B.C. (Laughlin, 1963, 633–34; Laughlin and Aigner, 1966; McCartney and Turner, 1966). The affinity of these finds with the Arctic Small Tool tradition is debated. On one hand they stand apart in the generally large size of the artifacts, plus the absence of projectile points, side blades, and burins (Irving, 1962, 61). However, the cores are small, and some of the micro-blades fit into the defined tradition. Allowing for subsequent changes over two or more millennia the Anangula materials may well serve as the Arctic Small Tool tradition base (Dumond, 1965, 1250). If the latter interpretation is closer to reality, then the Aleutian finds may be the products of proto-Eskimos and Aleuts.

As noted, the Pacific drainage sequence, when compared with that of the Bristol Bay region, stands as largely distinctive except for the period around A.D. 1200. The longest and clearest progression in the area is recorded in a publication by Clark (1966), whose work was on Sitkalidak and adjacent Kodiak is-lands. His material provides a major step forward in this area of long-standing obscurity and confusion. The earliest finds, Ocean Bay I at around 3500 B.C., contain a chipped-stone assemblage with flaked points having contracting stems, other bifacially chipped blades, a small pecked-stone lamp, and a few pieces of abraded slate. By Ocean Bay II times, 2000 B.C., sawed- and ground-slate tools predominated. Although the number of artifacts recovered is small, the technological differences are striking, and the earlier forms are not duplicated as a configuration elsewhere in Alaska. The more recent forms are similar only to isolated finds in southwestern Alaska, except perhaps for finds on the adjacent Alaska Peninsula. Furthermore, the slate manufactures do not match the slate work at Kachemak Bay I found along Cook Inlet. The next phase, near the end of the second millennium B.C., is poorly defined, but the earlier levels at the Three Saints site extend from the early Christian era to about A.D. 800. The ground-slate technology, which included double-edged knives with serrated bases, barbed and unbarbed stemmed points, ulu blades, and other objects, belongs to the Kachemak tradition. Between the end of this phase and the next, termed Koniag, there was a change in types, quality of workmanship, and artifact style. Little is known about the shift from the Three Saints to the Koniag phase, which began about A.D. 1550. Clark thinks that the shift was more likely gradual than abrupt, a contrast with Hrdlička's view of a meaningful break, but the picture is not clear at this point. It is safe to say, however, that the archaeology in the historic homeland of the Pacific Eskimo is largely separate from the sequences along the coasts of the Bering Sea and Arctic Ocean.

Recent Studies of Origins

It is concurred that within the circumpolar zone the Bering Strait region is the area in which the Eskimo developmental sequence has the greatest continuity and antiquity. It might be assumed that this was where Eskimos first arose as a distinct cultural entity. The excavators of the major Western Eskimo area sites, however, have been attracted to other areas when interpreting the origins of their finds. They are less concerned with ultimate origins than with the roots of artifact forms and technologies. The tendency has been to shift from seeking a hypothetical cradle to the analysis of trait distributions which coalesced among the Eskimos. Attempts to establish either the homeland of Eskimos or the origins of key Eskimo characteristics are presented in the pages to follow. These descriptions stress recent definitive statements with little or no attention devoted to subsequent restatements.

The first attempt to trace the geographical distribution of artifact types on a large scale was by de Laguna, who used the Kachemak Bay finds as a base. Her analysis was of limited scope because of the scarcity of comparative materials, but the general conclusion was that diverse ties reached in all directions. The bonds were most prominent with the Thule culture of northern Alaska and Canada, but strong cultural links existed also with the Aleuts, fewer with Kodiak Island Eskimos, and more remote connections with the southern Northwest Coast. It also seemed important that Kamchatka and Neolithic Japan exerted an influence on the emergence and development of Cook Inlet Eskimo culture (de Laguna, 1934, 211–17). The distributional ties cited have little specific meaning since the time factor could not be controlled. They do demonstrate, however, that the occupants of Alaska's Pacific coasts were influenced for almost 3,000 years by very diverse peoples from an extremely wide area. This in itself is important because it suggests a breadth of direct and indirect contacts among peoples of the north Pacific arc.

The most comprehensive interpretations of Eskimo archaeology, based on the comparison of specific forms, have been made by Collins and developed largely from the analysis of his excavations on St. Lawrence Island. The known St. Lawrence Island sequence mirrors Siberian developments far better than it does the pattern on mainland Alaska, but still the far-reaching comparisons by Collins are important. The significance of the Thule developments was for the first time placed in proper perspective. Many of

the key Thule forms, which are basic Eskimo traits, were identified as widespread in usage before Thule emerged and were found
to exhibit a great deal of temporal and spatial continuity from the
beginning of the Christian era. The distinctiveness of Thule originated out of a late Birnirk base in Alaska, and the culture then
spread to central Canada. In prehistoric but recent times a regional distinctiveness developed in Canada, and certain characteristics, such as the technology surrounding dog traction, were
carried back into Alaska. Collins commented on the idea of Boas
that a westward migration from Canada into Alaska occurred, but
he attributed it to the return movement of Canadian Thule Eskimos into Alaska. In the quest for Eskimo origins the Old World
was cited by Collins as the most probable region because of the
widespread Eurasian distribution of typical historic Eskimo characteristics such as skin boats, sleds, toboggans, the toggle harpoon,
lamps, and ground slate. If any area of emergence was visualized,
it was between the Kara Sea and Bering Strait where a people
may have moved from interior rivers to the arctic seas. The more
remote ancestors of the earliest St. Lawrence cultures were
thought to have perhaps lived between the mouths of the Anadyr
and Kolyma rivers of eastern Siberia (Collins, 1937, 361–83).

   The discovery of the Ipiutak site and the resulting descrip-
tive monograph by Larsen and Rainey (1948), as well as a later
paper by Larsen (1952), brought forth another effort to establish
Eskimo origins on the basis of the distribution of certain select
forms. That Ipiutak ties were strongest with Asia was obvious
from the flint technology, the animal style interpreted as Scytho-
Siberian, and the knowledge of wrought iron, but to localize the
area of possible origin proved more difficult. The authors, however, became convinced that the vicinity of the Yamal Peninsula
of western Siberia offered the most promise. According to their
interpretations, sea-mammal hunters who used harpoons from
kayaks and stressed hunting walrus had lived in this region. A
bronze object with a bearhead design from the Yamal area site
meant that these people had contacts with metal casters to the

south, and the bear was similar in form to an Ipiutak one made of ivory. The fact that the chains and openwork carvings of ivory at Point Hope Ipiutak might have been imitations of iron objects was taken as further evidence that contacts between the sea-mammal hunters gave rise to Ipiutak and metal-working peoples. Further similarities were found in decorative motifs such as skeletal designs and joint markers in bronze from the western Ural Mountain region. Thus we again have Eskimo, or at least Ipiutak Eskimo, origins sought deep within the Old World but without intermediary links with the Bering Sea region.

Another comprehensive theory based on a detailed site report is by Rudenko (1961). In 1945 the Uwelen site and others on the Chukchee Peninsula of extreme eastern Siberia were excavated. The earliest finds were closely related to the St. Lawrence Island period called Okvik, which was a flourishing Eskimo culture characterized by complex gear for hunting sea mammals, including toggle-headed harpoons employed by men using kayaks and umiaks. The origins of such a marine economy, already well established shortly before the time of Christ, should be sought somewhere to the south of extreme eastern Asia according to Rudenko. Since neither toggle harpoon heads nor Eskimo cultural remains have been found to the west of the Kolyma River mouth and since the shallow coastal waters to the west are uninhabitable for sea mammals, it is not logical that Eskimo culture could have originated in northern Siberia. On the Kurile Islands, however, toggle harpoon heads have been found, which leads Rudenko to expect that a maritime culture based on sea-mammal hunting will be discovered on Kamchatka. In summary Rudenko (1961, 176) stated: "Thus, it is to the south, across Kamchatka, to the island chain fringing the continent of Asia on the east, to the area where seamanship and the harpoon complex are developed from early times that we must keep looking to solve the problem of the origin of the ancient culture of the Bering Sea area."

One of the theories yet unmentioned that has a bearing on Eskimo origins concerns the continuity in the means for making a living in the circumpolar north, along with the occurrence of specific traits and complexes. In 1931 Bogoras wrote of the essentially homogeneous nature of arctic and subarctic climate, geography, fauna, and flora. In the same article a classification of economic adjustments to northern living was presented. One particular point of note is the remark that the north Eurasian coastal area is rich in sea mammals only at the extreme eastern portion and in the west around the Yamal Peninsula and White Island (Bogoras, 1931, 465–82). A distributional study of circumpolar cultural forms was made by Gjessing (1944), who later (1960) analyzed the continuities in social life among northern peoples. In the earlier study Gjessing recorded numerous examples of specific forms which were distributed from Norway to Greenland. Among the most widespread traits he listed were the open skin boat or umiak, toggle harpoon heads, side prongs for fish spears, slate end-blade forms, semilunar knife blades, gouges of slate, comb-marked pottery, and other less significant specific manufactures and art forms. In his discussion of circumpolar kinship systems and social structure Gjessing took the Lapp form as the working model. It was described as classificatory, extended bilaterally with sibling solidarity as well as unity of cousins and in-laws of the same generation. There was local or village exogamy. This system, with other features and innumerable variations, was thought to be very widespread in the north, and diverse peoples with systems similar to that of the Lapps were mentioned to validate the working hypothesis.

Of all the areas from which the wanderings of Eskimos are traced before they settled in northern America, the favored place of ultimate origins for Americanists has been northern Europe. This hypothesis has a great deal in its favor since it projects the movement of a people across the breadth of one vast ecological zone. The idea of Eskimo ancestors in Europe having "followed the reindeer northward" and then wandering east originated with Dawkins, was expanded by Sollas, and seemed to be manifest in studies by Gjessing. While Collins never went as far as some of the others, he was nonetheless drawn to the idea of a northern Asian cradle. It might be mentioned that the hazy linguistic ties thought to connect the Eskimo and Indo-European phyla at one time might offer additional substantive support for the theory of European origin.

One of the most serious impediments to the development of more sound hypotheses concerning Eskimo origins was the stress placed on circumpolar trait continuities. The idea of circumpolar unity in culture and society is inviting if arctic peoples and their ways are viewed as largely unchanging for great spans of time in a static environment. But with careful attempts to trace the spatial continuity for most complexes from people to people, or from one area to another, the thesis dissolves into an outmoded point of view.

In spite of the accumulated evidence it seems unlikely that there were direct continuities between Upper Paleolithic Europeans and the emergence of modern Eskimo culture. The European cradle may be refuted with diverse lines of evidence which become impressive when tallied. The only thorough test of the hypothesis was by de Laguna for Paleolithic and Eskimo art, but the results were negative. When this work is cited at all, it is usually noted that the study is not conclusive because of the finds made after its publication; however, the original study and its conclusions have not been disproved.

The Upper Paleolithic Solutrean phase in Europe, beginning about 17,000 B.C., although earlier than the Magdalenian from which Eskimo culture has often been considered to arise, deserves passing comment. The reason is that the source for early lithic industries in the New World sometimes has been sought in the Solutrean. Any connections in these lithic industries would tend to strengthen the possibility of Magdalenian and Eskimo ties. Smith (1962, 58–67) interprets the Solutrean as a brief phase of prehistory restricted to western Europe and doubts that the early New World manufactures in flint were derived from it. Virtually all of the traits of the circumpolar stone age cited by Gjessing are not only quite late, post-Mesolithic in Scandinavia (Moberg, 1960, 67–74), but furthermore, the distributional links are scattered widely and do not form a continuous chain. Even if geographical continuities were to be found, it is most doubtful that they would form associational units representative of a culture, which is an essential prerequisite. To find isolated traits is not enough; it must be demonstrated that a tradition of sea-mammal hunting as such spread across northern Eurasia. The traits comprising the hypothetical culture could not logically be forms which are more recent than the known beginnings of Eskimo culture. This would eliminate not only the ground-slate items cited by Gjessing but the pottery as well. Furthermore, as Bogoras noted, the low coastal shelf along the northern coast of central and most of western Siberia was and is largely unsuited for sea mammals, making it unlikely that the remains of sea-mammal hunters will ever be found in this area.

Another line of negative evidence is the failure of physical anthropologists to link the Eskimo physical type with Upper Paleolithic European populations.

In recent years Chard has dealt with Eskimo origins more often than any other anthropologist. He has not ignored trait distributions in his search, but he has concentrated more on the Old World background from which Eskimo and other New World peoples could have arisen. Chard's major contribution has been to summarize and interpret contemporary Russian sources, none of which derive Eskimos from the northern coast of Asia. It is with justification that Chard harshly criticizes other American writers who have built largely mythological ties across northern Eurasia to Bering Strait. Chard makes many telling points to destroy the theory. One critical fact is that the Eskimo sites between Bering Strait and Bear Islands in eastern Siberia, nearly 1,000 miles apart, are oldest in the east and become progressively more recent to the west (Chard, 1955, 168–69). Second, at the Yamal Peninsula sites, critical in the reconstruction of Ipiutak origins, there is no evidence in original sources for kayaks or toggle harpoons. The people did hunt sea mammals, but not necessarily on the seas in the Eskimo pattern (Chard, 1959, 82–84). It has been over ten years since Chard's first synthesis of Russian materials was published. In spite of the far-reaching implications of his conclusions, they have hardly dented tradition. It often is commented how conservative Eskimos have been through time; a less rational conservatism seems to prevail among Eskimologists.

If Eskimo culture did not arise in Europe, northern coastal Asia, or central Canada, and if it was rather fully developed by the Christian era in the vicinity of Bering Strait, then Eskimo origins might be sought somewhere along the Pacific littoral. An east Asian site with a bearing on the problem is along Lake Ushki in east central Kamchatka, where four separate time horizons have been isolated. The earliest level, which dates around 8700 B.C., contained a microlithic flint industry in which prepared cores and microblades were important along with small end blades and scrapers. Centering about 4000 B.C., burins were found along with delicately flaked end points. In a general way, these finds recall the Arctic Small Tool tradition. During the second millennium B.C. in eastern Siberia pottery appears, accompanied by ground-stone tools, labrets, and a continuation of fine flint-chipping technology. In the Chukchee Peninsula toggle harpoon heads did not appear until the first millennium B.C. In the middle of this span there was reportedly a lowering of local temperatures accompanied by a deforestation of the coastal area. According to Dikov (1965, 10–25), in the area where the Pacific Ocean and Bering Sea meet, there were large numbers of sea mammals, and it was here that Eskimo culture arose. In this interpretation it should be recalled that the Old Whaling remains at Cape Krusenstern, Alaska, date 1800 B.C. and reflect an already developed economy of sea-mammal hunting.

Resting the case for Asiatic origins, it is time to mention another contender which has been lingering in the shadows. Ethnologists and to a lesser extent archaeologists have recognized that cultural ties existed uniting the Northwest Coast Indians with the Eskimos, particularly the Pacific Eskimos. It has been assumed that the Indians came primarily under Eskimo influence, but it now seems more likely that Eskimos were the greater borrowers. Excavations made recently in southern British Columbia by Borden (1962, 9–19) indicate that by about 1000 B.C. the basic adaptations of Northwest Coast Indian culture already had taken place. The people had a maritime-based economy which included the use of harpoon darts as well as toggle harpoon heads. A ground-slate technology existed, the general Northwest Coast art styles were flourishing, and the people probably were skilled wood-workers, as indicated by some of their tools. Borden's thesis is that, prior to Eskimo times, there were important ties between the interiors of western Asia and western North America. The case is particularly good for the ground-slate industry. In the Siberian Neolithic, around 5000 B.C. or somewhat thereafter, slate forms were manufactured which are similar to those recovered at the Fraser River area throughout the first millennium B.C. In Eskimo sites, however, ground-slate tools did not become dominant until around the beginning of the Christian era. Thus, in studying the relationships between Eskimo culture and the cultures of other peoples, it is necessary to consider both sides of the north Pacific Ocean.

Chapter 3

Biology

Meaningful generalizations about Eskimos as a racial group are limited by the regional variations in their physical type. The earliest investigators were not greatly troubled by the problem because their sample came primarily from the eastern American arctic and they were unaware of the range in differences. Later studies have described the diversity, but no one has arrived at an acceptable theory to accommodate it. The classic Eskimo physical type is distinguished mainly on the basis of the head form, which is said to be among the most distinctive in the world. The skull is long, narrow, high, and topped with a heavy ridge. The face is not only high, but it is also broader than the width of the skull. The forehead is narrow, and browridges are weakly developed (Collins, 1951, 441). This head form, with other distinguishing features as well, is most typical of the Greenland Eskimos. Furthermore, when the generalization is made that Eskimos have blood type O to the virtual exclusion of other types in the ABO series, the statement applies only to what is assumed to have been a pure breeding isolate, the Polar Eskimos of northwestern

Greenland (Laughlin, 1950, 166–67). It is clear that the view once accepted of the Eskimo physical type applies best to the people of a limited area in the eastern arctic. Eskimos are said to be fat, but such is not the case. It is only their bulky clothing that gives them the appearance of being corpulent; typical Eskimos are lean, heavy-boned, and muscular. A more valid statement of their general appearance would first take cognizance of their Mongoloid characteristics: large head, broad mandible with very broad ascending ramus, medium to narrow nose, short to medium stature, small hands and feet, and relatively short legs in proportion to their total height (Laughlin, 1950, 168; 1963, 642). In the following text Alaskan Eskimos are considered briefly in terms of morphology and at greater length with reference to blood factors, physiological processes, and diseases.

Morphology

During the past twenty years most physical anthropologists have become cautious when comparing biological characteristics in human populations. There was a period in the recent past when the overt appearance of the living and the bones of the dead were compared boldly to derive far-reaching statements about physical relationships. At a later date it was felt that an analysis of blood from peoples around the world would provide a better index to genetic ties. While blood-group analysis has offered another broad dimension to the understanding of physical man, it has not provided the clear-cut answers once expected. The contemporary study of bones and soft tissue suffers from the problem of not being able to isolate either the genetic factors involved or the adaptive value of noted traits. This restriction does not mean that these studies are useless, but the inferences drawn are much more limited in scope than those which would have been accepted only twenty years ago. An analysis of skeletal characteristics for a given population may, for example, offer clues to the stability of the people in a particular geographical region, an extremely useful type of information. No attempt will be made here to trace the history of Eskimo biological analyses, and no stress will be placed on comparative studies of skeletal materials or living populations. What will be dealt with are certain critical archaeological finds that are important in influencing our overall view of those who are known racially as Eskimos.

CHANCELADE SKULL

Some early discussions of the Eskimo physical type stressed the morphological similarities with the Chancelade skull found in 1888 at a Magdalenian site in the Dordogne of France. During the Magdalenian, the final stage of the European Paleolithic sequence, numerous artifact forms were produced which have counterparts in aboriginal Eskimo cultures. From about 1870 onward, various interpreters of the Magdalenian, but particularly Dawkins (1874, 353–59, 425) and Sollas (1924, 577–84), suggested that the Eskimos represent a surviving Upper Paleolithic population which followed the retreating glaciers northward and then spread east to arctic America. With this view of Eskimo origins it is understandable that Eskimo skeletal material would be weighed with the Magdalenian skeletons in mind. The comparisons stressed the narrowness of the skull, the broad face, the powerful jaws, and the palatine torus or bony ridge at the roof of the mouth. After other human skulls from the Upper Paleolithic of Europe had been found, however, it could be seen that the Chancelade skull fit well into the series and did not represent a unique development. Additionally, while a feature such as the palatine torus is characteristic of some Eskimos, it is also found in Lapps and north Europeans, as well as among other peoples. These facts minimize the importance of similarities between Chancelade and Eskimos (Lasker, 1961, 124–25).

HOMO ERECTUS PEKINENSIS

It once was widely accepted that the Mongoloid racial strain first was notable in the fossil bones of *Sinanthropus pekinensis,* dating from the mid-Pleistocene of China and now classed as *Homo erectus pekinensis* (Campbell, 1963, 69). The points of similarity between these skulls and those of Eskimos include the midline ridge, mandibular torus or projection of bone on the lower jaw behind the canine teeth, large pulp cavities in the teeth, and shovel-shaped incisors, that is, teeth on which the inner surfaces have a scooped-out appearance. Although it is true that many Eskimos and Mongoloids in general have these characteristics, they have also been found in other populations. Additionally, no later finds in China suggest a clear line of development from *H. erectus pekinensis* to modern Mongoloids. The current evidence suggests to Laughlin (1963, 643) that the Mongoloid racial form did not become distinct until some time between 13,000 and 8,000 b.c. and no direct link is known to exist between Peking man, the emergence of the Mongoloid race, and Eskimos (Chang, 1962a, 758–59; Lasker, 1961, 95–98).

ALASKAN ARCHAEOLOGICAL FINDS

In Alaska the earliest skeletal remains of man from a clear context occur at the Chaluka site on Umnak Island in the eastern sector of the Aleutian Islands. The one Paleo-Aleut skull, dating around 2000 b.c. and mentioned by Laughlin, is longheaded and has a thickening of the vault which is characteristic of certain forms of anemia. The general trend in head form among the Aleuts is from an early, longheaded population to one which emerged in historic times as broadheaded. The evidence suggests that a gradual change from one head form to the other took place with no influx of an alien population strain (Laughlin, 1963, 638–45).

The most important collection of Alaskan Eskimo skeletal material is from burials found at Point Hope. One group of sixty skulls dates about a.d. 1–300 and is from a Near Ipiutak or Ipiutak cultural context. The Point Hope series includes also the skeletons of about two hundred thirty adults which date after about a.d. 1600 and were associated with Tigara cultural remains. An analysis of the entire collection by Debetz (1959) led him to several conclusions. Both the Ipiutak and Tigara skulls belong to the northern branch of the Mongoloid stock but stand apart from American Indians. However, the Tigara population is not viewed as having stemmed directly from the Ipiutak people. Furthermore, in the features of a low cranial vault, a bizygomatic breadth shorter than the cranial vault breadth, and a lack of prognathism, the Ipiutak skulls are most like the Baikal type represented by the Reindeer Tungus and their likely ancestors the Yukaghir.

The oldest Eskimo skulls date from around 200 B.C. and are from the Uwelen cemetery on the Chukchee Peninsula in Siberia. The skulls are longheaded, a characteristic also of the Old Bering Sea skulls from St. Lawrence Island and a trait to be expected since the Uwelen cultural materials fit well into the Old Bering Sea sequence (Levin, 1959). In Alaska the longheaded Eskimo type is best known from the Point Barrow burials at Birnirk which date between A.D. 400 and 900. The Birnirk skulls are long, high, and narrow, and are most similar to series from Greenland and Labrador. More recent Eskimo skulls from Point Barrow, as well as the Tigara skulls, tend to be more broadheaded than the earlier ones (Collins, 1951, 449; Hrdlička, 1930, 323; Stewart, 1959, 251).

LIVING POPULATIONS

A large number of general observations have been made about the physical characteristics of living Eskimos. Most of the systematic information was assembled and interpreted by Hrdlička (1930), but because of changes in methodology it seems to have little meaning among physical anthropologists today. A compilation of the available information by Shapiro (1931) offers a general view of Alaskan Eskimos in terms of the established measurements and observations. The mean measurements shown in the table are for adult males. Alaskan Eskimos are taller than non-Alaskan ones; for example, in a sample of eight Smith Sound Eskimos in Greenland the mean height for males was 157.4 cm. In

general, from northern Alaska southward and from north to east
the mean heights decrease. Cephalic indices have a general uniformity among Eskimos except that the Kodiak Islanders are
extremely broadheaded with an average cephalic index of 87.15.
Within Alaska the tendency toward broadheadedness increases
from north to south. There also is a slight decrease in facial index
and an increase in nasal index among Eskimos from the east to the
west (Laughlin, 1950, Table 5).

		Indices		
Sample and Size	Stature in cm.	Cephalic	Facial	Nasal
Point Hope (13)	166.5	78.3		
Noatak (11–12)	167.9	81.6	82.5	66.8
Seward Peninsula (39–40)	165.4	78.0	84.9	71.2
Southwestern Alaska (61)	162.4	80.7	84.9	69.3

In a sample of forty males, largely from western Seward
Peninsula, most of the men had straight black hair and brown
eyes. Epicanthic folds were absent in a quarter of the men and
marked for only one man, while the balance tended to have slight
or medium folds. Facial hair on the cheeks was slight in about an
eighth of the sample and absent in the others; facial hair on the
chin was absent in half of the number and marked for only two
persons. Facial hair above the lip was of a medium amount for
half of the men and ranged widely for the balance. In general,
unexposed skin areas were only slightly darker than among Europeans, but exposed areas had weathered to various shades of
brown (Shapiro, 1931, 356–58). Another characteristic which has
been noted for Alaskan Eskimos is the frequency of hypermobil-
ity of the joints, especially of the fingers and wrists (Blumberg et
al., 1961, 335). Learned behaviors which are commonly observed
include flexing from the hips when bending over and extending
the legs forward in a straight line when sitting.

BLOOD TYPES

In the ABO blood series it has been found generally that American Indians have no B allele present, whereas the Mongoloid peoples of Asia have the highest frequencies of type B in the world. As would be expected, Alaskan Eskimos have a type B, but in a relatively low frequency. A comparison of the ABO percentage frequencies for three well-sampled segments of the population is shown in the table (Laughlin, 1950, Table 1). Persons with

			Blood Type			
Sample	Number	Publication Year	O	A	B	AB
Point Barrow	329	1948	40.73	47.11	9.73	2.43
Nome	254	1944	43.31	42.52	11.81	2.36
Bethel	341	1949	36.95	44.87	11.73	6.45

type A all have the allele A_1, which is a characteristic shared by American Indians and Mongoloids of Asia (Laughlin, 1957, 9). No major difference appears between the frequencies for the Inupik speakers (Point Barrow and Nome) and the Yupik speakers (Bethel). This fact implies either that there were many matings across the linguistic boundary or that the time separating them has not been great enough to permit differences to emerge in the ratios of a once united population. The lack of time depth for the linguistic separation seems the more likely explanation. A blood sampling by Pauls and his associates (1953) for nearly 3,000 Alaskan Eskimos living from Kotzebue Sound to Bristol Bay and in adjacent inland regions gave the following results: O, 38.08; A, 44.08; B, 13.08; and AB, 4.77. Striking regional variations in B frequencies were noted, with the Nushagak locale having the highest frequency of 19.8 percent, and Kotzebue Sound the lowest of 10.3 percent. A separate sample revealed that at Hooper Bay Village the B frequency was 37.0 percent. It might inciden-

tally be added that in Pauls's blood studies for Bering Sea Eskimos, the people were judged to be full-blooded. While the ABO
frequencies are similar to those for whites, which has led some
observers to suggest white admixture, there were no A_2 individuals represented nor was the frequency of N similar to that for
white populations.

For the MN series, Eskimos usually have a low frequency of
N, which is characteristic also of American Indians. A sample of
some six hundred Alaskan Eskimos produced the following per-
centages: MM, 63.91; MN, 30.46; and NN, 5.62. Like American
Indians and Asiatics, the Eskimos are Rh positive. In one sample
of over 2,500 Alaskan Eskimos, only one person reported as being
of pure Eskimo blood was Rh negative (Laughlin, 1950, 167–68;
Pauls et al., 1953, 254–55). The Diego factor, which has a high
frequency in South America and appears in Asia, is absent among
tested Alaskan Eskimos and Indians. Among other American Indian populations at least 5 percent are Diego positive. Since the
Diego factor is present in China and Japan, a continuous distribution into the New World might be expected but is not reported
(Corcoran et al., 1959, 191–92).

A study of hemoglobin A was made after it was found that
genetic variants in hemoglobins existed for Asian populations. An
analysis of blood samples from slightly more than seven hundred
Alaskan Eskimos failed to reveal any abnormal hemoglobin forms.
Only hemoglobin A was found, and this consistency was true also
of smaller samples of Aleuts and Indians in Alaska (Scott et al.,
1959).

In general, Eskimo blood factors as a whole are distinct from
those of Asiatic peoples as well as from those of American Indians.
However, the Eskimos bear a closer general affinity to the peoples
of Asia than to the Indians of North America. One of the conclusions from blood-type studies is that in areas where Eskimos and
Indians met, there was very little mixture. The samples from
border areas do not, however, appear to have been great and are
not reported in enough detail to decide the clear ethnic identity

of the marginal communities. That there has been mixture is clear from the ethnographic findings, especially along the Kuskokwim River where mixed marriages have taken place since the early period of historic contact and most likely before this time. In this context and in others as well, there is the important problem of the precision with which any particular individual has been identified as being an Eskimo. For example, the Eskimos of Kodiak Island since around the turn of the present century have identified themselves as Aleuts, although most of them are Eskimos (Hrdlička, 1944, 15, 20; Petroff, 1884, 137; K. Taylor, 1966, 212), and the Chugach Eskimos also believe themselves to be Aleuts (Birket-Smith, 1953, 19). The Eskimos living at Perryville on the Alaska Peninsula think that they are Indians, and the Eskimos of Crooked Creek on the Kuskokwim River say that they are Indians.

Physiology

Explorers, missionaries, and travelers who came in contact with Eskimos often reported what seemed to be significant differences between white and Eskimo physiology. It was said that Eskimo females matured much earlier and bore fewer offspring than females in other parts of the world. Both of these assumptions now are regarded as false. Further, there is the widespread belief, based on observations under arctic conditions, that Eskimos have greater cold tolerance than whites. Understandably, this belief led to the assumption that Eskimos possessed inherited characteristics which made them more resistant to cold. The next step was to search for physical characteristics of Eskimos which would support the theory. Thus, it was assumed that Eskimos were fat, which gave them a layer of insulation like a seal, and that their short stature aided in the conservation of body heat. These deductions and others fit into the general framework of animal physiology and became accepted. When laboratory tests of Eskimo subjects were conducted, however, it became apparent that they had no single clear-cut physiological adaptation to cold. In order to better understand Eskimo physiology, a number of key processes and factors will be examined, along with summaries of recent research.

BASAL METABOLISM

Some observers have reported basal metabolic rates for Eskimos which are substantially higher than those for white populations. It has been suggested that this difference partially resulted from the inapplicability of the standard height-weight formula (DuBois) to Eskimos. However, a test of the formula was made by measuring the body surfaces of more than fifty northern Alaskan Eskimos, and it was found that the average difference between the lineal method and the height-weight formula was less for Eskimos than for a sampled group of whites (Rodahl and Edwards, 1952). Basal-metabolism tests for seventy-three Eskimo subjects revealed that those examined for the first time had rates significantly higher than those for whites. When the Eskimos' apprehension was overcome by successive testings and they were put on a white man's diet, their basal metabolic rates dropped to the same level as that for normal whites. Thus, this particular study concluded that there is no significant difference between whites and Eskimos in basal metabolic rates when the variable factors cited above were accounted for (Rodahl, 1952). It should not immediately be assumed, however, that the rate is essentially the same in all such studies. Milan et al. (1963) report that after four to five days on a hospital diet, six Eskimo men had a basal metabolic rate of 47.6 KcAL/M^z/hr at one time and 45.4 at another, whereas a white control was reported at 37.4. Furthermore, another series of tests (MacHattie et al., 1961) found that metabolism measured at night for five Eskimo men from Anaktuvuk Pass averaged 40 percent above the Boothby-Sandiford standards and: "There was no correlation between the rate of night metabolism and the protein or fat fuel-energy fraction. This implies that factors other than specific dynamic action of food were involved in the genesis of the elevated resting metabolism of these people." Additional experiments agree that basal metabolism is somewhat higher in Eskimos than in whites, but there is no general consensus about the causes (Hammel, 1964, 424–25).

CHOLESTEROL LEVELS

A study of cholesterol levels was made on more than eight hundred young to middle-aged Alaskan men, of whom nearly thirty were Aleuts, almost twenty were Athapaskan Indians, and the balance, Eskimos from the Canadian border to Bristol Bay. The largest concentration of communities represented was in the Bering Sea area, followed by Kotzebue Sound villages. The tests demonstrated that the cholesterol level in general approached the level for normal men in a sample from the United States. The mean cholesterol level for all of the tested men was 214, with the highest village mean level being 293 and the lowest about 171. Men from five Inuit villages (Buckland, King Island, Noorvik, Shishmaref, and Wales) had the highest levels. The lowest levels were recorded among Yuk men (Chevak, Dillingham, and Hooper Bay Village), Cux (Nunivak Island), and urban Inuit (Nome). These villages were not named on the published map, and their identification may not be precise. The higher cholesterol levels would seem to cluster in the north and the lower ones in the south (Scott et al., 1958). No obvious correlation with diet has been found, and yet this is the type of association which would be expected.

COLD ADAPTATION

Often observers who have lived among Eskimos have felt that these people had a hereditary advantage over whites in tolerating cold weather, but laboratory experiments indicate that cold adaptation among Eskimos is not striking. In 1956 an experiment in cold tolerance was conducted by Adams and Covino (1958), using six Eskimo men from Anaktuvuk Pass, seven white soldiers, and seven Negro soldiers. The research design was to insert a rectal thermocouple and attach numerous skin thermocouples to each subject. Each man was placed in a cold chamber set at 17°C. for an experimental period of two hours. The average skin and rectal temperatures of Negroes and whites were found to be essentially the same, but the Eskimos maintained consistently higher skin (shell) and rectal (core) temperatures. The metabolic rate of the Eskimos also was higher. Both Eskimos and whites increased their metabolic rates at considerably higher average skin temperatures than did the Negroes. Likewise, the Caucasians and Eskimos began shivering at approximately 29.5°C., while the Negroes began shivering at 28°C. The elevated Eskimo metabolic rates accounted for their ability to maintain higher skin and rectal temperatures during the tests. One of the concluding paragraphs by Adams and Covino (1958, 11) states that "although the Eskimo possesses a higher metabolic rate and elevated shell and core temperatures than the Caucasian, the pattern of response of these two groups to a standardized cold stress is the same as indicated by shivering and metabolic response reported here. There apparently exists no true physiological difference between the basic responses of the Eskimo and Caucasian to cold. The seemingly greater tolerance of the Eskimo to cold under field conditions is probably related to dietary, psychological, clothing, acclimatization, and other physiologically extraneous factors."

An experiment by Eagan (1966) involved measuring the tolerance of Eskimos to finger cooling in water at O°C. and in air at −22°C. In the experiment were four young Alaskan Eskimos who had spent the previous nine months in Oregon, five white males who had just returned from climbing Mt. McKinley, and nineteen white U.S. Air Force personnel. The results demonstrated that the Eskimos were better able to withstand both air and water cooling. The tolerance could not be explained by the investigator except as the result of genetic difference or acclimatization which was not of a seasonal nature.

An experiment by Milan et al. in 1963 involved Alaskan Eskimos and was designed to compare their physiological temperature regulation with that of whites and Indians. The male subjects included six Eskimos from Anaktuvuk Pass, six Athapaskan Indians, and six white American soldiers. The subjects were systematically exposed to temperatures of 30.5°, 33°, and 35°C. in a water-bath calorimeter to measure heat production and loss. All of the subjects had been placed on a hospital diet for four to five days before the tests, and the Eskimos, followed by the Indians, had the highest basal metabolisms. During the cold bath at each of the temperatures the white rate of heat production was the lowest, with the Indian rates 10 to 30 percent greater and the Eskimo rates 30 to 39 percent greater. Furthermore, it was found that the Eskimos have a lower degree of peripheral tissue insulation which is dependent partially on the amount of body fat (Eskimos 6.6 percent, Indians 12.3, and whites 15.6 as determined by the skinfold method). It was suggested (Milan et al., 1963, 381) that the "surface temperature gradients extended more deeply in the Eskimos since a greater mass of the peripheral tissue participated in the heat transfer of heat to the environment." This is the most sophisticated experiment to date, and it points to an Eskimo physiological response to cold which is apparently different from whites.

CUTANEOUS PAIN THRESHOLD

An above-average ability of the Eskimo to tolerate cold might be based on a high pain threshold for these people. In order to test pain tolerance in some aboriginal Alaskans, a study was made of twenty-six Athapaskan Indians, thirty-seven Eskimos from Anaktuvuk Pass, and thirty-two white controls. The technique for inflicting pain was thermal radiation on the back of the hand. The conclusion was that no significant differences separated the racial groups. Therefore, the ability to tolerate cold could not be correlated with a higher pain threshold (Meehan et al., 1954).

MATURATION, FERTILITY, AND INFANT MORTALITY

The information processed by Hrdlička concerning the onset of the menarche among girls and the fertility of women is the best available, although the fertility data are inadequately documented. The information was collected around 1930 by a nurse and a school teacher who were long-term residents of the lower Kuskokwim River area. Although the sample is for a comparatively recent time period, the diet and conditions in 1930 probably reflected the aboriginal conditions in a general manner. The menstruation records for sixteen Eskimo girls at Bethel indicate that their menarches began at about 13.3 years (Hrdlička, 1936b, 355–57). In Hrdlička's sample of twenty-nine women from the Kuskokwim River and adjacent areas, two women never bore an offspring. Of the twenty-seven others, all of whom were near the end of childbearing age or beyond it, there were from two to twelve births per woman. The average number of live births was 6.2, but only 2.3 children appear to have survived early childhood (Hrdlička, 1936a, 93).

In 1956–1958 there were 41.7 births per 1,000 aboriginal population in the Bethel area; the aboriginal peoples of this area are virtually all Eskimo. In 1957 a comparable figure for all races in the United States was 25.0. Statistics on births for 1956–1958 in the lower Yukon River area and adjacent regions to the north and south, all inhabited by Eskimos, possibly approach the aboriginal pattern. The people of this area have less access to medical facilities than any other Alaskans. Infant mortality in this Yukon area was 138.1 per 1,000, compared with 7.2 for all races of the United States (Baseline and Service Statistics—Bethel Transmittal #1, 1962, Tables 1, 2). The lower Yukon area figure is truly astronomical. Even though none of these figures are for the aboriginal period, they possibly reflect precontact times, in which there were many births and a very high rate of infant mortality.

Comments about family size indicate that the average family had two to three offspring who survived infancy and childhood (Ray, 1885, 44; Rosse, 1883, 34; Simpson, 1875, 254; Zagoskin, 1967, 108). For a woman to have more than six children who lived to maturity was most exceptional. At Point Barrow in the early 1850's it was noted by Simpson (1875, 254) that while the girls married at about fifteen years of age they did not usually have an offspring before reaching twenty and that there was an interval of four or more years between the ages of living children. The four- or five-year time lag between early marriage and the first conception is most likely the result of adolescent sterility (Montagu, 1946), and later spacing of children probably was due to a combination of infanticide and infant mortality.

Pathology

Apart from misadventure or accidents, the primary cause of Eskimo deaths in historic times has been diseases first introduced by whites. All virulent diseases among Alaskan Eskimos today appear to have been derived directly or indirectly from persons of European descent or extraction. According to the literature search by Aronson (1941), smallpox and tuberculosis, as well as syphilis, were unknown in aboriginal times. Syphilis, which probably was present among the Aleuts by 1792, had reached a peak in the Aleutian area by 1798. Intermittent reports about the presence of syphilis occur during the latter part of the Russian era (Romanowsky and Frankenhauser, 1962, 37, 62), but it appears to have been uncommon north of the Alaska Peninsula. In the Yukon-Kuskokwim area today it is unreported among Eskimos. Exposure unquestionably has existed, along with opportunities for its spread, and yet the disease has not established itself. Murdoch (1892, 39), who spent two years, 1881–1883, at Point Barrow, mentions that syphilis was not present in spite of the fact that sexual intercourse between whalers and Eskimo women was common. Contradictory evidence for the presence of syphilis among coastal arctic Eskimos is found in an 1890 physician's report that 85 percent of the Point Hope people tested had some form of the disease (Porter, 1893, 143).

Smallpox appears to have been introduced first into southeastern Alaska in 1775 or a few years later. An epidemic struck the Sitka area in 1836 and spread northward during the next few years, reaching as far north as Norton Sound (Ray, 1964, 64). It is reported that of the persons within the Russian sphere of influence in southwestern Alaska, including the Prince William Sound and Kodiak areas, nearly 1,000 died (Tikhmenev, 1861, 366–68). This appears to have been the only extensive smallpox epidemic.

The earliest reference to tuberculosis among aboriginal Alaskans dates from 1770, and by 1814 it was very common in the north Pacific region (Aronson, 1941, 31). To cite one current statistic on tuberculosis among aboriginal Alaskans conveys some idea of its prevalence. In the Bethel area in 1956–1958 the incidence of tuberculosis was 1,428.6 per 100,000 persons, compared with 51.0 for all races in the other states and 440.8 among Indians in the other states (Baseline and Service Statistics—Bethel Transmittal #1, 1962, Table 4-C).

The foregoing discussion of virulent diseases indicates that they were nonexistent in aboriginal times judging from both historical records and Eskimo receptivity. The absence of syphilis among southwestern Alaskan Eskimos today, and possibly other Eskimos as well, suggests a genetically based resistance to this contact disease. In the sections to follow, ailments which exist today and are assumed to have existed in aboriginal times are discussed in brief.

ACUTE INFECTIOUS DIARRHEA

A 1954–1955 study of intestinal infections was made at lower Kuskokwim River settlements, as well as at the arctic village of Wainwright; the total population involved was nearly 1,200. A conservative estimate of the incidence of diarrhea was 210 per 1,000, and the age group most often affected was that under four years of age. In the villages sampled, bacillary dysentery usually was caused by *Shigella flexneri* or *Salmonella typhosa*, both of which were endemic, and often the number of cases gradually built up in family groups during the summer (Gordon and Babbott, 1959). The same general situation was reported in subsequent studies, except that the incidence rate differed. In

1955–1956 more intensive investigations were initiated along the lower Kuskokwim River, and among the nearly 2,250 persons interviewed a third reported the occurrence of diarrhea during the preceding four months, with over half of the cases being among persons under ten years of age. In this study no relationship was found between the incidence of diarrhea and parasitic infections (Fournelle et al., 1958). A still later study for the Napaskiak area indicated that half of the one hundred seventy-four people had a history of diarrhea at some time during the year (Fournelle, et al., 1959). Infectious diarrhea has been and is an important factor in morbidity and mortality among infants and young children. One lower Kuskokwim physician, Dr. Harriet C. Jackson, estimated that 10 percent of the deaths among children were caused by diarrhea. As Fournelle et al. (1958, 1494–95) point out, however, the extent of diarrhea as a primary rather than a contributing cause of death is unknown. It seems reasonable to assume that in aboriginal times, when sanitation was far less adequate than in the 1950's, diarrhea must have been a contributing factor to, if not an important cause of, deaths among infants and young children. It is worthy of note that at Napaskiak, where the reported incidence of acute diarrhea is very high, the people employed a plant infusion to treat the disease in aboriginal times. The particular plant used, *Rumex sp.* or sour dock, is a genus widely recognized as an efficacious astringent (Oswalt, 1957, 24, 31).

ANEMIA

The first study of anemia was made on some seven hundred U.S. National Guardsmen who were Eskimos from settlements in western Alaska. The conclusion drawn was that the hemoglobin level in Eskimo men was slightly lower than that of whites. A second study was carried out in three villages along the lower Kuskokwim River. In two villages the hemoglobin levels were low, and in one the level was high. In the former settlements the men and most of the women were clinically anemic, and an attempt to raise the levels with iron supplements was in general unsuccessful. The lower hemoglobin levels in these villages were said to be nutritional, not hereditary, caused by an iron deficiency plus an unknown nutritional factor (Scott, et al., 1955). Since the lowest average hemoglobin levels are for the Yuit, this finding suggests that the foods needed to prevent anemia are most utilized in northern Alaska.

ARTHRITIS

The purpose of the one extensive study of arthritis was to establish the frequency of rheumatoid arthritis and osteoarthritis in a sample of Alaskan Eskimos. The most complete data were from Wainwright, with less comprehensive information gathered in the Bethel area. Serum also was obtained from aboriginal Alaskans who were at a training session for members of the U.S. National Guard. In general, the occurrence of positive reactions to the bentonite flocculation tests for rheumatoid arthritis was the same for Eskimos as for the white control group, except that the Wainwright sample had a higher positive reaction than did the other Eskimos or the control group. The results of the radiographs of hands and wrists, used as a gauge of osteoarthritis, did not differ significantly between northern and southern Eskimos. However, the radiograph results suggested a lower incidence of osteoarthritis among Eskimos than among whites. It was speculated by Blumberg and associates (1961, 339) that the lower prevalence of osteoarthritis may be due to a genetic selection because the stringent conditions of arctic living adversely affect persons with the disease.

HEART DISEASE

A pathophysiological study in 1950–1952 of Alaskan Eskimos concentrated in part on cardiovascular diseases and the seemingly high fat content of the diet. The diet of the nearly fifty adults of both sexes tested averaged 2,700 calories per day and 2.5 gm. of cholesterol per week. This intake corresponded to that of American men in the moderate habitual cholesterol level. Included in the sample were some Nunamiut, who live mainly on a meat diet. They had a cholesterol intake of 4 gm. per week, which corresponded to the highest normal level for American men. Arteriosclerosis, as established by clinical and roentgenological examination, and other cardiovascular diseases appear to be quite rare (Rodahl, 1954). Based on 1956–1958 statistics there were 65.6 deaths per 100,000 from heart diseases among the Bethel area native peoples, which contrasts with a comparable statistic of 369.1 for all races in the other states (Baseline and Service Statistics—Bethel Transmittal #1, 1962, Table 12).

HYDATID DISEASE

The agent of hydatid disease, a tapeworm of the genus *Echinococcus*, is worldwide in distribution and is infectious to man while in the larval stage. The common species in Alaska, *E. granulosus*, is hosted as an adult parasite in the small intestines of dogs, fox, and wolves. In man the larva is most likely to be in the liver, where it would remain undiagnosed, or in the lungs, where it has no known effects. If, however, the larva enters the kidney, spleen, brain, or bone marrow of man, it can cause death or crippling. Cases among aboriginal Alaskans are rather frequent, largely because of contacts with dogs, of whom 25 percent may be infected in some arctic Alaskan settlements. Considering the proximity of dogs to houses in most Eskimo villages, the frequent handling of dogs, and the contacts with dog feces, the opportunities for contamination are and were great (Rausch, 1952). It is probable that Eskimos in Alaska have been afflicted with hydatid disease for centuries, especially in light of the much more unsanitary conditions which existed in the past.

INFECTIOUS HEPATITIS

A worldwide distribution of infectious hepatitis is caused by an associated virus A. An epidemic at Kotzebue in August of 1955 involved twenty-one cases out of a total population of about 1,200 persons. There was no evidence for a source case, and of the persons affected all were under thirty-five years of age and most were males. The cases were associated with those geographical segments of the population drawing water from sources contaminated by human feces. A second outbreak, which took place the same year at the Kobuk River community of Kiana, was seemingly unrelated to the occurrence at Kotzebue. The conclusion drawn in both instances was that contaminated water was responsible, and fecal-oral transmission was probably via water (Davis, 1957). In general, epidemics of infectious hepatitis A result in comparatively few deaths, a statistic below the 0.2 percent level (Eichenwald and Mosley, 1959, 15).

TRICHINAE INFECTION

A 1949 study of trichinae in the Bethel area and another the next year at Kotzebue (Hitchcock, 1950, 1951) revealed that the number of persons who reacted positively to skin tests was 1.6 and 6.6 percent in the respective areas. The persons with positive reactions most often reported having eaten raw pork or else the raw meat of bears, seals, or whales. An analysis for the presence of *Trichinella spiralis* larvae in a sample of nearly 2,500 animals of diverse species, with the exception of ungulates, revealed that nearly 12 percent harbored larvae. The most likely potential source for infection in man seems to be raw bear meat. No larvae were found in walrus or baleen whales, and the frequency in seals and white whales was quite low. Contrary to common belief, the incidence of trichinosis among aboriginal Alaskans is low, although at Wainwright 28 percent of a sample of seventy-one reacted positively (Rausch, et al., 1956). In the rest of the United States, about 16 percent of the population have some encysted trichinae. Although trichinae infection in a mild degree is harmless, severe infestation causes trichinosis, a disease which is characterized by gastrointestinal disturbances followed by muscle soreness and may be fatal.

CAUSES OF DEATH

Clearly it is impossible to state with any degree of exactness the causes of death during the early period of historic contact. It is important to note, however, that all communicable diseases such as influenza, measles, tuberculosis, smallpox, syphilis, and whooping cough were introduced by whites. It is not possible to prove that any aboriginal diseases were fatal for many adults. Among infants and young children, however, infectious diarrhea contributed to the high infant-mortality rate. In searching for general causes of death among adults, it appears that accidents were significant, especially among males. This fact applied particularly to the arctic coast, where men hunted on open water and on the sea ice. Death from drowning, freezing, being carried away on the ice, or being attacked by a polar bear was an ever-present possibility (see Murdoch, 1892, 269; Nelson, 1899, 120; Rainey, 1947, 253). Even today the accident rate in Alaska is much higher than in other states. Calculated on a rate of 100,000 deaths for 1950, we find that accidents accounted for 59.3 deaths among whites in the states to the south, 151.0 deaths among Alaskan whites, and 206.7 deaths among Aleuts, Eskimos, and Indians (Parran, 1954, Section III, Fig. 4). Blumberg and his associates (1961, 334–35) make one of the few references to causes of death among modern Alaskan Eskimos, apart from the recently introduced communicable diseases. It is their opinion, based on their experience among Bethel area and northern Alaskan Eskimos, that "Trauma is very common among Eskimos and is considered to be one of the major causes of death."

The oral histories of Eskimos include accounts of fights between families, villages, or tribes. Male deaths by violence from this cause seem to have been moderately numerous. In the archaeological record are occasional examples of deaths by violence, such as the arrowpoints in two Ipiutak skeletons from Point Hope (Larsen and Rainey, 1948, 60). A violent death took place about

A.D. 1750 in an Eskimo house along the Kobuk River, but this may have been an example of senilicide (Giddings, 1952a, 122). There were also natural disasters such as a sea wave which struck the Nome area around 1830, washing away a Little Diomede Island village and destroying a Golovnin Bay settlement (Ray, 1964, 72). An earthquake in 1792 on Kodiak Island is described as having destroyed all the dwellings (Hrdlička, 1944, 8), and it seems reasonable that there were accompanying fatalities. Probably deaths likewise occurred when a landslide destroyed a Golovnin Bay settlement at an unknown but early historic date (Ray, 1964, 64). In the same vein a man within a house at Point Barrow was killed when beached ice crushed the house (Spencer, 1959, 51), and the same cause of death was reported for the area just north of the Kuskokwim River mouth (Nelson, 1899, 251). Accidental death might also be caused by fire. A fire in a house at Platinum, during an archaeological horizon related to Ipiutak, claimed the lives of two or three children (Larsen, 1950, 183–84).

Food poisoning also was a possible cause of death. Ray (1964, 64) writes that "botulism poisoning apparently was very high prior to European contact," and a 1901 example is cited of three families dying from it in the Golovnin area. Poisonous plants in Alaska are rare, but one which occurs in at least parts of south-western Alaska is *Cicuta mackenziana* or poison water hemlock, which in historic times has been known to cause deaths, particularly among children. A poisonous plant found along the Pacific Ocean front and Bristol Bay is *Veratrum eschscholtzii*, or the false hellebore, and the death camus, *Zyadenus elegans*, grows in sectors of western Alaska. However, whether poisoning from the latter two plants is fatal or not is unknown (Heller, 1953, 153, 161, 163).

From the foregoing information a number of conclusions are possible concerning Eskimos as biological beings. The morphological characteristics which are so distinct in configuration for early historic Eskimo populations in the eastern American arctic occurred with less frequency in Alaska at the same time period. This dissimilarity was due to the genetic isolation of the eastern breeding population and the survival in the east of Eskimos from a more homogeneous genetic strain than existed in the west. Furthermore, there is no current reason to regard the Eskimos as an ancient racial group, and any specific morphological similarities with ancient fossil finds are examples of parallel developments in separate populations.

We would expect to find clear physiological adaptations to cold among the Eskimos if they had first lived in a warm environment and then pushed into a cool temperate setting without adequate clothing. Their physiological response to cold would be expected to be similar to that of aboriginal Australians or Alacaluf Indians (Hammel, 1964). As tested, however, Eskimo metabolic rates generally are higher than those for whites but not consistently so. Their core-shell responses to cold, which differ from those of whites although not in any radical dimension, may be due to dietary, not genetic, factors. Thus I would deduce that Eskimos possessed clothing and, most likely, housing adapted to a cold environment before they moved into an arctic setting.

The biological aspects of an individual Eskimo's life cycle suggest that Eskimo women bore many offspring but that very few children reached adulthood. Infanticide was a factor in the number of children surviving, as will be discussed later, but the major factor in infant mortality was acute infectious diarrhea. No one can say with certainty that epidemics of deadly diseases did not spread through the Eskimo population in aboriginal times, but for the time of historic contact, no such diseases have been recorded. In a population pyramid for the Yukon-Kuskokwim area dating from 1890, by ignoring the unreliable figures for persons under one year of age, we find that in a sample of about 5,500 only fifty persons were sixty-five years old or older, and one half of the population was between the ages of one and nineteen (Porter, 1893, 175). Apart from infants who died from natural or artificial means, the most likely cause of death was trauma. Judging from family size the population barely replaced itself; with food stress leading to infanticide, with the high rate of infant mortality apart from infanticide, and with the abnormal number of accidental deaths, Eskimos maintained their numbers precariously.

Chapter 4

Settlement Patterns

In the ethnological analysis of Eskimo data, adaptations on which survival depends almost always have been stressed. A similar emphasis is found in the present study and seems unavoidable due to the nature of Eskimo living. In the present chapter and the four which follow, an explicit distinction is made between the cultural and the social information. Cultural behavior is viewed in terms of settlement, subsistence, and technological patterns, whereas the social side of living is concerned with community patterns, the individual, and the social institutions in which people participate. A classification of settlement-community patterns is offered, and it will be established that Alaskan Eskimos fall within a narrow segment. Settlement patterns are described first because they provide the foundation for social life. The six dominant subsistence patterns become the vehicle for presenting the house and settlement forms, followed by a comparative discussion of houses in particular. Finally the subsistence patterns, tribal populations, and tribal areas are analyzed for an introductory view of Eskimo adaptations.

Among Alaskan Eskimos the most common pattern of settlement was for tribal segments to establish winter villages, range from these during the summer months, and return to the same villages at the onset of winter. Normally two families occupied one house in a winter village, and in warmer weather the family groups dispersed to summer camps. The most common variations around this standard were the year-long residence of a few isolated families in a hamlet, the establishment of summer villages rather than camps, the occupation of particular campsites during both spring and fall, or a summer mobility with families ranging widely and camping at many different sites throughout the season. In certain instances a sizeable population might occupy a single site throughout the year, as happened among the Kingikmiut of Wales, the Unaligmiut of St. Michael, and perhaps among some of the Koniag on Kodiak Island.

The major factor which determined the location of a summer or winter settlement was the abundance of game and fish in the area. Ideally a summer dwelling site was situated on high ground to provide the residents with a view of the surrounding country in order to note the approach of game or enemies. High ground also was less likely to flood with coastal storms or overflowing rivers. Other major considerations were the availability of fresh water and wood, plus the presence of a beach or riverbank where boats could be landed easily and safely. In winter settlements the accessibility to wood was likely to be even more important, and an elevated site again was sought. The factors which most often led to the abandonment of a settlement were a scarcity of food sources, the cutting or building of a riverbank or beach line, or a local disaster.

The arrangement of houses within a settlement did not follow a preconceived plan, although related families tended to live near each other. On occasion there might appear to be a planned linear arrangement of houses, particularly along old beach lines, oblong knolls, or riverbanks, but such an ordering had no purpose except to take advantage of the higher and drier ground. The house entrances throughout a village might face one direction because of the prevailing winds, the contours of the site, the accessibility of sunlight, or the desire to face a body of water.

The most noticeable structure in a community was the communal house, also called a men's, club, or dance house. The Yupik term for this type of structure was *kazigi, kashgee*, or a close variant, while in Inupik the word was often recorded as *karigi*. To the Russians in Alaska such a building was a *kashim*. Not only was this community-oriented structure the largest in a settlement, but also it was located on the highest plot of ground or in the center of a village if possible. Kashgees were not built by the Chugach, but at least one was generally present in each large, stable settlement of the other tribes. In addition to the dwellings and to one or more of the men's houses, each village was likely to have drying racks for meat and fish, storage pits, caches on raised posts, and racks for boats and sleds. Parturient or menstrual structures might also be present.

Classification

The classification employed for an analysis of Alaskan Eskimo settlement-community patterns was originated collectively by Richard K. Beardsley, Preston Holder, Alex D. Krieger, Betty J. Meggers, and John B. Rinaldo (1956). A second classification has been designed specifically for circumpolar peoples by Kwang-chih Chang (1962b), but I prefer the former system. The primary reason for employing the approach of Beardsley and his associates is that it accommodates not only arctic hunters and fishermen, but also all the societies of the primitive world and much of the modern as well. It has a broad comparative basis not found in other anthropological classifications of peoples. The Beardsley classification is based on the concept of community mobility. Communities become increasingly large and stable as more food resources are available and as a people's abilities to exploit these resources increase. Some environments have an almost unlimited productive potential, whereas others are limited in productivity no matter how complex the sociocultural system might become. This classification, which is offered as an evolutionary approach, has seven levels with each defined in terms of community pattern and environmental factors. As the authors point out, extremely diverse societies fit easily into the levels. At the hypothetical beginning, the community members move often and without restrictions in their almost continual search for food. As more food becomes available through an increase of knowledge about exploiting the environment, such populations become more sedentary. Thus, community mobility is a function of subsistence resources, technological knowledge, and other sociocultural factors. The initial level in the system, the Free Wandering stage, occurs during population expansions into unoccupied areas and perhaps during population contractions. This stage is of no real concern to us, nor is the next level, Restricted Wandering. In it the people wander about an area defined as their own and to which they have exclusive rights. The next two levels, however, apply directly to Alaskan Eskimos. These are defined by Beardsley et al. (1956, 138, 140) as follows:

> *Central-Based Wandering.* A community that spends part of each year wandering and the rest at a settlement or "central base," to which it may or may not consistently return in subsequent years.
> *Semi-Permanent Sedentary.* A community, which can be identified with a village, that establishes itself in successive locations, occupying each for a period of years. The population is stable and continuously sedentary, but able to be so only by moving the village periodically.

Alaskan Eskimos are best accommodated in the Central-Based Wandering level. This level is reached when it is possible to harvest, store, and preserve a nondomestic crop; when a wild food is locally abundant; or when conditions of incipient farming exist. The number of people sustained at the central base is perhaps about two hundred, and they are reasonably well integrated when they are together. During part of the year, however, the people live in nuclear or extended family groups which are self-sufficient. The base as well as the composition of the social group may change, but community rights to resources within the base area are observed. While the people are at the central base, the accumulated foods are not for the exclusive use of individuals or families and thus are not the basis for division in terms of wealth. Community integration is not great due to the seasonal dispersal of families from the central base and the fluid nature of the membership. Thus, leaders may influence and symbolize a community, but they have no meaningful political power. Religious behavior includes the presence of shamans, who cure by magic, and a concern with the dead. Group ceremonies vary widely and may take place regularly, sporadically, or not at all. Examples of Central-Based Wanderers cited from the ethnographic literature include the Eskimos, the northern and central Californian Indians, the interior Salishan, and the Siriono, Timbira, Kaingang, Gilyak, Goldi, Maritime Koryak, and Kamchadal.

The annual patterns of movement for specific Eskimo communities have been sought, but often it is difficult to learn about the seasonal movements of a people in any form that approaches completeness. If information for a particular settlement is unavailable but the tribal data are reasonably good, then the latter have been utilized. To rank communities on the basis of mobility poses certain problems which arise from the variations within a tribe in seasonal movements. A single family, willing to endure long periods of physical isolation, might live at one spot throughout the year, whereas most other families of the tribe would cluster for part of the year but scatter at other times. It would appear that the norm is for most families to avoid extended periods of physical isolation, and yet single-family isolation is reported among the Unaligmiut along Norton Bay (Ray, 1964, 69), the Kuskowagamiut (Oswalt, field notes), and the Nunamiut. Nunamiut thinking recognized that an isolated nuclear family was more likely to succeed economically than a cluster of families. However, the

social monotony in family isolation led most families to seek
companionship with others (Gubser, 1965, 62).

It is important to consider the number of moves and the
number of months spent in the more stable settlements. It would
appear that there were "urban" and "rural" population segments
and probably most tribes included the combination. For example,
the Unaligmiut of the Koyuk-Golovnin area were as a whole
Central-Based Wanderers, and yet a few small settlements seemingly were occupied during most, if not all, of a year. Most of the
Unaligmiut settlements in this area were occupied for many years,
and yet in one locality the villages were moved every few years
(Ray, 1964, 66–71). Physical mobility at the level of Central-
Based Wandering may be ranked in terms of the longest time
spent at one locality during a year and the number of moves per
year. These factors have been considered by tribe or village and
compared with a ranking of the people by population density.

Group	Tribal Population Density per 100 km.²	Moves per Year	Most Months in One Settlement
Chugach	15	2	9
Nuniwagamiut	10	2	9
Ohagamiut	4	2	9
Napaskiagamiut	4	6	5
Malemiut	4	4	5
Tareumiut	2	2	9
Kovagmiut	2	2	9
Kiatagmiut	2	2	7
Nunamiut	1	4	4

The groups in the table are all Central-Based Wanderers. The
Nunamiut are not only at the bottom of the scale in terms of
population density, but they were also less successful than the
others in maintaining a central base. They moved often, and their
more permanent camps were composed of small numbers of
closely related families. Only in years of good caribou kills were
the settlements composed of larger social groups who were not

necessarily so closely related (Gubser, 1965, 353–56). A seasonal round for the Kiatagmiut and the Kuskowagamiut is presented by Elliott (1886, 381–82). Since there are more specific descriptions for the latter tribe, his observations will be applied only to the Kiatagmiut of the Nushagak. Elliott does not state the size or composition of a winter village, but such a settlement probably was similar to the type on the central Kobuk River. Among the latter people one or two nuclear families formed a winter settlement (Giddings, 1961a, 34–48). Among the Malemiut of the Buckland River, however, the winter village appears to have been larger and more permanent than those cited thus far (Lucier, 1954, 215). The Malemiut of the Deering region seem to have exhibited the general pattern found along the Buckland River, and the same was true for the Kauwerak of Imuruk Basin (Larsen, 1958, 580–81). For the other populations cited in the foregoing list, except the Napaskiagamiut, the settlements included some unrelated families and were stable for most of the year. This statement is clearly so for the Tareumiut of Point Hope (Rainey, 1947, 244–68) and Point Barrow (Simpson, 1875, 260–67), the Kuskowagamiut village of Ohagamiut (Oswalt, 1963a, 116–28), the Nuniwagamiut (Lantis, 1946, 171–81), and the Chugach (Birket-Smith, 1953, 52–55). In computing the length of stay at the most permanent settlement for each of these peoples, no allowance was made for hunting trips made away from the settlements. Frequently men hunted alone for a few days or even for more than two months in a typical year. The men who spent the most time on such trips were those along the Kobuk, central Kuskokwim, and Nushagak rivers.

One pattern of seasonal settlement at Napaskiak in the 1950's was said by residents to have been the same as in aboriginal times. In this economic round the people left their riverbank settlement in the spring and again in the fall to live for the season at inland tundra camps; in the summer they might establish fish camps at still other localities (Oswalt, 1963b, 79–98). I suspect that this type of mobility was more widespread than at Napaskiak alone

and is an intermediary between the small, kinship-based settlements of the Nunamiut type and the larger, more stable aggre-
gates of relatives as well as nonrelatives in settlements among the
Tareumiut, Nuniwagamiut, and others. Reports exist also for
settlements which were so stable that they qualify as Semi-
Permanent Sedentary communities. Wales, inhabited by Kingikmiut, was such a community (Ray, 1964, 80). The Unaligmiut of
St. Michael had separate summer and winter entrances to their
dwellings and kashgees, a fact which suggests year-round occupation of a single site. A similar residence pattern is also known
among some of the more northerly Unaligmiut (Nelson, 1899,
243–47; Ray, 1964, 69–71). Such physical stability, however, is
rare. The Wales situation might have come into being because
this settlement was an important center for Siberian trade, and
this importance possibly led to its development as a permanently
occupied trade settlement unlike any other in Alaska. Unaligmiut
stability is more difficult to explain. It may have arisen as a result
of their virtually unique occupation of a border area; which en-
abled them to receive ideas from two contrasting ecological centers. Perhaps it was by combining northern and southern ideas
that a way of life arose among them which had more than the
usual physical stability.

Summarily, tribes with population densities of fewer than
three persons per one hundred square kilometers remained at their
central bases for long periods but only in very small social groups
as compared with more populous tribes. The more dense populations were able to maintain themselves for long periods in villages
composed of two to three hundred persons. An alternative for
peoples with low-to-intermediate densities is suspected to be the
maintenance of relatively large winter settlements, with small
family groups moving repeatedly at other seasons.

Subsistence and Dwelling Types

Alaskan Eskimos fit best into a single level of the Beardsley
classification, and yet they had widely varying ecological adapta-

tions. Their settlement patterns will be further considered within divisions based on the different economic foci (see Map 5, p. 13). Although such divisions may seem arbitrary in some instances, they suggest meaningful subsistence distinctions within the Central-Based Wandering pattern of settlement.

CARIBOU HUNTERS

Eskimos who depended largely on caribou occupied the Brooks Range, the upper Kobuk and Noatak rivers, some sectors of Seward Peninsula, and Cape Newenham. The northern caribou hunters camped in tents at spots where many animals could be intercepted on a migration, or they built more substantial dwellings where caribou abounded. A second major concern in locating a settlement was that it should be near willow thickets which would provide fuel. Settlements might contain from one to twenty residences, depending on the number of caribou either expected or present. Although related families or friends lived close together in a settlement, there was no village plan as such. A family might move from one settlement to another many times during a single year, but most of a winter was spent in one location if possible. The number of persons in a settlement probably never exceeded three hundred.

Two different dwelling forms were common among the most northern caribou hunters: the dome-shaped tent and the four-post-center house covered with moss. A Nunamiut family, which might have as many as ten members, lived in a tent throughout the year if it planned to be mobile. These dwellings were framed with willow poles forced into the ground in opposing pairs and then bent and lashed together at the top to form an oval or a circle. Sewn caribou skins with the hairside outward were placed over the pole frame except at the doorway, smoke hole, and window. Over this cover was stretched another of dehaired caribou skins, and around the base of the tent were arranged blocks of turf. A layer of snow might be piled over the entire structure. At the entrance, a block of sod covered with caribou skin formed a threshold, and from a horizontal pole above the doorway hung the skin of a grizzly bear. On one side of the entrance was a wooden window frame covered with strips of bear intestine sewn together. On the floor were willow boughs, and toward the center was a stone-lined fireplace with a smoke hole above it. The rear third of a tent was floored with caribou skins, and here the family members lounged against rolled-up sleeping skins. A dwelling of this nature, with the wall poles moved outward and the ceiling lowered, could accommodate up to about sixty persons for a festive occasion (Gubser, 1965, 69–71; Ingstad, 1954, 38; Larsen, 1958, 576).

More permanent Nunamiut winter quarters were, like the tents, constructed on the ground surface but were covered with moss (Fig. 2, A). The central framework consisted of four fork-topped posts set at the corners of a square or rectangle forming the center of the dwelling; stringers connected these

Figure 2. (A) Nunamiut winter house of wood and moss.
(B) Kovagmiut winter house.

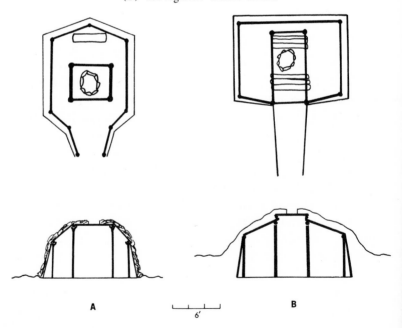

A   6'   B

posts. Shorter forked posts were placed at the corners of the side and rear walls, and stringers connected these posts with each other. Willow poles placed over the framework formed the side walls and roof. To each house was attached a flat-roofed entry-way with walls like those of the house. The roof and walls of the structure were covered with moss, save at the top where an opening for the skylight was left. The floor plans of such houses were of three forms: octagonal; rectangular, with the longer walls at the sides and an outward jog in the rear wall; or rectangular, with an entryway in one of the long side walls. Typically this form of house had a central fireplace and flooring of willow boughs. The flooring might be on either side of the fireplace or on the side away from the entrance in the case of the type having a side entryway. Along the back wall in each house was a shelf for the storage of meat. A house such as this might be occupied for only one season and would serve for the storage of equipment when no longer used as a dwelling. For the storage of meat, holes were excavated in the ground or in a rocky area, filled, and then covered with stones or perhaps skins (Campbell, 1962, 50; Gubser, 1965, 71; Ingstad, 1954, 158–60, 265; Spencer, 1959, 46).

Portable or temporary Nunamiut buildings included tepee-shaped skin tents used at the coast during summer trading trips, parturient structures framed with bent willow poles and covered with snow or moss, and a small, snow-covered winter dwelling less permanent than a tent. In making the latter structure, a willow-pole framework was constructed, and stones heated in a fire were placed inside. Then with a snowshoe used as a shovel, the frame was covered with snow. The heat from the stones caused an ice layer to form on the inner surface. After the frame was removed, the structure was ready for occupancy. A window of freshwater ice might be added, and at the entrance a skin was hung. A snowhouse of this type would be a logical prototype of the dome-shaped, snowblock houses constructed mainly by Eskimos in central Canada. Whenever a number of Nunamiut families lived at a settlement for any length of time, they erected a karigi.

This was a large, willow-framed tent to which each family contributed skins for the cover (Gubser, 1965, 72, 168–69; Ingstad,
1954, 39; Larsen, 1958, 576).

When there was no concentration of caribou, the families
moved independently to whatever area they regarded as potentially the best hunting country. The general pattern seems to have
been for a particular band or subtribal unit to range over a
one-hundred-mile sector of a river system in the pursuit of caribou. The four Nunamiut bands were concentrated in the central
portion of the Brooks Range, and their extensions beyond this
general area were to hunt briefly at an adjacent inland region or
to travel to the coast to trade (Gubser, 1965, 337–44).

The unstable nature of Nunamiut settlements was mirrored
in the pattern of Eskimos of the upper Kobuk and Noatak rivers.
The residents of the headwaters area wintered in multifamily
dwelling units. A willow framework was built over three or four
upright posts, and the structure was covered with a combination
of sod and moss. Each resident family had its iceblock window,
fireplace, and smoke hole (Stoney, 1900, 576–77). At Deering and
along the Buckland River the Malemiut permanent winter log
houses were semisubterranean and covered with moss, but there
were also temporary winter or summer dwellings. Their pattern
of settlement focused on intercepting caribou and thus required
the same type of mobility as that found among the Nunamiut. A
caribou-hunting way of life also occurred among the Kauwerak
of Seward Peninsula (Larsen, 1958, 580–81; Ray, 1964, 62). The
only other people with a great stress on hunting caribou were the
Chingigumiut, a Togiagamiut population who lived near Cape
Newenham, but nothing specific is known about their way of life
(Petroff, 1884, 135).

ARCTIC HUNTERS AND FISHERMEN

The settlements of arctic hunters and fishermen cut across
tribal boundaries and blend into some areas occupied by people
with a caribou-hunting emphasis. The best-known arctic hunters

and fishermen are the Kovagmiut of the central and lower Kobuk River. Although they hunted caribou, they depended most heavily on dog salmon during the summer and on whitefish during the other seasons. The choice of a winter settlement site was not dictated by accessibility to caribou, and among the known selections were islands, riverbanks, or areas inland a short distance from a riverbank. Along the central and lower Kobuk are three excavated archaeological sites dating between A.D. 1730 and 1880, and from them as well as from ethnographic accounts may be determined the winter-house form and seasonal pattern or population movement. The dwellings (Fig. 2, B), like the more permanent houses of the caribou hunters, were semisubterranean, rectangular structures with four-post roof construction, short tunnels at the center of one long wall, stone-edged fireplaces toward the front, and sleeping areas at ground level on either side of the fireplace (Giddings, 1952a, 11–19, 119; Oswalt, 1949, 7–8).

In the Kotzebue Sound area, possibly among the Malemiut, were winter houses of a form called the Mackenzie type because of its prevalence in that Canadian area. The shape was that of a cross, with four posts supporting the roof at the central section of the structure where there was a fireplace. On three sides were alcoves, and on the fourth side, the tunnel entrance. Such a house at Hotham Inlet was occupied by six families (Simpson, 1875, 258). This type of dwelling is related to the Utukok River mouth Nunamiut house with a recess (Larsen and Rainey, 1948, 48), and is similar also to a house excavated near Ambler Island (Giddings, 1952a, 119).

A temporary winter structure for the central river Kovagmiut had a pair of posts spanned by a beam against which upright poles were leaned on both sides and at one end. An opening for smoke was left over the interior fireplace. This lean-to was covered with moss and had a skin to cover the entrance at one end. The central Kobuk dwellings used temporarily in spring or summer were dome-shaped, willow-framed, and covered with either caribou skins or moss and spruce bark. Among the Selawik Eskimos a similar type of summer house was covered with brush, grass, and earth. More permanent central Kobuk summer housing had four posts at the inner corners with beams placed along the tops of these uprights. The walls were covered with a network of willows, and both the walls and roof were topped with flattened and aged spruce-bark slabs. All cooking was done out-of-doors, and a smudge fire was built at the entrance to discourage mosquitoes from entering the dwelling. A bark structure for the storage of foods probably was of the same design as the house just described (Giddings, 1961a, 35, 48, 125–27; Stoney, 1900, 546).

From what is known of the settlement pattern of these people, their mobility was nearly as great as that of the caribou hunters; their winter settlements were small and consisted of a few nuclear families. The largest known settlement was at Ambler Island and had fifteen houses, possibly built during two construction periods. Probably more typical of the settlements was one on Squirrel River where three houses apparently were occupied at the same time. The houses were used only for a single winter, judging from the known length of occupation for a winter settlement historically and from the amount of debris on the floor of an excavated house (Giddings, 1952a, 13–19, 108; 1961a, 41, 125–26; Oswalt, 1949, 7–8).

In the diet of the central and lower river Noatagmiut, salmon were very important, but these people also traveled to the seacoast to hunt seals and beluga whales in the spring. The Selawikmiut obtained salmon along Hotham Inlet, and these plus whitefish probably were more important in their diet than caribou. Both tribes had much the same settlement pattern as was found among the central and lower river Kovagmiut, and all of them were likely to visit a Kotzebue Sound trading center during the summer months (Cantwell, 1889b, 79–80; Simpson, 1875, 236).

ARCTIC WHALE HUNTERS

The largest and most organized settlements of whale hunters were at prominent points of land or on small islands in northern

Alaska. Whale hunting was the focal point of their economy, but they also fished and hunted other land and sea mammals. The whale hunters maintained large winter villages in which they lived for many years. The largest village was Wales, with around five hundred persons (Ray, 1964, 79), and the next in size was Point Hope, with possibly about four hundred. At Point Barrow in 1850 possibly three hundred fifty residents lived in about sixty houses and utilized two or perhaps three karigis. The Point Barrow settlement, according to an 1852–1853 account, was noted to form "a scattered and confused group of grassy mounds, each of which generally covers two separate dwellings, with separate entrances." Some mounds, however, were single houses, whereas others covered three houses grouped together. Behind each house on upright poles were horizontal platforms for the storage of boats, sleds, and food. On slightly higher ground than the house area were the karigis, which appeared as mounds larger than the houses (Simpson, 1875, 237, 256–59).

The Tareumiut of Point Hope and Point Barrow used drift-wood to build shallow, semisubterranean winter houses with long entrance passages to which separate rooms were attached. By combining the Point Barrow area house descriptions by Simpson (1875, 256–57) with those of Murdoch (1892, 72–75), the house form emerges with clarity (Fig. 3). The earth- and sod-covered rectangular houses were entered from a long, subterranean passage at the middle of one long wall. The ground-surface entrance to the tunnel was framed so that it could be covered in foul weather, and wooden blocks might serve as steps to the tunnel floor. The tunnel ended at a hole in the house floor, and about halfway along the passage, rooms were appended to either side. One room served as a kitchen and had a cone-shaped roof open at the top. The opposite room or rooms were smaller and used mainly for storage. The gabled house roof had a single ridgepole and a long pitch at the front, where a section of gut covered the framed window. Against the rear wall was a wide bench on which the family members slept or sat. The dwellings were walled with vertical planks, and the inner ceiling was of smoothed

beams or planks. Oil-burning soapstone lamps along each side wall
provided light and also heat for the structure as well as for some
cooking. Each of the two families occupying the dwelling had a
lamp.

Large Tareumiut winter villages had one or more karigis
built either in the same style as a dwelling or with a less permanent roof, larger dimensions, and a low bench serving only as a
seat around the walls. Here the karigi served as ceremonial center
as well as workshop for men and training place for boys, but it
was not the normal sleeping place for men nor a hostelry for
travelers. Temporary winter housing for hunters away from their
villages and sometimes for visitors in a village was built of snowblocks. The blocks were piled on top of each other around a
rectangular plan and were roofed with skins. A passage and
adjoining kitchen, plus storage rooms, might be added to such a
structure (Murdoch, 1892, 79–81; Simpson, 1875, 259–60).

Winter houses used year after year were vacated during the

Figure 3. Tareumiut winter house.

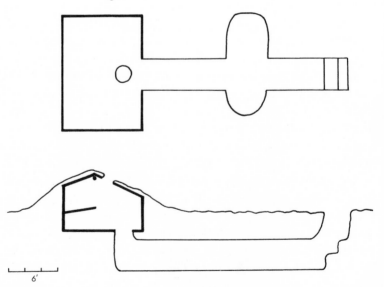

summer by the Tareumiut because they were damp and the tunnels collected standing water. The cone-shaped tents for summer occupancy accommodated individual families. The frames, which were long poles bound together at the top, were covered with seal or caribou skins. Inside the tent a wooden hoop was lashed to the heavy pole framework at a height of about six feet, and additional support was provided for the lower portion of the tent with short poles placed against the outer edges of the hoop. The hoop served also as a storage rack for long artifacts. A summer residence sometimes had a translucent window, but it had no smoke hole since all cooking took place outside. During the summer months the Tareumiut often traveled widely to trade or hunt, and their skin tents were ideal for this type of mobility (Murdoch, 1892, 83–85; Simpson, 1875, 260).

The Wales people probably occupied houses similar to the one described by Collins (1937, 262–63) and located along the coast about twenty miles north of Wales. It consisted of an irregularly shaped entry room, a passageway, and the dwelling proper. The entry room, with four center posts for roof support and alcoves with sloping roofs, bore a resemblance to the Mackenzie type. The inner room was like that described for Point Barrow except that the roof, supported by two beams about equidistant from the front and rear walls, was flat on top.

The most aberrant summer-house form was present among the Kauwerak of King Island. These people lived on a steep rocky slope and cleared away the rocks to build winter houses which were much the same as those on the adjacent mainland. Their summer dwellings, however, differed markedly from any described thus far. They were rectangular, flat-roofed tents built on pole frameworks and covered with sewn walrus hides. The floors were planked, and a circular opening in the wall facing the sea served both as an entrance and a window. To make the structures level, the Kauwerak built them on posts which were long at the front of the house and short at the back (Nelson, 1899, 255–56). The Kauwerak and other whale hunters often traveled long distances during the summer months, most often to an Alaskan trading center, and they camped in tepee-style tents on their summer trips.

BERING SEA HUNTERS AND FISHERMEN

From the vicinity of Teller on Seward Peninsula southward including Nunivak Island and the Alaska Peninsula, the regional economy was more diversified than has been noted previously. In this large area the only peoples who do not fit into the pattern of diversification are the riverine fishermen and a small group of caribou hunters. In the economy of the Bering Sea hunters and fishermen, seals, especially the bearded seal, were likely to be important. These Eskimos also hunted caribou, fished for white-fish rather intensively, and did not hesitate to take blackfish, stick-lebacks, salmon, or other species whenever possible. Their settlements seldom included more than three hundred persons. Villages rarely were as stable as those of the arctic whalers, but they were more permanent than those of the arctic hunters and fishermen. The sites chosen for winter villages included points of land along the coasts, sheltered bays, and spots at which streams joined.

The winter houses of the Bering Sea hunters and fishermen, which are best reported for the Unaligmiut, shared certain major characteristics with the permanent arctic houses. A semisubterranean rectangular dwelling room was entered from an underground passage which originated at ground level or inside a storage chamber. In both areas also there might be a raised wall bench at the rear of the house and perhaps a fireplace in the house floor. The most important differences in winter-house forms were that among the Unaligmiut the roofs were cribbed and the platforms might be at two levels and extend around three sides. If there was year-round site occupancy, some Unaligmiut houses (Fig. 4) had not only subterranean winter entrance passages but also ground-level entrances for use during the summer. The Unaligmiut kashgee at St. Michael resembled the local house form, which had summer and winter entrances; however, the winter entrance in the kashgee opened at the fire pit. The kashgees of these people and of those to the south were in general square, up to about twenty-five feet on a side, and had a single raised bench around the walls. Larger kashgees occasionally built by the Unaligmiut were surrounded by frameworks made of horizontal poles held in place by uprights. The space between the framework and the building itself was filled with earth. In this region a kashgee served not only as the ceremonial structure and workshop but also as sleeping quarters for men, boys, and male visitors to the community (Nelson, 1899, 242–46, 250–53; Zagoskin, 1967, 115).

An aboriginal Nunivak Island house, in which two families probably lived, had a small, square living room with raised side and rear wall benches and a stone-edged fireplace. The roof construction was four-post center, and from the main room a short tunnel with a floor level lower than that of the house led through an anteroom into a small entryway (Fig. 5). In a winter

Figure 4. Two styles of Unaligmiut winter houses. The lower house was also used in the summer.

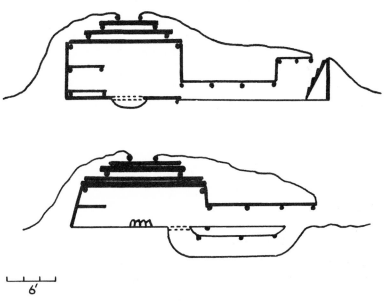

6′

village a single tunnel might join three or four houses and a
kashgee. The summer settlements, although somewhat different
from the winter ones, had the same general plan. In what was
perhaps a typical aboriginal settlement on Nunivak Island there
were two communal houses, ten dwellings, and seventeen caches.
The latter were storage structures, each built on a platform of
wood supported by four posts (Collins, 1937, 258–60; Lantis,
1946, 156–57, 162–64).

The summer living pattern of Bering Sea hunters and fishermen varied somewhat. The winter dwellings at St. Michael were
also occupied during the summer, but the Nunivak Islanders had
winter as well as summer villages, with permanent houses in each.
Elsewhere summer houses might be ground-surface forms built of
planks and logs with a gabled roof but no interior fireplace. Other
variations included dome-shaped bark tents, skin-covered tents, or
houses made from sod blocks. The general impression is that
families did not normally range widely from their winter villages

Figure 5. Nuniwagamiut summer or winter dwelling.

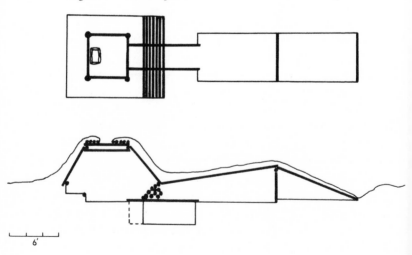

on extended trips. They might, however, move into tents and live at the same community or frequent summer fishing camps. They did not travel to large summer trading fairs since these did not exist in their area.

SALMON FISHERMEN

Considering the great runs of salmon in many Alaskan rivers and their dependability as a source of food, salmon would be expected to play a key role in the economic lives of many Eskimos. It is true that in the Bristol Bay area, where the runs are almost unbelievable in magnitude, the Eskimos were heavily dependent on them, but even here other foods were sought as important supplements. Nonetheless, it is possible to characterize certain riverine Eskimo populations as dependent primarily on salmon in their subsistence cycles. Scattered along the banks of the Yukon and Kuskokwim rivers in the Eskimo area were numerous villages of salmon fishermen, but none of these settlements were comparable in size to those of some northern coastal dwellers. Only in one instance was such a village recorded as having more than three hundred persons. Although the settlements along the Yukon, Kuskokwim, Togiak, and Nushagak rivers were not large, they were located closer together than were the sizeable Eskimo settlements discussed previously.

The early historic settlement form for salmon fishermen is best known from Crow Village on the Kuskokwim River and from Tikchik, located where the Tikchik River enters Tikchik Lake. At Crow Village, occupied in the late 1800's, ninety persons lived in five houses and maintained a single kashgee. The houses were excavated, and apart from one with four-post-center roof construction and the walls of a log cabin, the other four houses were semisubterranean and square with central fireplaces. The bench arrangement, when it could be established, was always low, just above the floor level, and was along the side walls alone or along the side and rear walls. Tunnels, except for one, were shallow, and three of the four semisubterranean houses had entry rooms. The type of roof construction is uncertain, but it seems to have ranged from flat to cribbed with four center posts. These winter houses sometimes were occupied during the summer. Temporary housing for hunters or village residents included dome-shaped structures with grass or bark coverings over a bent willow framework (Oswalt and VanStone, 1967, 91–92). The ten house foundations at Tikchik had been deeper than those at Crow Village, but the forms shared a roof construction of four center posts, low sleeping benches along two or three sides, central fireplaces, and shallow or deep tunnels. Six houses had entry rooms; one of these entry rooms had four posts supporting the roof plus a tunnel leading into it from the outside. One of the two kashgees at Tikchik was excavated deeply in the ground and had a steep tunnel entrance. The roof was cribbed, and a bench extended around all the interior walls. The second kashgee was similar but larger and may have had a flat rather than a cribbed roof (VanStone, ms. 2).

In the coastal area around the Nushagak River the semisubterranean houses had a plan forming an irregular square or circle, with a fire pit and a smoke hole above. Along the walls were raised benches, and a short tunnel led to the outside or into an entryway (Petroff, 1884, 15). One communal structure described was partly beneath the ground and had a tunnel that ended in the fire pit. A cribbed roof might be assumed for such a building (Swineford, 1898, 164–66).

One winter house in the lower Kuskokwim region was described as having an entry room which was a kitchen, and in it a fireplace with a smoke hole above it. A low tunnel led from this room to the house, which was twelve feet square and probably had a double-pitched roof. Light was provided by clay lamps since there was no interior fireplace. The residents slept on the floor, probably along the side and rear walls. From the illustrated stories still told by girls and women who live along the lower Kuskokwim we learn that house interiors usually had sleeping benches along the side walls. These benches had short logs at the head and foot and were separated from the central walking area by longer logs. On the tundra adjacent to the lower Kuskokwim River the summer houses were about ten feet square and walled with sod. The roofs were supported at the four corners with posts, and across these were beams over which was set a layer of sod. Such residences were at ground level as were the entrance passages when they were present. Food was cooked over an outdoor fire or behind a lean-to (Oswalt, 1963a, 29–30, 119; 1964, 312–13).

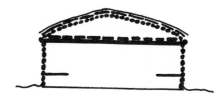

Figure 6.
Ikogmiut summer house.

Among the Ikogmiut along the Yukon River winter houses were probably similar in form to those at Crow Village or at St. Michael, but there were also separate and substantial summer dwellings. In the summer houses upright planks formed the front and rear walls, but the lateral walls were of horizontal logs held in place partially with uprights placed outside the house. Further stability was achieved by placing ceiling stringers between the lateral walls. Over the gabled roof of hewn poles were boards and then a layer of bark. Entrance was through an oval hole in the front wall, but its exact location is unknown. Along the inner walls were raised benches, and light came through small holes cut into the wall planks (Fig. 6). A dwelling of this nature sheltered from one to three families (Nelson, 1899, 247–48).

PACIFIC WHALE HUNTERS AND FISHERMEN

By far the area of most concentrated Alaskan Eskimo occupancy was along the shores of Kodiak Island. The Koniag on the other islands and the adjacent mainland, the Unixkugmiut, and the Chugach were not nearly so numerous, although the population densities here were among the highest. Whale hunting was prominent in the economies, followed in importance by the hunting of other sea mammals plus fishing for salmon and halibut. The sites selected for occupancy usually were sheltered bays or areas where a stream or river entered the sea. The Kodiak Island houses were multifamily dwelling units with two or three families occupying each sleeping compartment off a common main room. Portions of the main room were partitioned with boards to serve as storage places. The structural complex, or at least the sleeping section, was beneath the ground surface. The main room was used for cooking and as a general work room. It had a central fireplace, an opening above it to allow light in and smoke out, plank walls, and corner posts which supported beams along which the wall planks leaned. The family compartments had low ceilings and side wall sleeping areas marked with logs placed about three feet from the walls. The side rooms were warmed with heated stones carried in from the fire pit and had ceiling openings for light. The roofs were flat, vaulted, or dome-shaped, and one was noted to be domed with whale ribs. A sleeping compartment might be used for a steam bath, or a small bath room heated by stones might be built off the main room. No diagram of an early historic Kodiak house is known; the one in Figure 7 is a reconstruction from the descriptions, with all the reported roof forms illustrated. The Koniag built communal houses, but the details of their form are unknown. Sketches of houses at an Olga Bay site probably dating from around the period of historic contact have the general form described above, although some of the structural complexes were more elaborate. One recent Koniag house differs in roof construction by having four primary supports for the main room and may reflect the aboriginal form (Clark, 1956, 95; Griggs, 1922, 26; Hrdlička, 1944, 26–29; Lisiansky, 1814, 213–14).

The early observers of Chugach houses reported comparatively little about the forms. The winter dwellings appear to have been small, rectangular, plank-sided buildings with low ceilings. Summer residences ranged from shelters beneath large skin boats partially tipped over to bark-covered shelters and substantial multifamily, rectangular wooden houses. The latter form had vertical plank walls over an interior framing of posts and beams. The roofs perhaps were more or less flat and were, except for a smoke hole opening at the center, covered with bark slabs held in place

Figure 7. Koniag winter dwelling.

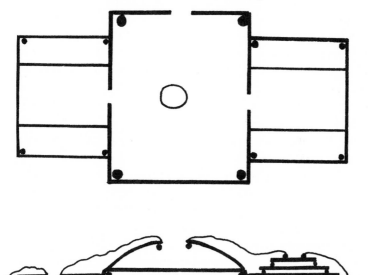

6′

with stones. Inside was a fireplace, and small sleeping rooms and a steam-bath room opened off the main room. These houses are described as being for summer and fall use only, but in general the design seems most similar to the winter houses of the Koniag (Birket-Smith, 1953, 53–55; de Laguna, 1956, 58–59).

COMPARISON OF HOUSES

All Eskimo houses provided protection against the elements, but with different degrees of adequacy based on their structural characteristics. It is worthwhile to compare the house forms without attempting a detailed analysis of types. Three architectural features critical because of their areal variety and functional utility were the presence or absence of a fireplace, the positioning of benches, and the depth of the tunnel. A dwelling with a fireplace could be heated with spruce wood or less satisfactorily with willows. In houses lacking a fireplace, one or more lamps provided heat. Sleeping benches, if raised above the ground, were free from floor drafts, and a tunnel prevented cold air from coming directly into a house. A deep tunnel, particularly one with a roof level below the house floor level, trapped the cold air, and as a result comparatively little artificial heat was required. For five winters in a subarctic setting, I lived in a semisubterreanean house with a roof construction of four center posts and with a long and deep tunnel. The tunnel roof was not below floor level, and the resultant partial cold trap did not prevent the house floor temperatures from dropping below freezing even when the room was warm at waist height. For sleeping comfort the only satisfactory arrangement was to have a high bed.

Among the Tareumiut, where wood was too scarce to use as fuel for heating a house during the winter, fireplaces were absent, but houses had deep tunnels and raised sleeping platforms. This would seem to be the ideal house style here since fireplaces could not provide heat. Among the Unaligmiut, the high wall benches, usually deep tunnels, and fireplaces provided the ideal combination for greatest warmth. South of the Unaligmiut area, the most common pattern was to have house benches just above the floor, a fireplace in the main room, and a short, shallow tunnel. In this warmer environment, it would seem that the heat provided by the fire more than compensated for sleeping near the floor and not having the most efficient means for keeping the cold out.

In areas where dome-shaped houses with pole frameworks were reported, as among the Nunamiut, inland Kuskowagamiut, or Kobuk Eskimos, the builders were in close proximity to Athapaskan Indian tribes and may have borrowed their house form. Even among the Nunamiut, where the form was most important, the domed tent competed with the more typically Eskimo permanent house with a roof construction of four center posts. The willingness of the Kobuk and Brooks Range Eskimos to construct such a house each year stands as significant in itself. It means that "permanent" house construction was considered worthwhile even if the dwelling were to be used for only one season. The willingness of these people to build a nonportable house each year may have been based on the type of environment in which they lived. Here the cold necessitated a well-constructed dwelling, even though the limited resources necessitated semiannual moves.

Summer houses with plank or bark coverings over a framework of posts were reported as far north as the Kobuk River, although north of Norton Sound the conical tent was the dominant summer residence. The people who spent their summers fishing for salmon, which included many Yuit and a few Inuit, built the substantial wooden houses. If they moved about a great deal, as was true of most Inuit, the tepee was obviously more desirable.

It is reasonable to view house forms as adaptive to localities since environmental accommodations were essential; yet it is not always possible to understand why certain materials or forms were not employed. For example, the use of sealskins for tent coverings was rare. It must be assumed that this material, since it was widely available, proved unsatisfactory for such a use. Perhaps it is worth commenting, too, that while sod houses were built when no other building material was accessible, as in certain central Yuit localities, they could have been constructed over a broader area. The fact that sod was used only rarely is difficult to understand. Sod dwellings not only were warm, but the building material was also available nearly everywhere. The only conclusion is that the cultural tradition of an adequate dwelling must not have included sod structures.

After viewing the subsistence areas as units and sometimes anticipating details later to be expanded, we see significant differences in settlement-community patterns begin to emerge. The settlements which were most distinctive belonged to the arctic whalers; in these large but scattered permanent villages, the winter houses had ridgepole roof supports, rear wall benches, and deep tunnels. Other characteristics of the arctic whalers were their use of tepee tents for their far-flung travels on summer trading trips and their comparatively well-organized community life. Large, stable villages also were found among the Koniag, who were whalers, but the Koniag type of whaling differed from the arctic form, their summer travels were not nearly as extensive, and their house forms were less unique. The Chugach, of the same subsistence pattern as the Koniag, stand apart in their house-construction technology, which was more characteristic of the Northwest Coast Indians. If we set aside the whalers, there is a rather striking degree of similarity in the housing pattern among the other Alaskan Eskimos. Settlements were small, and houses had four-post roof construction, benches just above the floor level, and shallow tunnels. In the north, settlements of small family groups predominated, and dwelling sites were highly unstable. Villages occupied by sizeable groups of kindred were more the norm in the south; here settlements tended to be nearer one another and more stable than in the north. These differences in settlement pattern indicate the flexibility of Eskimos in exploiting any particular environmental setting. Because of this variability they defy neat classification by settlement type.

Population Densities

Another way to view settlement patterns and subsistence orientations is through an analysis of population densities. The tribal areas are plotted by biotic provinces on U.S. Geological Survey Map E for Alaska, scaled at 1:2,500,000. Measurements for each tribal area are made with a planimeter scaled at one hundred square kilometers (100 km.^{2} equals 38.6 square miles), but the water area of large lakes such as Iliamna, Selawik, and Becharof are excluded, as is Baird Inlet. The glacial ice mass and rugged mountains adjoining Prince William Sound also are treated as uninhabitable. Table 1 lists the tribes, the tribal areas by biotic province and totaled, the total populations, and the rounded population densities. In addition, densities are calculated for language groups.

The Alaskan Eskimo average of four persons per hundred square kilometers is low, as would be expected, but the range is greater than would be anticipated. In arriving at densities of comparable value, it must be assumed that each tribe utilized the land within its boundaries to an equal degree, even though this clearly was not the case for the Koniag. They do not appear to have frequented the mountainous interior of the island. Thus, the density of the island Koniag might be increased to bring it up to about one hundred persons per hundred square kilometers. This figure is an estimate since the exact area of exploitation is difficult to establish. The other tribes seem to have exploited all their lands at least seasonally.

The population density of the Inupik speakers approached two per hundred square kilometers and encompassed three different subsistence patterns: caribou hunters, arctic hunters and fishermen, and arctic whalers. The first two subsistence orientations led to small, scattered populations, whereas the arctic whalers had large, concentrated populations. Given the conditions which

TABLE I. ESKIMO TRIBES, BIOTIC PROVINCES, AND POPULATION DENSITIES

| | Tribal Areas and Biotic Provinces (in hundred square kilometers) | | | | | |
	Sitkan	Aleutian	Eskimoan	Hudsonian	Total	Population†	Density†
TRIBES							
Aglegmiut		80	20	15	115	500	4
Chugach	110				110	1,600	15
Ikogmiut			240	25	265	1,500	6
Kaialigamiut			220		220	1,200	5
Kauwerak			250		250	900	4
Kiatagmiut		15	10	180	205	400	2
Kingikmiut			40		40	650	16
Koniag	30	190			220	6,500	30
Kovagmiut			260	55	315	500	2
Kuskowagamiut*			480	280	760	3,100	4
Magemiut			150		150	400	3
Malemiut			150	20	170	600	4
Noatagmiut			370	40	410	400	1
Nunamiut			2,000		2,000	1,500	1
Nuniwagamiut			40		40	400	10
Peninsular Eskimo		510			510	1,600	3
Selawikmiut			140	25	165	300	2
Tareumiut			610		610	1,500	2
Togiagamiut			150		150	1,000	7
Unaligmiut			250	80	330	850	3
Unixkugmiut	40				40	600	15
LINGUISTIC GROUPS							
Inupik			3,820	140	3,960	6,350	2
Yupik							
Cux (Nunivak)			40		40	400	10
Suk (Pacific)	180	190			370	8,700	24
Yuk (Mainland)		605	1,520	580	2,705	10,550	4
Totals	180	795	5,380	720	7,075	26,000	

* Includes an area of combined Eskimo and Indian occupancy. † Figures rounded.

gave rise to this variability, we would expect greater continuity in the arctic-whaling way of life than in the other two subsistence orientations. Peoples representing the latter patterns would be less likely to maintain their culture over a long period of time. The Yupik speakers, with an overall population density of six, would be expected to have had greater long-term stability than the Inuit. The tremendous population density of the Koniag is so far removed from all the others that some sort of explanation for their separateness must be sought. One important factor is that they lived on islands, for island populations (Nunivak and King islands furnish examples) consistently are denser than those of adjacent mainlands. As was noted in the discussion of prehistory, the cultural continuum of Kodiak shortly before A.D. 1500 was different from that of the Bering Sea Eskimo region. Then the Koniag came under direct Bering Sea area influence for a short period of time. Suggestively they might have increased rapidly in numbers after 1500 by their success in combining their established north Pacific economy of sea-mammal hunting with the intrusive Bering Sea hunting and fishing pattern.

These overall figures, crude though they are, illustrate several points. The Eskimos north of Bering Strait and those of the Pacific drainages stand at the two extremes in population density with the Bering Sea hunters and fishermen falling between. The Bering Sea peoples had a flexible economy not possible in the arctic and yet one less capable of expansion than that of the north Pacific whalers. In settlements where salmon fishing was stressed, high population densities had not been realized, suggesting that these economies were not extremely old, at least not among the recent ancestors of the Yuit. Alaskan Eskimos did not permanently inhabit the inland side of any mountain divide. Furthermore, there is no straightforward increase in population densities when moving from north to south; instead, there are scattered pockets with higher densities.

Chapter 5

Subsistence and Clothing

The extreme northern latitudes of North America challenge and almost defy occupancy by man. Under these circumstances, as found in northern Greenland and the Canadian District of Franklin, the limited resource potential focused human energy on daily and seasonal methods for survival. The high arctic conditions did not exist in Alaska, and a lessening of the environmental stress is reflected well in the cultural developments of the Eskimo inhabitants. The types of settlements, house forms, and subsistence orientations discussed previously were major adjustments to northern living. Now we may turn to the details of subsistence activities, particularly with reference to food and clothing, to describe another aspect of physical survival. The subsistence patterns presented are for six representative peoples and convey the contrasting ways in which food and clothing materials were obtained. Trade relationships are discussed since they directly

117

influenced the total resources available. Only then may food and clothing be described, for often it was not the skins of indigenous animals but rather those obtained through trade which provided the garments so essential for arctic living.

At one extreme the Nunamiut settlement pattern reflected potential mobility at any season and a primary dependence on caribou to satisfy food as well as clothing needs. The Nunamiut represent a people who developed a high degree of specialization in survival methods because of their limited resources, whereas the Koniag are at the other extreme. In the relatively mild environment of the Pacific Eskimos, clothing need not provide extreme warmth, food resources were plentiful, and people rarely faced the critical problems of basic survival. The other tribes are scattered between these two extremes. In general, people were as sedentary as their subsistence welfare permitted, but there were exceptions. In some years families might place their economic security in jeopardy by remaining in large settlements even though their food supplies had dwindled dangerously, whereas they could have prospered if they had retired to small, isolated social units. At other times they moved because they were bored with a particular setting. These variations, however, were not the norm, which was to move only as the need arose.

Representative Subsistence Patterns

CARIBOU HUNTERS

The environment of the Brooks Range did not offer the Nunamiut the potential for a balanced economy. The subsistence round was of necessity focused on caribou, and other game was sought either after the need for caribou had been fulfilled or when it could not be fulfilled. Barren Ground caribou were life and living for these people, and the yearly cycle centered on caribou hunts. Although caribou might be accessible throughout the year, they were most likely to be abundant during the early summer when they wandered northward and in the fall as they moved south. In the winter small herds might remain in the mountains, even along the northern slopes, but their local movements defied prediction (Gubser, 1965, 303–10).

The Nunamiut knew of the patterned spring and fall caribou migrations as well as the erratic movements of the herds at other times, and this knowledge led to intensive hunts during the migrations. The most successful means for securing migrating animals was through the cooperative efforts of a number of hunters and their families. A location was found where caribou were likely to concentrate, and here the hunters erected two converging lines of cairns made of rock or sod. These cairns looked like men to the caribou, and near the base of this funnel earthen mounds might be constructed to form a shield for the hunters. Beyond the mounds, snares were set in from one to four partial circles. The wandering caribou became anxious when they saw the cairns but continued forward cautiously. Then women and children appeared behind the herd, and the frightened animals bolted forward. Men armed with bows and arrows shot the caribou as they approached; the ones which they did not bring down were likely to be caught in the snares and could be killed with spears. Another method was to use cairns for guiding caribou into lakes at certain spots where they were then speared by hunters in kayaks as they attempted to swim across the water. A hunter also might stalk an individual animal or a small herd, but this was a far less rewarding hunting technique. Caribou meat usually was fit for consumption at any season, but the best skins were from animals taken in the late summer or early fall. When caribou were taken cooperatively, the kill was divided equally among the hunters, although an individual who already had cached a great quantity of meat might give some of his share to a less successful man. After the meat had been taken to a settlement by the hunter or his wife, the wife took charge of its distribution. She considered first the needs of her household, next those of her parents or grandparents, then her siblings, and finally her husband's parents (Gubser, 1965, 61, 77–81, 97; Ingstad, 1954, 59–62).

The means for taking other animals reflects the Eskimos' extensive hunting and trapping knowledge. Diverse species ranging in size from ground squirrels to wolves and Dall sheep were captured in snares. Meat from sheep was considered by some Nunamiut to be the best of all foods. Sheep also were taken with bows and arrows or driven over cliffs by trained dogs. If caribou could not be located, the meat from sheep might save families from starvation. Species obtained on hunting trips in timbered country included black bears caught with snares or shot with bows and arrows and wolverine taken in rock deadfalls. Moose were numerous in willow thickets along the south side of the Brooks Range, but hunting parties went to this area only when there was little prospect of obtaining food locally. One summer moose-hunting technique was for a hunter to trick an animal into passing near a second hunter armed with a bow and arrows. In the winter moose were wary and could be taken only by skillful hunters. Musk-oxen were harassed with dogs until they formed a protective circle, and then they were shot with arrows or dispatched with spears. One of the most dangerous animals was the arctic grizzly bear, which was snared or hunted with spears; whereas the black bear was regarded as a dull creature, the power and intelligence of the grizzly bear was respected (Gubser, 1965, 267–89).

A widely reported Eskimo hunting device for killing wolves or fox was usually termed a spring bait. This implement, as employed by the Nunamiut, consisted of an eight-inch willow stick sharpened at the ends or a strip of baleen fashioned in the same manner. The piece was coiled, bound with sinew, and covered with liver or blood. The mass was frozen and left at a place frequented by the species for which it was set. An animal swallowed the frozen ball and soon the coating, followed by the sinew, disintegrated in the animal's stomach. When the baleen or willow stick sprang back to its original shape and punctured the animal's stomach, it caused death from internal hemorrhage (Gubser, 1965, 96).

Ducks and geese migrated through the Brooks Range on their way northward each spring and returned, perhaps in lesser numbers, in the fall. During these seasons snares were set in lakes just beneath the water surface so that the birds would tangle their feet as they landed. They also were felled with bolas as they flew overhead in flocks. More important were ptarmigan, for in a year when big game was absent or scarce, the presence of Nelson's rock ptarmigan meant survival itself. These birds were captured individually in snares throughout most of the year (Gubser, 1965, 246–47).

The fish taken from lakes and rivers included arctic char, grayling, herring, lake trout, ling cod, and whitefish. They were taken in gill nets, in cone-shaped traps of willow, with leisters, and with hooks. Contrary to what might be expected, however, they were less important in the diet than ptarmigan and during a normal year constituted only about 10 percent of the food taken. The people did not care for fish as a steady fare, and fish were never reported to have staved off starvation (Gubser, 1965, 100, 252–54).

The plant species available were not diverse, nor were plant products more than supplementary to the primary diet of meat and fat. Berries, one type of tuber, and roots were collected for food. Plants were more important for their use in manufactures. The species most readily available and having the most versatile uses were the willows. They served as dwelling frames, kayak ribs and stringers, floors for houses, and most importantly as fuel. The people were obliged to range farther for the birch, spruce, and other woods which they employed in their manufactures (Gubser, 1965, 103–04, 239–42).

Familiarity with sea mammals resulted from summer trading trips to the coast; in addition, the Colville River segment of the population speared, but did not harpoon, ringed seals and a smaller number of harbor seals in the river. In rare instances an inland-ranging polar bear was killed with arrows and spears. If a walrus or other sea mammal was seen on the coast, he would be hunted, but systematic hunting of sea mammals was not a part of Nunamiut life (Gubser, 1965, 255–59).

The Nunamiut hunter used a bow and arrows to confront animals directly only if they were numerous and gregarious, as generally was true of caribou and ptarmigan, or if they were extremely large meat animals, such as moose. At most other times the people employed snares or deadfalls. The latter method, utilizing fixed, untended traps, provided a very different means for obtaining game from searching it out directly. Taken in their entirety, the hunting methods and settlement pattern of the Nunamiut permitted a relatively full exploitation of the environment. One final dimension was their travel to the coast by umiak to trade for those things which they could not obtain locally.

The Nunamiut shared their caribou-hunting emphasis with the Noatagmiut of the upper Noatak River and the Kovagmiut of the upper Kobuk River, and the seasonal round for the latter bands was the same as for the Nunamiut. Among the Malemiut of Deering caribou hunting also was the primary economic pursuit, but in addition they hunted seals along the coast in the spring. Seal hunting was done either at breathing holes or from kayaks in open water. The Deering pattern prevailed, too, among the Malemiut along the Buckland River and at Candle, and among some of the inland Kauwerak. The Malemiut also might visit the Kotzebue area trading centers during the summer. The caribou-hunting emphasis of the Togiagamiut of the Cape Newenham area, the Chingigumiut, has led to their placement in this subsistence orientation, but the details of their way of life are not known (Larsen, 1958, 580–81; Lucier, 1954, 215; Petroff, 1884, 135; Ray, 1964, 62).

ARCTIC WHALE HUNTERS

The Tareumiut of Point Hope moved from their winter houses into conical tents at some time in July after the sea ice disappeared. The most important summer hunting activity was for families to travel by umiak up the Kukpuk River to hunt caribou, particularly fawns, to provide clothing and bedding skins. After reaching the upper river, the families walked overland, and the men hunted in small groups. They stalked caribou or herded them into ambushes, where the animals were killed with arrows or were speared from kayaks if they were in the water. During the summer ptarmigan were hunted or snared; fox, hoary marmots, wolverine, and wolves, taken for their pelts, were snared or killed in deadfalls.

In the fall most families returned home with their accumulated skins and meat, but some remained inland until freeze-up and then returned, hauling their umiaks on dog sleds. Other families prepared in early summer for journeys to coastal trading centers, while still others camped near the village and set nets for beluga whales. Local excursions might be made to cliffs where seabirds nested. Here eggs and young birds were collected for food, and mature birds were taken mainly for parka skins. Any caribou wandering along the beaches to escape from mosquitoes were hunted, and along the shore salmon, salmon trout, and whitefish might be netted. Another source of food which might be found along the coast was walrus which had hauled up on a beach (Rainey, 1947, 265–67).

In the late fall men went out in kayaks to hunt seals in the open sea before the ice pack appeared, but the unpredictable local currents and the possibility of shore ice forming while the hunter was out made such trips dangerous. The shore ice, which formed rapidly, might be too thick to penetrate with a kayak and yet too thin to support the weight of a hunter carrying his kayak. During this season people most often ate sea-mammal meat cached from the previous spring plus any available caribou meat. The sea ice consolidated and thickened near the end of October, but it was never stationary except along the shoreline. The seals searched for open leads where they could breathe, and as ice formed over the leads, the seals maintained breathing holes. Any particular seal had a number of such holes at which he could be killed, but there was no way of predicting when a seal would return to a particular hole. Thus, the hunter located a hole and waited. This seal-hunting method often is called *maupok* in the literature. For such hunting a slender ivory rod known as a seal indicator was stuck into the snow covering the hole. The rod moved when a seal pushed his nose into the hole, and this movement notified the hunter, who was standing nearby or was crouched on a small three-legged stool, that a seal was present. In a matter of seconds the hunter had a toggle-headed harpoon poised, and he struck the seal as it pushed up through the hole for a breath. The harpoon used at breathing holes was designed specifically for this type of hunting. Seals were taken in this manner until April (Murdoch, 1892, 233–34, 254–55; Rainey, 1947, 253–54).

When the ice pack was offshore and local conditions were right, polar bears were common. The bears hunted seals along the leads and were in turn hunted by men. If a man found a recent seal kill, he knew that nearby was a bear who, having eaten his fill, was likely to be asleep and thus could be hunted with less risk. Polar bears were thought to be left-handed and therefore could more easily be approached and speared from the left side. In January tomcod were caught through holes chipped in the shore ice. To jig for tomcod a cluster of unbarbed hooks was placed on a baleen line weighted at the bottom. The line was attached to a short stick and jigged with another short stick. The fish which became impaled were lifted from the water by wrapping the line quickly around the sticks. Somewhat later in the season crabs were taken through holes in the offshore ice. A net baited with a seal's nose was fastened across a hoop-shaped piece of baleen. The trap was lowered horizontally into the water and allowed to rest near the bottom for about a quarter of an hour. When it was raised slowly to the surface, small crabs would be clustered around the bait. Both crabs and tomcod were frozen and then eaten raw (Rainey, 1947, 255–56).

By early April the first bowhead whales appeared along the offshore leads, and the *umialiks* (whaling crew captains), who had fulfilled a long series of ceremonial and social obligations which began the previous fall, were ready for the whale-hunting season. The ten to fifteen whaling crews, each with about six men, sledded to the border of a lead and poised their umiaks at the edge of the ice so that they could be launched quickly. Some men slept as others watched, but they used no sleeping bags and had no shelter except a windbreak of ice blocks. The harpooner, with his heavy, toggle-headed harpoon poised in a crotched rest at the bow of the umiak, often sat in the bow and waited. If a whale surfaced close enough, a boat was pushed onto its back by the crew. The harpooner drove his weapon point into the whale's back and immediately tossed overboard three inflated sealskin floats attached to the harpoon line. The whale dove, the harpooner paddled back to the lead edge, and the remainder of the crew, singing songs, boarded the umiak to pursue the wounded whale. Nearby boats were launched when the songs were heard, and each umialik directed his crew to the spot where he thought the whale would surface. As the whale rose to breathe, the floats bobbed to the surface first. Each boat crew paddled hastily to the spot to launch other harpoons, and the whale finally was dispatched with flint-pointed spears. The first eight boats to arrive and join in the kill shared the take, which was towed to nearby ice and butchered (Rainey, 1947, 257–60).

By early June most bowhead whales had passed Point Hope, and during the summer, or earlier if no whales were near, other game was sought. Migratory birds were taken with slings or bolas by hunters secluded behind blinds along points of land, but more important was the intensive hunting of seals, particularly the bearded seals. As the seals' breathing holes increased in size with the warmer rays of the sun, the animals climbed onto the ice and slept nearby. One method for taking them was to set a net horizontally in the water a short distance beneath the breathing hole. The weighted net was kept in place with lines suspended through four holes around the breathing hole. A seal would surface through the hole successfully, but in diving back it became entangled in the net and drowned. A seal basking in the sun beside its breathing hole was approached cautiously by a hunter, who slid forward on a piece of polar-bear skin. When the seal became uneasy as he neared, the hunter acted like a seal and scratched the ice with a seal call, a handled implement with seal claws at the end. Reassured, the seal rested again until finally the hunter was near enough to launch a toggle-headed harpoon with a line attached to retrieve his kill. Because of the strength of a bearded seal, men often hunted in pairs and helped each other land a harpooned animal, which then was killed with a special club. This method of hunting seals, termed *utok*, was widespread among coastal Eskimos (Murdoch, 1892, 253–54; Rainey, 1947, 262–65).

Tareumiut emphasis on whale hunting was shared by people on the islands of the Bering Strait area. The Eskimos of Diomede, King, and possibly Sledge islands hunted great and lesser whales, walrus, and seals intensively during much of the year, but during the summer they traveled to the mainland to fish or trade. The same generalization applies to Wales, although some residents remained in the village throughout the summer since it was a trading center (Ray, 1964).

ARCTIC HUNTERS AND FISHERMEN

Among the arctic hunters and fishermen, who hunted neither great whales nor caribou as a major economic focus, the subsistence patterns were quite variable. The Noatagmiut of the central and lower Noatak River, as opposed to those of the upper river, might move to the coast to hunt bearded seals and beluga whales in the spring and return to the river to fish for salmon and whitefish during the summer. Eskimos of the middle and lower Kobuk River stressed seining or gillnetting salmon during the summer. This fishing, combined with fall caribou hunting, formed the essential core of their subsistence cycle. In the late fall both of these riverine peoples set funnel-shaped whitefish traps in association with weirs. Among the Selawikmiut, where caribou were scarce and salmon absent, whitefish were the most important staple, although these people might travel to Hotham Inlet to fish for salmon. Families from any of the tribes in the Hotham Inlet area might summer at a nearby coastal trading center (Cantwell, 1889a, 71; Giddings, 1961a, 39–48, 129–32; McLenegan, 1887, 75; Stoney, 1900, 572, 837–38).

BERING SEA HUNTERS AND FISHERMEN

The Unaligmiut of the Norton Sound area employed diverse techniques throughout the year for taking caribou. They set snares or killed the animals with bows and arrows after first deceiving them into passing near concealed hunters, or drove them into narrow valleys where they could be killed, or ran them down in the case of fawns. During the fall, both before and after sea ice formed, seals were caught in nets set off points of land. Another technique for taking seals after sea ice had formed was to place nets beneath their breathing holes. When leads developed in the ice in late winter, seals were harpooned in the open water; in the spring they were taken as they slept on the ice. Smaller land animals were captured in a variety of traps, snares, and deadfalls, and wolves were also taken with spring bait. One of the most important animals snared was the hoary marmot, whose skin was valued for summer parkas and as an important trade item (Nelson, 1899, 118–31; Zagoskin, 1967, 112).

Comparatively little is known about the economic pattern of those Yuit tribes living along the coast or on the inland tundra in the area between the Yukon River and Bristol Bay. At certain points of land along the coast, such as at Hooper Bay Village, the people appear to have concentrated on seal and caribou hunting, but they did not ignore migratory birds and fish. The Eskimos of the tundra country between the Yukon and Kuskokwim river mouths apparently fished intensively for whitefish, blackfish, and sticklebacks. This area also abounded in mink and muskrat, which were trapped, and sometimes caribou herds were to be found. Because this region was the most important Alaskan nesting ground for ducks, geese, and swans, the summer hunting of these birds provided meat as well as skins. The Togiagamiut and the Kiatagmiut fished for salmon, sealed, and hunted walrus, which frequented the Bristol Bay region (Petroff, 1884, 126–36).

From spring through fall the Nunivak Island Eskimos hunted seals intensively, and they might travel inland to take caribou during the summer. They captured no great whales, probably because these mammals did not enter the relatively shallow water around the island, but they did take beluga whales. In the spring they successfully hunted walrus and bearded seals; the latter usually were unavailable at other times. The most important method for taking seals was by harpooning them from kayaks. These people did not hunt seals as they rested on the ice, nor do they appear to have hunted them at breathing holes during the winter. Additional characteristics which differed from those of the more northerly coastal peoples included the absence of bolas for taking birds, the absence of formal cooperative hunts, the relative unimportance of fishhooks, an emphasis on nets for taking seals and birds, and a diversity of weapons for hunting from kayaks (Lantis, 1946, 158–72).

SALMON FISHERMEN

The subsistence rounds of the Eskimos along the Yukon, Kuskokwim, and Nushagak rivers shared the same basic emphasis. Each stressed fishing in the main river channels, along adjacent streams, and in lakes. The most important fish taken were species of salmon, which were caught in gill nets or in traps set in association with weirs; in addition, individual fish were taken with barbed harpoon dart heads. Whitefish, too, were trapped as well as netted. Ptarmigan were snared and netted, while migratory birds such as ducks and geese were snared, shot with arrows, or captured during drives at molting season in some localities. Long trips often were taken in the fall to obtain clothing skins, particularly those of caribou. Those Eskimos living near the coast hunted seals in open water, particularly during the spring of the year

(Nelson, 1899, 118–66; Oswalt, 1963a, 116–28; Oswalt and Van-Stone, 1967; VanStone, ms. 1).

PACIFIC WHALE HUNTERS AND FISHERMEN

The Pacific whale-hunting and fishing tribes maintained themselves in an environment which contrasted with the settings for the other tribes because of the vast resource potential. In the Chugach area, king salmon began to arrive in early May, and from this time until August the other species of salmon which ascended streams included red, dog, humpback, and finally silver salmon. As these species swam up spawning streams where log weirs had been built to restrict their movements, they were taken with darts which had barbed heads. Another salmon-fishing technique was to build a trap, probably in association with a weir, at the mouth of a spawning stream which had a tidal flow. Salmon entered the trap on the incoming tide, milled about, and were stranded when the tide went out. Throughout the year the land animal most hunted was the mountain goat, which was prime in the fall and was taken with bows and arrows. Bears were caught in snares or deadfalls and might also be hunted by a man wearing a bearskin and a helmet which looked like a bear's head. Small land mammals such as fox, river otter, marten, or mink were caught in spring pole snares. A form of deadfall might be employed also for river otter or mink (Birket-Smith, 1953, 23–41).

Sea mammals were hunted in open water by men in one- or two-holed kayaks using some form of harpoon as their principal weapon. Hair seals, sea otter, and whales were hunted throughout the year, whereas most sea lions were taken in the fall and fur seals in the spring. The harpoons for seals, sea lions, and small whales were headed with a toggle or more often with a barbed harpoon head. In either case a line from the head led to a float, and after an animal was harpooned the float served as a drag to tire him and force him to the surface more quickly than would have been normal. Then the quarry was either harpooned again or lanced and finally killed with a wooden club. Since sea lions were large, hunters cooperated in pursuing them and aided each other in towing them ashore. Hair seals sometimes were hunted at their breathing holes in the ice, but rarely, if ever, were they stalked when they slept on the ice (Birket-Smith, 1953, 23–27).

Both large whales and sea otter were pursued in open water by hunters using kayaks with two holes. The forward opening was occupied by the hunter and the rear one by a paddler. For sea-otter hunts many kayak teams cooperated since these animals were shy and difficult to kill. The standard weapons were bows and arrows or light harpoon darts launched with the aid of a throwing board. The latter was headed with a barbed point which fit directly into a socketpiece. The head had a hole at the side for the attachment of a line to the feathered shaft. The bows used were self bows, that is, without backing. The copper arrowpoints were barbed and detached from the shaft in the same manner as a harpoon dart head. The arrows were held in a cylindrical wooden quiver which was attached to the kayak deck (Birket-Smith, 1953, 23–31).

For the Chugach to hunt whales of large or small species, a great deal of esoteric knowledge was required. Pairs of men in two-holed kayaks cooperated in hunting whales, which were sought in bays rather than in the open sea. For the smaller species toggle harpoon heads were employed, but great whales were hunted with slate-bladed lances. In all likelihood the lance heads first were rubbed with a mixture of aconite poison and nontoxic ingredients. After a whale was lanced, it was not pursued. A ritual was performed, and the hunters returned home to wait for the animal to die and drift ashore. Other whaling techniques are reported, but the one just recounted seems most likely to have been the local aboriginal form (Birket-Smith, 1953, 33–34).

The most important sources of food were sea mammals and salmon, but these were supplemented with other foods obtained by hunting, fishing, or collecting. In the early summer cod and halibut were caught with barbed and weighted hooks. Both candlefish and herring were obtained in large numbers, possibly in dip nets. Birds were taken with bows and arrows as well as with gorges, while cormorants were caught in nets or clubbed to death while resting at night. A wide variety of shellfish, including clams, cockles, mussels, sea urchins, and sea slugs, were collected from the beaches and were an important source of food when other forms could not be obtained. The plant foods included species of kelp and seaweed plus diverse berries, roots, tubers, and leaves (Birket-Smith, 1953, 38–42).

Among the Koniag, the most important food sources were salmon and whales, supplemented with a wide variety of other species. During the summer halibut were hooked, and salmon were netted or speared. At this time, too, the Koniag used lances or harpoons to kill hair seals and sea lions. Whale hunting in open water was, as among the Chugach, a specialized activity of only certain men who knew the accompanying rituals. The hunting of sea otter and fur seals, again in open water, was most intensive during the spring. Plant foods as well as birds were a part of their normal diet, and during times of stress shellfish were collected (Hrdlička, 1944, 52–55; Lisiansky, 1814, 174, 202–10).

Food Preparation

The manner in which foods were prepared for consumption varied comparatively little throughout the Eskimo area of Alaska. The most important method for cooking meat or fish was boiling. The food to be cooked was either placed in a container of water to which preheated stones were added, or else it was cooked over a fire in a pottery or stone vessel. Less frequently, meat or fish might be roasted over a fire. Partially frozen raw meat or fish was eaten, but it was not usually consumed raw if it had thawed completely, an exception being whale skin. In preparing food for storage, both meat and fish were butchered and sun-dried. Small fish, however, were simply strung whole on ropes or willow shoots and dried. Meat and fish might be buried separately in pits or placed together in meat cellars where they decomposed slowly; later they were consumed without further preparation. A widespread practice was to dip dried foods into a container of seal oil before eating them, but oil was not drunk alone as a normal part of the diet. Eskimos are described sometimes as consuming great quantities of water or the most common early historic beverage, tea. Mealtime might be at irregular intervals, or light morning and noon meals might be followed by a principal meal in the evening (Birket-Smith, 1953, 43–44; Gubser, 1965, 74–75; Murdoch, 1892, 63–64; Nelson, 1899, 267–68).

Trade

The literature includes accounts of the trading ties which bound the Inuit tribes of Alaska with each other, with the Eskimos and Chukchee of Siberia, and to a lesser extent with Athapaskan Indians, Canadian Eskimos, and the northern Yuit. Trade goods from northeastern Siberia appear to have been received in arctic Alaska rather steadily soon after the Anadyrsk post was established in 1649 (Rainey, 1947, 267–68). It is probable that the routes along which European trade items passed were the same as those existing earlier, and historic trading centers were no doubt the meeting places of old. The most important centers for trade were at Wales, at Kotzebue and Sheshalik at the head of Hotham Inlet, at the Utukok River mouth, at Negalik at the Colville River mouth, and on Barter Island. The most important late prehistoric trade routes linked Alaska with Siberia across Bering Strait, with Russian metal goods and Chukchee reindeer skins being favored Siberian exports. By the early 1850's traders from Siberia took four or five loads of trade goods annually from East Cape to the Diomede islands, on to the market at Wales, and later to the head of Hotham Inlet. The Noatagmiut carried the products to the upper reaches of the Noatak, from which they were passed on to the Nunamiut, who in turn offered the goods to the Tareumiut from Point Barrow at the trading center of Negalik. The Tareumiut traveled to Barter Island, where they met Canadian Eskimos with English trade goods from the Mackenzie River posts of the Hudson's Bay Company (Simpson, 1875, 236, 265–67). The Point Hope Eskimos went either to a Hotham Inlet meeting place or northeast to another at the Utukok River mouth where they met Nunamiut from that river drainage (Rainey, 1947, 267–68).

The early historic trade items, apart from those of European origin, included both raw materials and finished artifacts. The intertribal exchanges were between established trading partners, with coastal products traded for inland goods. Materials offered by coastal peoples were bearded-seal skins for boat covers, strong ropes, and waterproof boot soles; walrus skins for umiak covers and rawhide ropes; and whalebone or walrus ivory for diverse small artifacts. Key materials from the interior were caribou and other skins for clothing and wolverine skins for parka ruffs and trim. The most important food product was sea-mammal oil or fat traded from the coast to the interior. More specialized items of trade originated in particular areas or localities and were exchanged widely. These included whetstones and adz blades of jade from the Kobuk River as well as copper knife blades and soapstone lamps from the Canadian arctic. The number of persons involved in trading was not insignificant. At the trading center of Negalik as many as six hundred persons might congregate, and in 1884 an estimated 1,400 persons met at a Kotzebue trading rendezvous (Cantwell, 1889a, 72; Gubser, 1965, 160–63, 231–33; Murdoch, 1892, 48–49; Stefansson, 1914b, 9–12; Stoney, 1900, 820–21).

Visiting a trading center provided an opportunity to obtain exotic products, but in addition it was an occasion to renew friendships, to entertain, and to be entertained. These meetings, which lasted for days or weeks, were in many ways exciting gatherings. Among some tribes it was essential for families either to visit a trading center or to have access to the goods received by other tribal members if they remained in their home country. Those Eskimos who depended on caribou meat as the mainstay in their

diet, among whom were the Nunamiut, the upper Noatak and
Kobuk Eskimos, and perhaps some of the Malemiut, had to obtain
additional fat for a balanced diet. This point was made for the
Nunamiut by Gubser (1965, 160–63). The dependency of inland
Eskimos in northern Alaska on coastal Eskimos for blubber or seal
oil seems clear, but the extent of this trade between coastal tribes
and the Noatak, Kobuk, and Selawik Eskimos is not as straightforward. The information is best for the Kobuk, and here Giddings (1961a, 128) did not regard the coastal trade for fat as
essential since substitutes were available locally. He cited the
production of oil from fish viscera and from land animals as
alternatives. We know, however, that comparatively little fat is
available from caribou, the greatest potential land-mammal
source. Among the Kuskokwim Eskimos, where relatively fat
salmon were abundant, seal oil still was considered a dietary
essential, but this might reflect a cultural preference. I would
regard a trade with coastal peoples as essential along the Kobuk
and cite the generalization by Stoney (1900, 843) that "Seal oil is
the condiment used with all foods," to suggest its importance (see
also Zagoskin, 1967, 115).

If trading contacts with northern coastal Eskimos were essential for the inland peoples to survive, the reverse also was true.
Above all else, coastal Inuit required caribou skins as parka material. Sometimes they could obtain the skins on inland hunting
trips or by hunting caribou when they ranged to the coasts, but
if these conditions did not prevail, they were obliged to trade for
the skins. The sea-mammal skins available to the coastal peoples
were not regarded as suitable for most clothing. For example,
although the Point Barrow Eskimos recognized the advantages of
sealskin for boot soles and used the skins in this way, only rarely,
according to Murdoch (1892, 109–10), did they resort to the use
of sealskins for trousers or boot tops. For all clothing needs other
than boot soles they preferred caribou or Siberian reindeer skins.
The substitution of other skins was known, but sealskin was not
one of the likely substitutes. Simpson's (1875, 241–44) description

of the clothing for the same Eskimos confirms Murdoch's gener-alizations. Nelson (1899, 31) described parkas from the Bering Strait area as being made from Siberian reindeer or caribou skins; he mentions sealskin as a possible trouser material. The wide-spread use of caribou or Siberian reindeer skins as the primary material for winter clothing leads to the conclusion that these skins provided the best protection against the environment. Other skins could be substituted, but they were smaller, heavier, less durable, or provided inadequate protection. Thus, the one inland product which could be supplied by caribou hunters was an essential need of the coastal peoples. Caribou skins and blubber or seal oil were the key trade items for those who lacked local access to these products. In late prehistoric times the coastal Eskimos found that the Siberian traders were a more dependable source of skins than were either the inland caribou hunters or their own inland caribou hunts. Siberian traders had the added advantage of being able to provide tobacco, tea, and metal products. The overall trade complex indicates that in the north self-sufficient inland Eskimos did not exist and that coastal Eskimos in turn could maintain themselves without trade only if the caribou nec-essary for clothing skins happened to be available locally.

The assumption that the skins of caribou and reindeer were the perfect arctic clothing material is important in considerations of early contacts between diverse groups. If coastal sea-mammal hunters in northern Alaska required these skins in late prehistoric times, the same condition probably existed earlier. The impor-tance of caribou in the economy of the Inuit people of A.D. 300 at Point Hope has been established clearly. It would seem, too, that dependence on caribou skins for clothing dated long before Ipi-utak, possibly to the earliest occupation of the arctic coast and interior arctic.

Trade between Inuit tribes and Athapaskan Indians occurred, but it was of little importance. These people had access to essen-tially the same products, and in addition their mistrust for one another tended to make trading relationships strained. The most persistent trade among these groups probably was between the Koyukon Indians and the Kovagmiut and Nunamiut, as well as between the Nunamiut and the Kutchin Indians (Giddings, 1961a, 30, 124; Gubser, 1965, 44–50, 343–44; Nelson, 1899, 34).

The Yuit tribes did not develop great trading centers such as were found among the Inuit at Kotzebue Sound and at the Colville River mouth. Possible reasons for their less intensive trade were that the resources were more evenly balanced in the Yuit tribal areas and that the more frequent hostilities between Yuit tribes discouraged congenial trading contacts. Most Yuit trade centered in the northern region and consisted of the exchange of sea-mammal fat for caribou skins. Additional items of importance, such as hoary marmot and ground-squirrel skins for parkas, were traded widely as was walrus ivory in the form of finished artifacts or as a raw material. For Siberian reindeer skins the Yuit tribes offered beaver and river-otter pelts, but this trade seems to have dated mainly from the early historic period (Hrdlička, 1944, 80–81; Nelson, 1899, 228–32; Oswalt, 1960, 107–09; 1963a, 11, 102; Petroff, 1884, 124–26; Tikhmenev, 1863, 225–27; Zagoskin, 1967, 97, 100, 124).

In one reported instance, Yuit trade was handled mainly by owners of umiaks, assisted by relatives. The owner of an umiak on Nunivak Island, for example, made up his crew of male relatives and friends to trade with friends or relatives at Nelson Island and Hooper Bay Village. His trading did not take him to more distant points nor was it very intensive, again perhaps because of the balanced resource potential of the island (Lantis, 1946, 169–70).

The people most devoted to trading as a livelihood or to tribal specialization were the Malemiut of Kotzebue Sound. They always were described as shrewd and aggressive in their business relationships. Furthermore, they were active colonizers of non-Malemiut Eskimos during the early historic period. By the 1880's they had pushed to the south side of Seward Peninsula and on to Unalakleet as traders and settlers. One reason the Malemiut were so successful at trading over an extensive region was that they had a great deal of experience in their home area, which was the most important trading rendezvous in aboriginal Alaska. They were willing to leave their home country because the caribou herds there had been depleted by the early historic period, and they were able to settle in the northern Yuit area since the smallpox epidemic of the 1830's had decreased the population in many Yuit settlements (Nelson, 1899, 229; Petroff, 1884, 125–26; Ray, 1964, 66–67).

Trade between the Yuit tribes and adjacent Indians was formalized at the Kuskokwim-Holitna river junction. Eskimos who were on friendly terms with the Georgetown Ingalik seem to have joined these Indians, and together they met the McGrath Ingalik and some Tanaina Indians at the summer trading center. The Tanaina of the Cook Inlet area traded with the Eskimos around Bristol Bay and even with the Eskimos on Kodiak Island when relationships with the islanders were friendly. The Cook Inlet Tanaina desired whale meat and sealskins, for which they offered the Eskimos moose and wolverine skins. The Ingalik Indians of the Anvik subtribe, who traded with the adjacent Unaligmiut, offered wolverine skins and small, well-made wooden containers for seal oil and sea-mammal skins. The same items were traded between the Indians and Eskimos on the Kuskokwim (Nelson, 1899, 70; Osgood, 1937, 73–75; 1958, 61–63; Oswalt, 1960, 107–09).

Clothing

Eskimo clothing has been praised, with justification, as the most suitable apparel ever developed for a cold climate, and the basic, best-known item is the parka. The ideal materials for parka manufacture were either prime caribou skins or Siberian reindeer skins. Both were light in weight, provided optimum warmth, and did not wear out quickly nor tear easily. In general parkas were manufactured from two skins, one for the front and another for the back. They were sleeved with portions of separate skins, and there was an opening for the head, to which a hood might or might not be attached. A parka for a woman of childbearing age had a bulky recess at the back to accommodate a young offspring. All parkas fit loosely enough for the wearer to draw one or both arms inside during cold weather. Both men and women wore trousers, which often extended to the knees or below, and sometimes short underpants or a pubic apron. Boots usually were separate from trousers, and footwear included socks as well as insoles. Head covering was provided by a parka hood or by a variety of other forms. Mittens were worn, but gloves seem to have been post-contact in manufacture. Since Eskimo garments were without pockets, it was common for a man to wear a belt from which was suspended a tobacco pouch or knife. The further particulars of clothing styles and their variations are best exemplified with descriptions for two tribes, one representing the Inuit and another the Yuit. After these major regional styles are presented, variations among other Alaskan Eskimos will be cited.

NUNAMIUT

Among the inland Inuit the best parkas and pants were made from the skins of caribou fawns, with the skins of other caribou utilized only if the ideal skins were unavailable. The same skin preference applied to most other garments, with the partial exception of some outer parkas. Clothing which was next to the body had the hairside facing inward; when two sets of garments were worn, the hair or fur of the outer set faced outward. The outer parkas of men were sleeved, probably reached to just below the hips, and had an attached hood trimmed with a strip of wolverine fur to provide a frost-free ruff. The fitted pants of men extended from the hips to just below the knees. A second set of garments often was worn by men, although a single pair of pants might complete even a winter outfit. The inner parka of men, which included a hood with a wolverine fur ruff, reached to just below the waist. A fox-tail boa might be worn about the neck, and hats were of beaver, river otter, or other fur animal pelts. Protection for the hands was provided by mittens, preferably made from sheepskin. Winter boots were entirely of caribou skin and reached just above or slightly below the knees. The upper portion had the hairside in if designed for wear in extremely cold weather, and the soles were from dehaired caribou skin. The best summer boots were soled with dehaired, bearded-seal skin. Cushioning insoles of skin or grass were needed with sealskin soles, and inside any boots skin socks were worn with the hair facing inward.

The inner parka of a woman was bulky and reached below the knees. The roominess provided space for an offspring to be carried against the mother's naked back, with the child held in place by a belt which looped from the middle of the woman's back over her breasts. Her inner parka had a hood trimmed with strips of wolverine and wolf fur. The women also wore trousers that probably reached to just below the knees. The boots of women appear to have been of the same general forms as those of the men. The outer parkas for all age groups might be from caribou or one of a wide variety of other skins, such as bird, ground squirrel, hare, or hoary marmot. An outer parka was sewn carefully and set off at the cuffs and lower border with trim of dehaired skin, some of which had been dyed by soaking it in alder bark to derive colors which ranged from dull brown to shades of red (Gubser, 1965, 83–85, Ingstad, 1954, 135–36).

CHUGACH

Persons of both sexes among the Chugach wore parkas of animal or bird skins. The parkas reached the knees or the ankles, and below the sleeves were side slits through which the bare arms of the wearer could be extended. Beneath his parka a man wore a dehaired caribou-skin shirt obtained in trade from other Eskimos or from Athapaskan Indians. An inner apron from the skin of a newborn seal was worn by both sexes. Insoles of fur, grass, or moss were used with long boots made from sea-lion skin. The

Chugach also made boots with salmon-skin tops and sealskin soles, as well as hip-length boots from the entire leg and paw, with the claws intact, of a brown bear.

Protection against rain was insured with a variety of garments. One hoodless form that reached the ankles had short sleeves and was made of eagle skins from which the feathers had been removed. Another style, made from an almost complete black-bear skin, had an opening in the front which was laced closed after the wearer put it on. The bear's head was the hood; the forelegs were the sleeves, although the paws had been replaced with sealskin insets; the hind legs formed the trousers; and the clawed paws covered the feet. The Chugach also manufactured hooded rain parkas of flattened strips of sewn bear intestines. Although they were seldom used, mittens were manufactured from bear paws. Conical hats with flat tops were constructed of woven spruce roots and decorated not only with painted designs but also with dentalium shells and sea-lion whiskers (Birket-Smith, 1953, 64–68).

COMPARISON OF CLOTHING

Clothing among the inland Inuit tribes was much the same as for the Nunamiut, but coastal peoples such as the Tareumiut had distinctive variations. Their parkas for men reached below the thigh, were belted at the waist, and had triangular insets of white fur extending down each side of the neck opening at the front. The pants of men were of caribou skins if they were available; alternative materials were dog skins or sealskins. Baleen shavings or grass was used for insoles, caribou-skin socks were worn, and polar-bear skins or sealskins were used for boot soles. Mittens of polar-bear skin or dog skin were used in very cold weather, as were cloaks of deerskin. A woman's parka reached below the knees and had rounded front and rear flaps separated nearly to hip height. Women's parkas were more complex in cut than those of men and included decorative panels at both the front and back. However, the trim at the shoulders and the lower border was similar for the outer parkas of both men and women. A woman's parka was belted with sewn strips from the feet of wolverine with the claws hanging down from the belt at intervals. Another characteristic of Tareumiut women's clothing was that their trousers had boots sewn on at the bottoms. Over the summer parka a hip-length rain parka of sewn gut strips with a close-fitting hood was worn if needed by either men or women (Murdoch, 1892, 109–38; Simpson, 1875, 241–45).

The clothing forms of the arctic coast prevailed at least as far south as the Unaligmiut area of the northern Bering Sea coast. The most important northern Yuit departure was in the use of more diverse animal skins as parka materials. Not only were caribou and Siberian reindeer skins employed, but also the skins of hoary marmots, mink, muskrat, or birds were rather common. Bird-skin parkas had the advantage of being extremely light and warm, but since they were not durable, they were worn usually by poorer persons. From the vicinity of the Yukon River mouth southward to include the Kuskokwim River there were greater differences in clothing forms, particularly in parka styles. Parkas were long, often hoodless garments reaching at least to the knees and sometimes to the ankles. They most often were of hoary-marmot skins ornamented with marmot tails, but sometimes ground-squirrel skins with the claws and tails intact were used. Beneath a parka were worn belted trousers which reached the knees. If a long parka impeded a man's work, he gathered it up and folded the middle portion over a belt around his waist. If a parka was not hooded, a separate hood, hat, cap, fur headband, or ear flaps were worn. A small visorless cap of bird skin was reported for the Yukon delta area, and in the Kuskokwim region a goose skin with a slit in the breast for the wearer's head might serve as a hat. The parkas of women were somewhat shorter than those of men and were cut up the sides so that there were front and rear flaps. They were trimmed elaborately with skin tassels or animal tails and also had decorative front and back panels. In the Yukon-Kuskokwim region the usual mitten was of animal skins, but this style was supplemented with others of salmon skin, bird skin, or grass. Woven-grass socks might be substituted for those of skins, and boots of fish skin seem to have been rather common. For summer use, trousers and parkas were sometimes of fish skins (Edmonds, ms. 22–32; Nelson, 1899, 30–38, 43; Oswalt, 1963a, 26–27; Petroff, 1884, 134; Zagoskin, 1967, 212).

On Kodiak Island the parkas were long and were alike for both sexes. The sleeves were often short and sometimes nonfunctional, since there were slits beneath the sleeves from which the arms could extend. Parkas were made from a wide variety of skins including sea otter, bear, fox, or bird, but hoary-marmot and ground-squirrel skins were most preferred. The clothing of the Koniag was in many ways similar to that of the Chugach and other Yuit, but it also exhibited certain differences. The Koniag wore no trousers and usually did not wear boots or other footwear. The headwear of the men took two different forms, both of which were shared with other Yuit. One type, which was essentially cone-shaped with a flat top, was woven from spruce roots and had designs painted on. The second form had a peaked top and a broadly flaring visorlike extension over the forehead, was made from a bent piece of spruce wood, and probably was most often decorated with sea-lion whiskers. Women's hats were cylindrical with flat upper brims extending beyond the crown and were made from sewn intestines with added decorative trim (Birket-Smith, 1941, 126–32; Hrdlička, 1944, 37–41; Petroff, 1884, 136–40).

A comparative statement about subsistence patterns must take into account two factors above all others. First, Eskimos were flexible in exploiting a wide range of food resources, and second, the ethnographic accounts rarely provide an index into the quantitative importance of the species killed. Among the arctic whale hunters, great whales were the prime focus of the economy. If none were killed during a particular year, however, the people probably could have survived on seals, walrus, and beluga whales. The same alternatives were open to the Pacific whale hunters. The economies of the Bering Sea and the arctic hunters and fishermen stand somewhat in contrast, with greater balance in their subsistence pursuits, although it could be argued that among these people the seal was most likely to occupy a dominant role. The most specialized economy was among the caribou hunters, who could not have survived for a full year without great numbers of these animals. Another economic specialization was based on salmon fishing along the rivers with great runs. The population supportable during a normal year was high, but there are indications that some years the poor catch led to famine and thus limited population increases among these peoples.

An over all interpretation of the subsistence patterns leads to a number of specific conclusions. The arctic-whaling pattern is old, extending back at least to 1800 B.C., but there might have been breaks between the population today and that of early historic times. In any event, hunting great whales in northern Alaska was possible only at a few localities. Thus, what the northern whalers did in terms of their specialized technology or social patterns was not likely to be expandable nor to have a great impact on nonwhalers. The Pacific whalers had a greater commitment to maritime resources; to them land animals were not as important as they were farther north. As has been suggested earlier, the Eskimos of this area were comparative newcomers into an alien environment. Once again I would contrast the whalers in general with other Eskimos in Alaska. The flexible and diversified land-sea adaptations of the hunters and fishermen of the arctic and the Bering Sea are older, with roots in the Arctic Small Tool tradition and a continuity into the historic period. The population departing from this pattern became salmon fishermen, caribou hunters, or whalers, and these splits from the land-sea balance probably occurred repeatedly during the past 4,000 years.

A number of secondary comments round out the comparative view. First, just because a species was available locally did not mean that it had the potential to contribute to the subsistence welfare in a significant manner. This statement applies especially to fish such as pike, burbot, and trout. The technology for taking them existed, but it was not worthwhile to do so since they provided so little nourishment. Furthermore, Alaskan Eskimos had food prejudices which limited their diet somewhat. They rarely ate fox, pine marten, wolves, or wolverine. Finally, plant foods were insignificant in their normal subsistence patterns.

A comparative statement about Alaskan Eskimo clothing leads to a number of conclusions if the concern is with only the general patterning. The Nunamiut garments were the ones best adapted to extremely cold temperatures, and these were made of caribou skins except for some showy outer parkas. The same general forms were found among the other Inuit tribes and among the Yupik-speaking Unaligmiut. The latter people possibly adopted the Inuit styles in historic times as the result of Malemiut influence from the north. For the Yuit area in general, the clothing was more varied than among the Inuit. The garments often fit loosely and lacked the tailor-made appearance which we have come to expect among Eskimos. The Yuit clothing offered adequate protection against the cold but lacked the refinements known in the north. Finally, there was more variety in Yuit styles, in ornamentation, and in the diversity of materials utilized.

Chapter 6

Technological Patterns

Eskimo material culture, which is renowned among primitive technologies for its sophistication, reached its greatest development in Alaska. Eskimo artifacts customarily are exhibited as classic examples of technological ingenuity, and they justly deserve praise. Sometimes, however, the fact is ignored that the Eskimos of Alaska had more resources available to them than did other Eskimos. In Alaska, too, there were many opportunities to borrow ideas from non-Eskimos. When considering the technological ingenuity of these Eskimos, it is well to remember that many of the problems they faced in their environment were so different from those found in other regions that any solution might seem remarkable to outsiders. Furthermore, similar adaptations to arctic survival were made by non-Eskimos in Europe during the late Paleolithic.

Most of the systematic information about early historic material culture among the Eskimos of Alaska is in the monographic studies by Murdoch (1892) and Nelson (1899). These volumes are devoted largely to descriptions of artifacts and their uses.

Murdoch dealt primarily with the Tareumiut of Point Barrow, and Nelson's work centered among the Unaligmiut, although he included information about Eskimos as far north as the Bering Strait region and southward to the Kuskokwim River. The studies by these two men have been criticized for their stress on artifact descriptions and rather superficial remarks about most other facets of Eskimo life. The truth of such criticisms cannot be disputed, but without their inventories the richness of Western Eskimo technology would be less clear. The technological descriptions to follow deal first with the media worked and the most common tools employed. Following this, the manufactures of select tribes are described.

Materials and Production Tools

The products of nature include materials which may be divided conveniently into classes on the basis of their most important inherent qualities. The major categories of raw materials are solids, flexibles, plastics, and liquids, with an overwhelming significance of solids and flexibles. Among the solid materials worked by Eskimos were wood, particularly from spruce trees; caribou antler; walrus ivory; stone, with slate more important than flint or any other stones; and finally, bone from land or sea mammals and birds. Other solids processed primarily in restricted areas included sheep horn, ivory from prehistoric elephants, amber, ocher, and ice. Flexibles, which most often were brought together to create discrete items, were skins, either complete or cut into sections; sinews, particularly from caribou; plant products, including spruce roots, the inner bark of willows, birch or spruce bark, and grasses; mammal organs, including bladders, stomachs, and intestines; and baleen. Only clay was employed as a plastic, and pottery, although rare among the Pacific Eskimos, was elsewhere rather common. The liquids of greatest significance were water, urine, oil, and blood.

More diverse flexibles were employed than solids, and more

variation was found in the manufacturing methods for flexibles. The tools for processing flexibles usually were different from those employed with solids. Furthermore, men shaped the solids into finished artifacts, whereas women more often made articles from flexibles. The only plastic, clay, was processed by women, whereas liquids usually were handled by men.

In the descriptions to follow, only the material most often used is mentioned. For example, to state that wedges were of spruce wood means only that it was the most common wedge material. Wedges might also be from other woods, caribou antler, ivory, bone, or stone. Most of the information about materials and tools has been taken from such standard sources as Birket-Smith (1941, 1953), Giddings (1961a), Murdoch (1892), and Nelson (1899), but no effort has been made to cover the range of available information nor to reference each citation of a source. For the reconstructions of processing methods it has not been possible to derive all the pertinent details from published ethnographic accounts. In some instances I have drawn my conclusions after studying raw materials partially processed for later refinement and partially manufactured artifacts in archaeological collections from the recent prehistoric past.

SOLIDS

Wood was utilized wherever it was available, and spruce wood was preferred for most items. Spruce is relatively knot-free and is capable of being bent; also straight-grained spruce trees split with comparative ease. For certain items, such as net floats and shallow containers for liquids, spruce roots were the most desirable material since they tended not to crack when coming into intermittent contact with liquids. The usual source of spruce wood, even if spruce trees were growing nearby, was driftwood logs which floated seaward in the spring and fall when flooding river waters eroded the ground beneath riverbank stands. More driftwood logs probably were derived from the Yukon River system than anywhere else, but most rivers with spruce along their banks contributed to the supply. After a stranded log had dried, it could be used at any time during the next fifty or more years. When driftwood was plentiful along coastal beaches, river-banks, or river islands, it was possible to select precisely the piece needed to make a particular artifact.

The most important woodworking tools were the stone-bladed adz for cutting a section of wood free from a log, and the maul used together with wedges to split the wood along the grain into smaller portions. A polished-stone adz head was lashed with thongs directly to an antler handle, whereas a ground adz blade was fitted into an antler socket, which was bound to a handle. The wedges, of varying sizes, were most often spruce wood. Before a wedge was inserted, the wood was grooved with a bone or antler tool which had a round point.

A piece of wood was worked into an approximation of the finished form with an adz; the final form was produced with the aid of a crooked knife. These knives had slightly curved antler or wooden handles into which small curved blades fit along the top of the distal end. Such a knife was gripped with the palm facing upward, and the blade was drawn toward the user. Crooked-knife blades almost always were of metal in historic times. Metal blades for crooked knives appear to have been introduced about A.D. 1400 along the Kobuk River (Giddings, 1952a, 71) and at Point Barrow (Ford, 1959, 161, 243). They were more common at Kotzebue some fifty years later (VanStone, 1955, 106, 127, 137), suggesting that metal might have become more plentiful about 1450. It is possible that in northern Alaska the blades of some historic crooked knives were curved pieces of flint (Gubser, 1965, 80; Murdoch, 1892, 160). If a wooden artifact, such as a spoon, were to be hollowed out, the tool used was a knife with a blade consisting of a beaver incisor tooth fitted into the end of a short wooden handle.

To polish the surface of a nearly completed object, the curved outer surface of a beaver tooth was rubbed against the wood or the wood was smoothed with an irregularly shaped piece of antler. Small holes were made in wood by using hand drills with a tooth or stone point; for larger holes, one of two types of rotary drills was employed. A wooden shaft for a rotary drill was fitted with a stone point bound into an opening at its base. The rounded upper end of the shaft fitted into an antler bearing held in the hand or into a bit held between the teeth. The drill was propelled either with a thong strap which had handles at each end or with a slightly curved bow.

Caribou antler and walrus ivory were processed in much the same manner as wood. Antler was more important than walrus ivory because of its widespread occurrence and its favorable qualities of being less brittle than ivory as well as more easily worked into diverse forms. A cross section of antler is not the same throughout, the core being porous and rather easily gouged out or drilled. By contrast, walrus ivory has a marbled core along much of the tusk's length that is more difficult to work than the outer layer of enamel. Since items of ivory which did not have a balanced opposition between the core and outer enamel layers were prone to warp, the use of this material for artifacts was limited. Artifacts from the core alone are not common, and those with only the enamel layer represented could be neither thick nor wide.

Raw antler and ivory were first soaked in urine to soften them and then cut by ringing a cross section with uniform adz blows in one direction and by repeating the operation after turning the piece around. The result was a v-shaped cut around the material. Next the antler or ivory section was tapped until it broke free. The cutting process was repeated to obtain a section of the desired length. The next operation involved the use of a gouge. This tool, with a short antler handle and a small chisel like stone end blade, was ultimately derived from the Aurignacian type burin. A line was cut with a gouge along the length of the antler or ivory at a slight angle and was deepened until a groove was produced. A second groove was made paralleling the first but at an angle slanting toward that of the first cut. After the

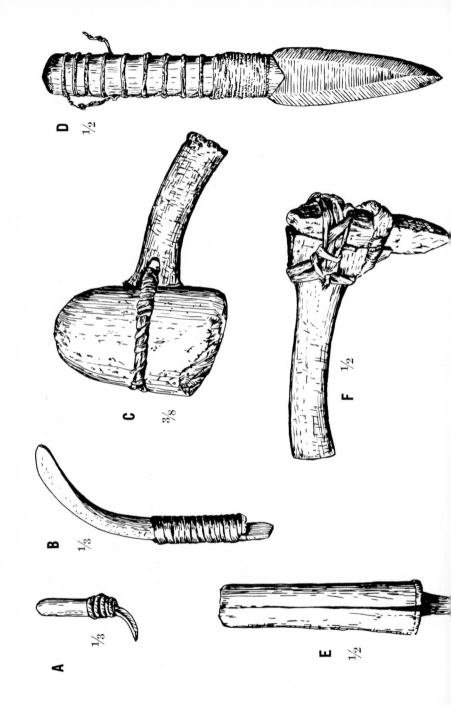

A ⅓

B ⅓

C ⅜

D ½

E ½

F ½

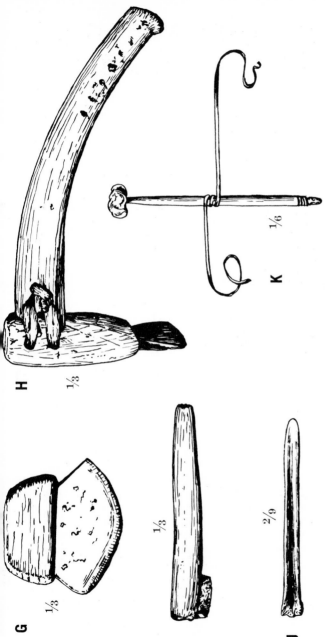

Figure 8. Tools (after Nelson, 1899; and Murdoch, 1892). (A) Beaver-tooth knife (redrawn from halftone). (B) Flint flaker with an antler handle and bear-bone flaker point. (C) Stone maul with an antler handle. (D) Slate-bladed knife. (E) Chisel with antler haft and iron blade. (F) Jade-bladed adz with an antler handle. (G) Ulu, or woman's knife, with a slate blade. (H) Slate adz blade set into an antler adz head lashed to an antler handle. (I) Flint-bladed crooked knife. (J) Split-bone bark peeler (redrawn from halftone). (K) Strap drill with caribou astragalus bearing and a flint point bound to the wooden shaft (detail supplied).

wedge-shaped piece was snapped free, the form was shaped further with a crooked knife and finished by a scraping with flint
flakes. If the object manufactured was to have a hole in it, either a
stone-pointed strap drill or a bow drill was employed.

The technology necessary in working bone was much the
same as that for working antler and ivory; however, bone was
used less often. The most important bones processed were from
whales, birds, and caribou. The porous quality of whalebone
made it a desirable material for certain uses, but bird and animal
bones were in general brittle and lent themselves to only a narrow
range of forms.

The process used to reduce any lithic mass depended on the
qualities inherent in that particular stone. Those which produced
concoidal fractures, such as the varieties of flint and quartz, were
flaked. Slate and basalt were first chipped or sawed, with both
techniques employed at times, and then they were polished to
finished form. Softer stones such as sandstone were pecked and
then polished. To approximate the form of an object from stone
which produced a concoidal fracture, the raw stone was first
flaked with a hammerstone or a maul and later given a finer
shaping with a flint flaker. This implement had a curved antler
handle with a groove at the forward end, into which was bound a
flaker point of antler or ivory.

Slate must have been reduced to usable pieces at quarry
locations since large unworked pieces rarely are found in dwelling sites. If small sections did not occur naturally, the pieces were
first fractured into flat slabs with hammerstones. The slate was
worked into artifact blanks by percussion fracturing or by sawing
with a sandstone saw, which had a straight cutting edge and a
v-shaped cross section. The next step was to grind the irregular
surfaces against stones of increasingly fine texture, and finally the
implement was polished with whetstones or polishing stones. To
produce a hole in a soft, thin piece of slate, the stone would be
drilled from one side only; if the piece was thick, it might be
drilled from both sides with the drill holes meeting in the center.

Another method used for thick stone was to saw grooves and then drill through the deepest ones. Sandstone and diorite might be processed by pecking away at the surface with a hammerstone until the desired form was created. The surface might not be modified further, or it might be smoothed with polishing stones. Again judging from the scarcity of large pieces of unworked raw materials in recent sites, the pecking process was performed away from dwelling areas.

The most difficult solid to process and the one traded most widely was jadite, available at a single source in Kobuk Eskimo country. Jadite was cut with saws of sandy schist and abraded further on flat grinding stones of sandstone or sandy schist. The grinding was performed with a rotary motion which in time left a raised area at the center of the grinding stone (Giddings, 1952a, 66–67).

FLEXIBLES

Of all the flexibles, skins were used most often and were prepared in a variety of ways. After an animal had been killed, the skin was cut free with a knife which had a double-edged flint or ground-slate end blade lashed to a wooden handle. To remove and save any fat which might remain on the under surface, a small, oblong, cup like scraper of ivory was drawn toward the user. Such a cup-shaped scraper might be the only type used on skins of birds and small animals, but larger skins were scraped a second time with a wooden-handled scraper having a ground- or chipped-stone end blade. This scraper was pushed away from the user. Along the arctic coast a woman who used this tool held the skin being worked on her thigh. In the Bering Sea coast area the men usually processed skins of larger animals, but elsewhere this seems to have been a woman's duty. The scraped inner surface was made more pliable by rubbing it with a piece of sandstone, pumice, or some other slightly abrasive stone. If the hair was to be removed, as it most often was from seal or walrus skins, the skin was soaked in water or rolled up and stored in a warm place until the hair began to fall out. After it was scraped again, it was stretched on a wooden frame to dry and then was folded and stored. If the hair or fur were to remain intact, the skin usually was soaked in stale urine and later stretched, scraped, rubbed, and stored.

The most important skin-cutting tool used by a woman was a knife with a ground-slate, semilunar blade fitted into a wooden handle. This knife was the *ulu* of Inupik or *uluak* of many Yupik speakers. For sewing, eyed needles of bone were threaded with twisted or braided caribou sinew, the leg sinews of caribou being preferred for this use. The sinews were dried, pounded to loosen the fibers, and then separated with heavy-tined combs. Stitches were carried from right to left, and the needle, held between the thumb and middle finger, was drawn toward the user. The type of stitch employed depended on the material and its use. A blind stitch prevailed for waterproof seams; other stitches were either overcast or running. Hard spots in skins might be chewed to render them pliable, and the edge of a skin might be chewed to soften it for sewing. When heavy seams were to be sewn, holes were first punched in the skins with an awl, and a threaded needle was drawn through these holes. A thimble, which consisted of a small oval piece of sealskin with a cut along one side, was used on the forefinger.

One of the important uses of dehaired sea-mammal skins was for rawhide line. Among the Tareumiut a skin to be cut into line was first wetted and then was held taut by one man as another began to cut from an outer corner. The man held his knife so that the blade was vertical and cut away from himself, working in circles toward the center of the skin. In the Bering Sea coast area the skin was trimmed to an oval form before the cutting was begun.

Roots from spruce trees were split initially with mauls and wedges. They were divided into smaller sections by using the rounded point at the proximal end of a crooked-knife handle or the rounded point of an antler barking tool, and they might be smoothed with a knife blade. Just before they were used, they were soaked in water to render them pliable. The inner bark from willow shoots was in some areas an important flexible. Along the Kobuk River it was removed from live willows in either summer or winter. In the summer, long sections of bark were peeled off with the aid of a sharply pointed, bone barking tool. The same process was followed in the winter except that the willows were cut and thawed before the bark was stripped. The outer layer of bark was removed, and two inner bark strands were twisted together and used.

Of the three tree barks employed as flexibles, the most important was birch. Along the Kobuk River large sheets of birch bark were collected in the spring before the snow was off the ground. A tree was selected if the trunk was relatively free of knots and limbs and if the bark surface did not rub off when handled. The tree was ringed through the bark layer at the top and bottom of the section to be removed, and then a vertical cut was made. The bark was peeled free by using a bone tool with a rounded point. Spruce bark was removed from a living tree during the summer in the same manner and with the same type of tool. Spruce bark was flattened, dried, and then used.

Grass needed for weaving was collected in the fall after a killing frost. For making mats three or four individual strands were twisted together, and a series of these was suspended at right angles from a stick. This stick may be considered as a one-bar loom, and the strands hanging from it were the warp elements. Grass strands similar to the warp were twisted and passed over and then under as weft elements to produce flat mats. In the manufacture of grass bags with pointed or flat bottoms, two or more stems of grass formed the warp strands. These strands were twisted as were the double-strand weft elements which passed over and under the warp. The weave was either loose or relatively tight, and at the basket top the warp strands were braided to form a rim. The coiling technique was employed to construct small baskets. A bundle of grass strands formed the core of the coils, and flattened strands were wrapped around the core and passed through it individually to bind the coils together.

Long, flexible strips of baleen were cut from bowhead whales with a slate- or flint-bladed knife. Along the ends of these strips were hairlike strands which served to strain food materials from the water as it was taken into the whale's mouth. To remove these strands a small, semilunar, chipped-stone blade set into a bone handle was drawn back and forth rapidly to produce shavings.

The intestines to be used, most often those from seals, were first emptied, then inflated to dry, and afterwards split and rolled up for later use. Treated in a similar manner, except for the splitting process, were the bladders and stomachs of animals. Among the most important containers were entire animal skins or portions of skins. Large containers were made from nearly complete skins of hair seals by first cutting off the head of the seal and removing the flesh and fat through the opening. Afterwards the skin was dehaired, and the neck opening was sewn at the edges to keep it from tearing. An oval plug with a central groove along the side was inserted, and a rope was bound into the groove to seal the container. If the skin was to form a clothing bag, the hair was left intact, the opening was sewn closed at the head, and a cut was made on the ventral side between the flippers. Holes were punched on either side of this slit and a rope was passed through them to close the container.

PLASTICS

Pottery most often was manufactured by women from clay found locally, although either clay or finished pottery might be traded from one village or tribe to another. In making pottery the clay was moistened and kneaded, and different materials might be added as binders or temper. The tempering materials most widely reported among the Iniut were blood, sand, and feathers, particularly those from ptarmigan, and all materials were used in combination. After the clay and the intrusive materials had been mixed thoroughly, a vessel was produced either by working one lump of clay into a molded form or by making a base and then adding small hand-flattened patches or coils to form the sides. The surfaces of the vessel were smoothed, and it was dried before being fired in an oxidizing atmosphere.

LIQUIDS

The liquids utilized served diverse purposes in the processing or decorating of material items. The most important liquid probably was human urine, which served to break down the grainy inner surface of skins. The inner bark from alder trees might be added to either plain water or urine and the skins soaked in this solution to produce a rust to red color. Red for this or other uses also was produced by pulverizing red ocher and mixing it with water or oil. Another source of red coloring was human blood, sometimes let by puncturing the inner surface of a nostril with a sharp stick. The blood might be mixed with urine and was applied with a squirrel-hair brush. Ground charcoal provided black coloring; an ocher of yellow was employed less often, as was white from clay.

Tribal Technologies

The raw materials and the tools for their processing which have just been presented are found among most Alaskan Eskimos. More specific manufactures are described by considering forms from tribes with contrasting settlement and community patterns; those peoples selected are the Tareumiut, Unaligmiut, and Chugach. Stress is placed on hunting and fishing equipment, containers, and items associated with transportation. Other manufactures which have been described or will be considered later are clothing, toys, items of personal adornment, and objects associated with ceremonial life.

TAREUMIUT

The Tareumiut spent most of each year at a central base and employed diverse methods to make their living primarily from the sea. The abundance of their manufactures reflected their relatively high degree of physical stability, and the diversity of material forms indicated their varied activities. The spruce-wood hunting bows were four feet long and curved away from the bowstring at the ends. Bows were backed with two bundles of braided sinews which were drawn taut. The spruce arrow shafts were two feet long and had two split and twisted feathers bound with sinew at the nock end. Arrows for caribou had heads of antler with barbs along one side and tangs designed to slip from the arrow shafts when the animals were struck. One variety of arrowpoint used against polar bears had a flint end blade at the tip of a barbed antler arrowhead, but others consisted of tanged flint arrowpoints, triangular or oblong, bound at the distal end to an arrow shaft. Blunt arrowpoints of bone or ivory were used against small game, and arrows were carried in an oblong quiver of sealskin stiffened at one side with a wooden rod. Tied to one wrist of an archer was a sheep-horn or an ivory wrist guard. Spears for killing polar bears at close range or dispatching swimming caribou from kayaks had six-foot spruce shafts to which were attached triangular, tanged flint points.

Traps included log deadfalls set for fox, baleen spring bait for wolves, pitfalls in the snow for caribou, snares set at the nests of birds, and gorges tied to a stake for seagulls. Birds might also be taken with clusters of ivory bola weights or with bird spears. A bird spear consisted of a five-foot-long spruce shaft, at the end of which was set a single barbed point of ivory or two slightly flaring points of ivory with barbs along the inner edges. Some two feet from the base of the shaft three ivory prongs with wedge-shaped tangs were fitted into the wood and bound in place. Such a spear was thrown with the aid of a throwing board and had an effective range of about thirty yards. If the end point or points missed the bird, it still was possible that a lateral barb might strike it.

The most diverse, as well as the most complex, weapons were for hunting sea mammals. These fell into two major categories, but both were designed to injure an animal and impede its escape.

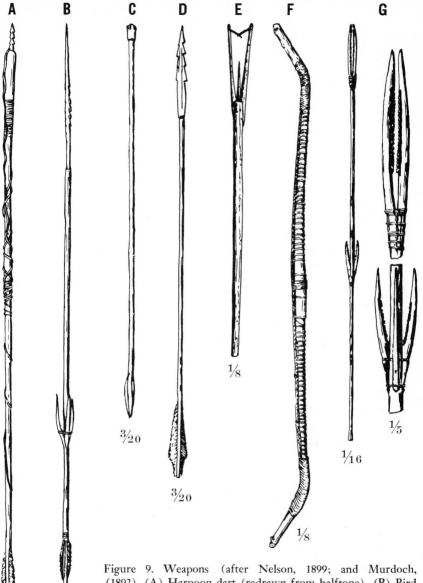

Figure 9. Weapons (after Nelson, 1899; and Murdoch, (1892). (A) Harpoon dart (redrawn from halftone). (B) Bird spear with side prongs, basal feathering, and a single end point (redrawn from halftone). (C) Blunt arrow (redrawn from halftone). (D) Arrow with barbed arrowpoint (redrawn from halftone). (E) Double-pronged leister spear. (F) Sinew-backed bow. (G) Bird spear with side prongs and a double end point.

The weapon point either was barbed to hold the animal or else formed a toggle beneath the animal's skin. The first type, which will be referred to as a harpoon dart, had a head of ivory, with a sharp point and a pair of lateral barbs. Near the base was a line hole and then a tang which fitted into an ivory socketpiece; the latter in turn was attached to a wooden shaft. This weapon was propelled with the aid of a throwing board and was used against small hair seals. A length of line passed through the dart-head hole and was tied to the base of the socketpiece. Attached to this line was another, which was fastened to the shaft at about a third of the distance from the base, with the rest wound loosely around it. The two lines formed the sides of a triangle and the shaft an extended base. This type of dart was thrown by a man from a kayak. After the head struck a seal, it detached from the socket-piece. As the seal sounded, the line unwound, and the shaft was dragged beneath the water at right angles to the dart head.

Weapons with toggle harpoon heads were either thrown by hand or thrust. At the base of a toggle harpoon head was an offset barb with a drilled hole at one side to receive the end of a foreshaft. Near the midpoint of the head was a transverse line hole, and in the top was a slot to receive a triangular slate or flint point. The foreshaft, with a line hole for attachment to the shaft, fitted into a socketpiece which was hafted to a spruce shaft. Such a harpoon was used for taking walrus or bearded seals. Through the line hole in the head was passed a loop of rawhide which was tied to a single line with an inflated sealskin float at the end. The harpoon was held in a throwing position by placing the forefinger against a small ivory projection bound to the shaft. After an animal was struck, the harpoon head toggled, and the sounding animal dragged the float beneath the water as the shaft floated free. The harpoon shaft could be fitted with another head and launched again when the animal surfaced. A spear was used to kill the animal when it had become exhausted. A similar but smaller form of toggle harpoon was employed when hunting small hair seals from the edge of a lead in the ice. The only differences between this weapon and the foregoing form were that this one had an ivory ice pick at the base and a line that was held in the hand. The ice pick served mainly to test thin ice over which the hunter might walk and to aid him in walking over broken ice fields. For hunting seals at their breathing holes a toggle harpoon of the same form but with different proportions was used; the shaft was short, the ice pick and foreshaft were long, and the line was attached to the shaft. A whaling harpoon, which was not thrown but was thrust into the whale's back, had a long shaft and a fixed foreshaft. From the harpoon head, which had a blade at right angles to the line hole, a line extended through the hole to two inflated sealskin floats. A harpooned whale was killed with a weapon composed of a long spruce shaft and a triangular, tanged lance blade.

In the vicinity of Point Barrow, fish were not plentiful in either fresh or salt waters. At tidal cracks in coastal ice tomcod and sculpins were taken in the fall. The tackle consisted of a barbed lure-hook of ivory, a baleen line, and a wooden rod, which served also as a reel for the line when not in use. In the late winter, holes were chopped in the shore ice with an ivory-pointed ice pick, and they were kept open by removing any newly forming ice with a scoop made with an antler frame, baleen mesh, and a wooden handle. A cluster of barbless hooks around a single shank was lowered, jigged to attract tomcod, and then raised to the surface abruptly in order to impale any fish that were near a hook. Gill nets made of baleen or sinew strips were set beneath river ice for whitefish or along open lagoons for salmon. Rawhide nets were set beneath the sea ice in the winter and along the seashore in the summer to capture small hair seals. The final fishing implement of note was the leister, which had a central barbless point and two lateral prongs.

Among the containers were skin pouches for tobacco, skin bags for tools, and oblong wooden tool boxes with fitted lids, as well as small wooden boxes, often in the shape of an animal, for harpoon head points. Buckets, which were round or oblong, had

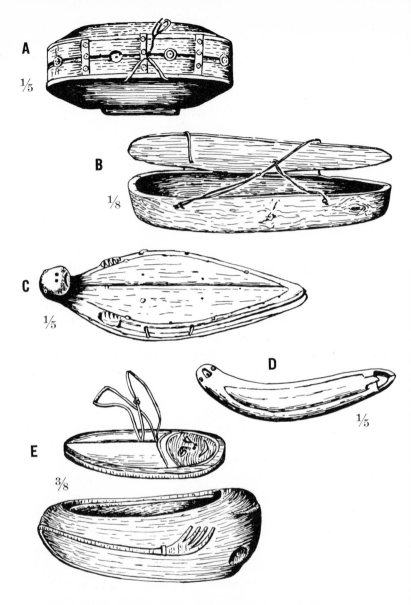

Figure 10. Containers (after Nelson, 1899; and Murdoch, 1892). (A) Wooden box (redrawn from halftone). (B) Large wooden tool box. (C) Tool box (redrawn from halftone). (D) Wooden paint box (redrawn from halftone). (E) Wooden paint box.

baleen or wooden bottoms and fitted sides made from a single piece of wood or baleen bent and then sewn together at the overlap. Meat bowls and trays or dishes were carved from single pieces of wood, and there were soapstone lamps as well as pottery vessels.

For travel over water two forms of skin-covered boats were employed, the kayak and umiak. The spruce-framed kayak was designed to carry a single individual who sat amidships. The vessel, about nineteen feet in length, had a beam slightly wider than a man's hips and a cowling in front of the manhole. The foredeck was flat as was the decking behind the manhole. The framework was built around two longitudinal gunwales; along the bottom of each were mortises to receive rounded ribs, and inside the framework were bound spruce laths. The first cowling piece in front of the manhole was rounded, whereas the others rose to a point amidships and decreased in size to a flat foredeck. The vessel was covered with dehaired, hair-seal skins. Either a single- or double-bladed spruce paddle propelled a kayak; the double-bladed form was used only for speed. The umiak or large, open skin boat was built with a mortised and lashed spruce frame. An umiak was thirty feet long with a six-foot beam and measured two and a half feet at its maximum height. Dehaired bearded-seal skins were preferred for the covering, and these vessels were propelled with single-bladed paddles.

The dog sled was ten feet long and had spruce runners which were separated by about three feet and were turned up at the front. The runner bottoms were fitted with strips of whalebone attached with wooden pegs. The runners were joined with four bow-shaped crosspieces which were mortised into the runner tops. Four uprights, which increased in length from front to back, were mortised into each runner between the crosspieces and the tops of these uprights were connected with longitudinal strips of wood. Horizontal stringers were lashed on the inner sides of the uprights at the highest point adjacent to the crosspieces. Small planks were lashed between the stringers to form the bed. This

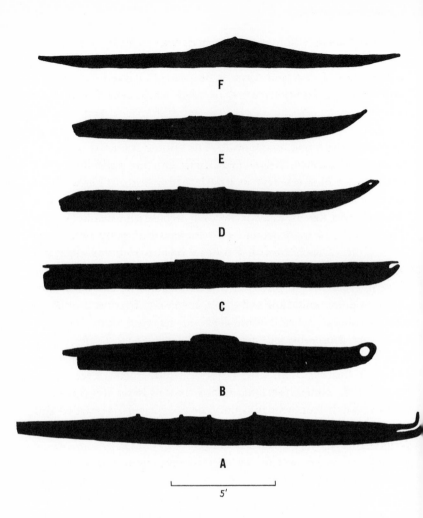

Figure 11. Kayak types. (A) Koniag. (B) Nuniwagamiut. (C) Unaligmiut. (D, E) Kauwerak. (F) Tareumiut.

form of built-up sled was used for transporting bulky objects and might have a distinctive form of ice shoe. These were made from two sections of clear pond ice, eight inches thick, ten inches wide, and as long as the runners. A depression was gouged in the top of each strip into which the sled runner was placed. The runners were frozen to the ice shoes and then the shoes were trimmed. Another sled form for carrying loads of meat and umiaks was ten inches high and had six-foot runners set two and a half feet apart. Crosspieces between the runners were lashed into place through drilled holes. Similar but smaller sleds some two feet long were designed to transport compact loads and were pulled by one or two persons. The larger sleds were pulled by as many as ten dogs attached on alternate sides of a main line. A dog harness had a head loop and a loop for each of the forelegs; a single line led across the dog's back and ended at a toggle fastened to the main trace. Due to the packed snow conditions in the vicinity of Point Barrow, snowshoes were not worn.

Some Tareumiut manufactures in addition to clothing, toys, and objects with religious or ceremonial associations were embellished. Tools, weapons, and containers of wood often were covered entirely with red ocher or sometimes had bands or stripes of red set off by black stripes. On tools or handles of ivory, and to a lesser degree of antler because it was used less frequently, the most common motifs were a compass-made circle around a dot, a single line along a portion of the artifact, parallel and sometimes ticked lines encircling an object, or converging lines with fillers. The most elaborately decorated items were bag handles and drill bows. They were usually of ivory and might have circle-dots, one or more engraved lines along the length of the curved shaft, or lines and circle-dots used in combination. Representations of men, caribou, bearded seals, or whales were etched on other handles or bows. Figures of men and animals were engraved on tablets of ivory on occasion; these appear to have been representations of hunting scenes or perhaps catch-records for larger animals. Carvings of animals and men in ivory or sometimes in soapstone from lamp sherds were known, but their function was unrecorded. The sculptures were poorly executed, the representative engravings were organizationally simple and not well done, and the skills in working wood or flexibles were not impressive when compared with those of more southerly Alaskan Eskimos.

UNALIGMIUT

Of the thirteen Yuit tribes, the Unaligmiut material culture is the best known, although the recorded inventory does not seem complete. It would be better to describe the manufactures of a more centrally located Bering Sea Eskimo tribe, but it is impossible to do so since their products are not reported systematically in the published literature. A comparison between the Unaligmiut and Tareumiut material culture reveals that the artifacts made by the Tareumiut were likely to be less elaborate than those of the Unaligmiut, but comparatively few forms were clearly unique to only one of these tribes. Since the arctic coastal Inuit and northern Bering Sea Yuit shared the same basic technological knowledge, only the more significant variations from the forms already described for the Tareumiut will be detailed.

Either the self- or sinew-backed bow was used with a wide variety of arrowpoints. An arrow for large game might be headed with an oblong flint point having a diamond-shaped cross section and a short tang. Long, barbless bone points which were triangular in cross section might also be used for large animals. Birds were shot with blunt arrowpoints which were beveled at the end, and antler arrows for fish had three points at the end, each with small barbs. The arrow quiver had a stiffening rod and was probably in other respects like that of the Tareumiut. To straighten an arrow, the shaft was inserted into an oblong hole made through a piece of antler and then was gently bent. A similar but smaller implement was employed for straightening arrowpoints of organic material.

The traps for game included fixed and spring-pole snares, and spring bait for wolves. Birds, particularly ptarmigan, were taken

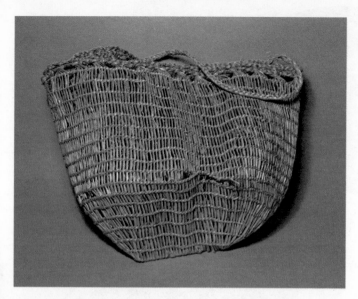

1. Ikogmiut grass basket.

2. Gut window from the central Bering Sea region.

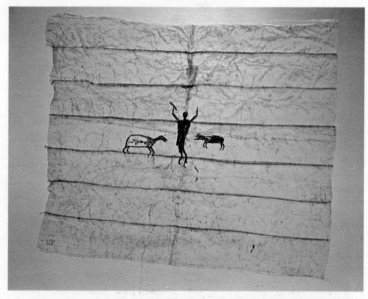

3. Pottery vessel and lamp from the central Bering Sea coast.

4. Wooden dish from Nunivak Island

5. Wooden container reportedly from the Nome area.

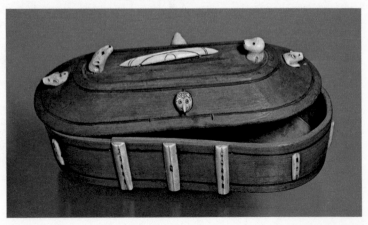

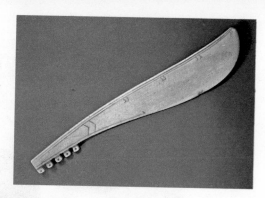

6. Storyknife from the
central Bering Sea coast.

7. Finger mask from
Hooper Bay Village.

8. Central Bering Sea coast mask.

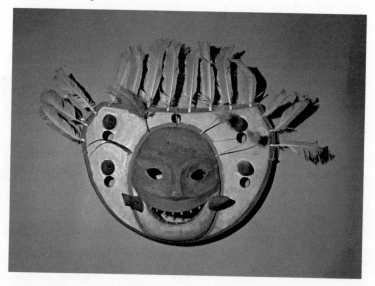

9. Wooden masks from Point Hope.

10. Shaman's animal effigy, or kikituk, from Point Hope.

in fine-meshed nets of sinew staked upright. Cliff-bird eggs might be collected with the aid of a rawhide seal net fastened to the edge of a cliff and lowered over the side. A barefoot man climbed down the net and gathered the eggs, placing them inside his parka which was belted at the waist. Fish-baited gorges were set for seagulls, but bird bolas appear to have been uncommon. A bird spear might have a cluster of three barbed points at the end, or a single end point and three more points about a third of the distance from the butt end. In either case the spear was thrown hard and fast by using a throwing board in an overhand manner.

Barbed harpoon darts were more common than toggle-headed harpoons, probably reflecting the importance of hunting small hair seals. The harpoon darts, with barbed antler or ivory heads and four-foot shafts, were fitted as among the Tareumiut so that the shaft was dragged at right angles by the seal. Among the Unaligmiut, however, the base of the shaft might be feathered. Similar but longer and heavier harpoon darts were used against bearded seals, walrus, and white whales. These weapons were thrown with the aid of a finger rest lashed to the shaft about a third of the distance from the base. An inflated bladder float might be attached to the shaft. An alternative means for playing a seal was to coil the dart line in a harpoon line board fitted on the kayak deck in front of the hunter. This board consisted of an oblong piece of spruce with two basal lobes which were slipped under a thong tied across the deck of a kayak. Around the upper portion of the board was an oblong rim, and within this rim was the coiled line. The line extended from the dart head through the coil to an inflated sealskin float at the rear of the manhole. After the harpoon was cast, the line uncoiled from the board and the float was thrown overboard. For use against larger sea mammals, the toggle harpoon head with accompanying foreshaft and socketpiece was fitted to a shaft that was somewhat longer than the foregoing form and had a finger rest to aid in propelling the weapon. A harpoon used in association with hunting on ice fields had an ice pick at the base of the shaft. A seal call was employed when hunting seals which were basking on the ice. Wounded seals often were killed with a braining club, which consisted of a round or oblong piece of bone or stone in which one or more holes had been drilled for the attachment of a handle or a rawhide thong. For killing wounded walrus or white whales, a spear with a triangular, tanged point attached to a spruce shaft was used.

The diversity of equipment connected with fishing clearly reflects the importance of fish in the Unaligmiut economy. Tomcod were caught by jigging beneath the shore ice in the spring and late fall. A hole was chipped with an ice pick, and the newly forming ice was removed repeatedly with a wooden-handled scoop which had an antler rim and rawhide netting across the inner section of the rim. Two poles were used, with a reel on one for winding the hooked line. The other short pole had a split antler eye at the end for inserting the line of rawhide, sinew, or bird quills which had been split, made flexible, and knotted together. Near the lower end of the line were a sinker and a hook shank with multiple barbless hooks attached. For grayling, loach, blackfish, pike, and whitefish, barbless hooks were attached to lines. Seines were employed for herring, but gill nets were set for whitefish and salmon. The netting material was rawhide or sinew, and mesh sizes were measured with gauges. Net floats were wooden and sinkers were stone or antler. Nets of heavy rawhide line weighted with heavy stones were set for white whales and seals. In small streams funnel-shaped traps were set in association with weirs to catch whitefish and blackfish in the spring, whereas in the fall whitefish and pike were speared through holes in the ice with leisters. Salmon or whitefish might also be speared with a barbed harpoon dart head fitted into a wooden shaft. Through a hole in the dart head was a rawhide line which was held coiled by the fisherman and fed from his hand after he threw the spear. By means of this line the harpooned fish was played and then landed.

Containers were pottery, basketry woven by twining or coiling, skin bags, and a host of small wooden boxes, buckets, and dishes. The lamps were made of stone pecked into a sad-iron or circular shape. The latter form also was produced in clay, as were shallow, saucer-shaped lamps.

The kayaks were seventeen feet long with rounded bottoms and decks arched at the same height for the full length. They were propelled with either single- or double-bladed paddles. A single-bladed paddle was used also with an umiak, which was of the general Alaskan Eskimo form described for the Tareumiut. Also similar were the sleds for carrying bulky but comparatively light loads and the dog harnesses. Ideally the dog teams consisted of seven animals and pulled loads of three hundred to four hundred pounds. Snowshoes were rounded and slightly upswept at the front, but the webbing was loosely woven. Short sleds to be hand-pulled for portages often were carried on the stern section of kayaks. These sleds were about four feet long with short upright stanchions attached to the longitudinal strips which reached from the front to back. Crosspieces between these strips held the runners together.

When compared with similar Tareumiut artifacts, the forms discussed for the Unaligmiut seem better made. Red ocher was the paint predominately used on diverse implements. The artifacts most likely to be decorated elaborately were bag handles and drill bows. Handles were etched not only with representations of animals but also with scenes from village life. Sometimes sculptured heads of animals were carved on the bag handles. The circle-dot motif was less common than in the north, while toggles decorated with animal heads were more common.

CHUGACH

As is true of other aspects of Chugach culture, the information about manufactures is best known from the reconstruction by Birket-Smith (1953). Sinew-backed bows of spruce were used, and arrows were vaned with three radially arranged split feathers. The barbed, ground-slate arrowpoints had long rectangular tangs. For sea-otter hunting, small unilaterally barbed dart heads of pounded copper were set into bone socketpieces. A line which went through a hole in the dart head was wrapped around the shaft and tied to the nock end, which was feathered. Cylindrical quivers were either of skin with a stiffening rod or of two pieces of wood sewn together and topped with a circular lid. Land animals and birds often were caught in snares and deadfalls. The former were set for small land mammals, bears, and birds, with deadfalls most important for bears, river otter, and mink. Seagulls or ducks might be taken with three-pronged gorges.

Harpoon heads of the dart form were more common than those which formed a toggle, but both were used against seals, sea lions, and small whales. A toggle harpoon head of bone was fitted with a triangular slate end blade inserted at right angles to the harpoon line hole. Fitted into the harpoon head socket was a wooden foreshaft with a wedge-shaped tang which was fastened directly into the weapon shaft. A rawhide strip extended from the line hole to the shaft, where it was tied, and an inflated seal-stomach float was fixed on the shaft. A harpoon dart head was fitted into a bone socketpiece, and possibly there was a float on the shaft. For killing small sea mammals a short-handled wooden club was employed. Large whales were taken with lances on which broad-bladed, tanged points of ground slate were mounted in detachable foreshafts which in turn were attached to the weapon shaft.

For halibut fishing a barbless hook was fastened to a line attached to one end of a two-pronged stick; a rawhide line weighted with a notched stone sinker was tied on the second projection. A similar type of hook was used for catching cod. Snares were set for fish, and sharp-tined rakes with long handles impaled herring, which then were shaken off into a boat. The fish leister with three barbless wooden prongs at the end of the shaft was an additional means of taking herring. After salmon were confined by a weir of poles set in a stream, they were harpooned with barbed dart heads to which a hand line was attached. Fish likewise were taken in streams in which the tide entered; a trap of roots, grass, or bark held the fish as the tidal waters withdrew.

The containers commonly used included bowl-shaped lamps

of pecked stone, wooden buckets with bent and sewn plank sides and pegged-on wooden bottoms, food bowls and storage containers shaped from single pieces of wood, and small baskets with flat bottoms and slightly flaring sides made from spruce roots. Large bags might be made from sealskins and smaller ones from sections of skins or animal bladders.

For travel over water the typical umiak and kayak were employed in addition to a kayak form with two manholes, usually called a *bidarka*, and wooden dugout canoes. The paddles for all of these vessels probably were single-bladed and had crutch handles. For travel on land a plank toboggan was pulled by three or four dogs harnessed in tandem. The dog harness was composed of three loops of rawhide thongs, one for the head and the other two for the forelegs. When used as pack animals, dogs carried skin pouches on both sides of their backs.

In the artifact categories discussed, most items were well made but lacked decoration. The notable exceptions included baskets into which geometric designs were woven and oblong eating bowls cut from a single piece of wood. The bowls, which were boat-shaped with rim insets and grooves, might be painted in sections or all over. The wooden spoons and dippers of wood or mountain-goat horn had curved handles, often with motifs which recall Tlingit forms.

COMPARISON OF TECHNOLOGIES

A comparative analysis of raw materials and artifacts by area reveals both broad and restricted regional variations. Some tribal differences in the use of materials were affected by the availability of raw material, but this fact alone does not explain certain differences. Considering the areal diversities in materials, however, makes the significance of similarities and differences in forms more apparent. In general the artifact inventories of the arctic and the Bering Sea Eskimos shared more similarities with each other than either did with the Pacific Eskimos.

Wood was scarce among the northern Tareumiut and Nunamiut, and alternative materials served most purposes. However, wood was essential for weapon shafts, bows, and arrows since there were no recognized substitutes, and every tribe was able to meet these needs. The Pacific Eskimos had an abundance of diverse woods, and their woodworking was skillful, although only a limited number of forms seems to have been produced. It must be remembered, however, that the record of Pacific Eskimo material culture is far from complete. The best and most diverse forms of wooden objects described from any Eskimo area were produced on Nunivak Island and the mainland region between the mouths of the Yukon and Kuskokwim rivers. These people relied on driftwood, but even it was unavailable locally on the inland tundras. For this reason the Yukon-Kuskokwim-Nunivak triangle would not be considered a logical choice for an area of woodworking intensity, and yet it was here that the Eskimos excelled in this craft skill. The imagination of these craftsmen in designing and manufacturing small containers was unsurpassed. A further reflection of their abilities is found in the frequency with which decorative elements were added to wooden objects. The containers might be painted entirely, representative figures painted on, the entire vessel shaped to represent an animal, a section sculptured, or decorative grooves, inlays, and openwork handles added.

Artifacts from antler were utilized everywhere but were least common among the Pacific Eskimos of Prince William Sound and Kodiak Island, where caribou were absent. It would be difficult, however, to single out any particular locality as exhibiting the greatest development of antler utilization. The Bering Sea and arctic Eskimos shared the same general ability to work antler well. Walrus ivory was accessible to the arctic coastal Inuit as well as to the Yuit of Nunivak Island and in the Bristol Bay region. Along most of the Bering Sea coast walrus were rare or absent, and they were uncommon in the Pacific Eskimo area. It is clear that ivory was worked among all peoples who killed walrus and was traded widely both as a raw material and as finished artifacts. To single out the area in which ivory-carving skill was greatest is difficult. According to Petroff (1884, 135–36), one center was in the Bristol Bay region among people I would identify as Aglegmiut, and according to Nelson (1899, 196), another was between the mouths of the Yukon and Kuskokwim rivers. If, as seems reasonable, the Aglegmiut entered the Bristol Bay region in late prehistoric times from the north, they must have carried their ivory-carving tradition with them. The Inuit of King and Diomede islands are famous carvers today and possibly were equally skilled at the time of historic contact.

Stonework artifacts were produced nearly everywhere at the time of historic contact by chipping, grinding, or pecking and then polishing. Flint chipping was least likely to be found among the Pacific Eskimos, where grinding and pecking dominated. The Bering Sea Eskimos knapped flint much less often than they ground slate, whereas for the arctic Eskimos the reverse was true. Pecked stone, reported everywhere, was of diminishing importance in the cultures ranging northward from the Pacific drainages. By and large pecked- and ground-stone artifacts were most elaborate among the Pacific Eskimos, and manufactures from flint were best among the arctic tribes.

The most widespread material in the category of flexibles was skin, and skins were important everywhere. More diverse skins were worked by the Bering Sea Eskimos than by those of the Pacific or arctic regions, whereas the most complex skin garments were produced by the Inuit. The most varied and sophisticated uses of spruce root were found among the Pacific Eskimos. Of the three tree barks utilized, birch bark was the most important and was worked with greatest skill among the inland tribes. These Eskimos had ready access to the material and had contacts with Athapaskan Indians, who were skillful in their use of birch bark. The most elaborate objects of grass were from the central Bering Sea coast and adjacent inland regions. Working of baleen was most common along the arctic coast, where bowhead · whales were killed often. In the final category of flexibles, intestines were utilized everywhere as a material for waterproof garments, and sealskins made into containers were found as trade or locally produced items throughout the Eskimo area.

Pottery was made everywhere except among the Chugach and possibly the Unixkugmiut, although it was not plentiful among the Koniag. The most complex and diverse forms were produced by the Eskimos of the central Bering Sea coast, and here, too, the elaborations in surface treatment were greatest.

In summary, two centers of craft skills are identified: the Pacific Eskimos were the best stoneworkers and produced excellent items from wood or woven spruce roots; the central Bering Sea tribes were the best wood and ivory workers, as well as the best potters and weavers of grass. Thus, Alaskan Eskimo craft skills climaxed among those Eskimos of southwestern Alaska. The least complex material culture was reported from the Nunamiut, and the traits they possessed were shared with adjacent coastal Eskimos.

From the Tareumiut of Point Barrow to the Unaligmiut of Norton Sound the material culture was much the same, although there were regional and local variations. The people of this area produced the tools and weapons we are most likely to consider as typically Alaskan Eskimo. South of Norton Sound some of the more typical items begin to drop from the inventories. Along the central and southern Bering Sea coast there was an emphasis on open-sea hunting from kayaks and less stress on hunting seals either at their winter breathing holes or as they basked in the sun on the ice in the spring. With open-water hunting, harpoon darts and throwing boards were used more frequently than was the hand-thrown, toggle-headed harpoon. By the time the Pacific Eskimo area is reached, additional losses, such as the absence of multiprong bird darts, wound plugs, and seal nets, are noted. Among the Pacific Yuit the characteristic forms of Eskimo material culture occurred with far less frequency than they did from Norton Sound northward. In other words, northern Alaska produced the more typically Eskimo technology, but the greater skills and elaborations of technology were found among the southern or southwestern Eskimos.

Chapter 7

Community Patterns

The presentations of settlement and technological patterns were concerned with cultural adaptations leading to biological survival. Community patterns, by contrast, view the social relationships of village inhabitants. A typical community was composed of about two hundred persons who lived in ten to fifteen houses, with two families per house. The obligations of an individual were first to his nuclear family, then to his residence unit, and third to his personal kindred or patrilineage. Thus kinship ties primarily within the community dominated social life. A community might also include voluntary associations transcending formal kinship bonds, and these usually had their physical base in a village ceremonial structure. Formal community-wide social institutions embracing all individuals did not exist. Apart from relatives in other communities, the most important extracommunity ties were between friends, many of whom regarded each other as partners. Other extracommunity contacts were hostile ones with Indians or other Eskimos.

The discussion of community patterns will emphasize the household, the community, and the intercommunity levels, whereas the individual is placed in his social and cultural context in the chapter to follow. Since the household was the major focus for an individual, information on household composition is important. The largest number of persons per household was around twenty. This number was recorded for four Kuskowagamiut villages (Zagoskin, 1967, 306). An estimate of eighteen persons per household was made by Lisiansky (1814, 193) for the Koniag, and the same number was noted for ten Ikogmiut villages (Zagoskin, 1967, 306). In the Kuskokwim district, which included primarily Eskimos in the Yukon-Kuskokwim area exclusive of those on the south bank of the Yukon River, the average number of persons per house was thirteen (Porter, 1893, 174). One Kuskowagamiut settlement, Crow Village, had ninety persons living in five houses during early historic times. These houses, which were excavated in 1963, totaled 1,209 square feet of floor space, for an average of one person per 13.4 square feet of floor. In contrast with the Yuit household numbers just cited, the Inuit as a rule lived in smaller dwelling units. For the Tareumiut of the Point Barrow area the number of persons per house averaged six in the early 1850's (Simpson, 1875, 237–38). The upper-river Noatagmiut averaged eight persons per house (Stoney, 1900, 569), and this figure could be extended to the Nunamiut.

Alaskan Eskimo communities with more than three hundred individuals were unusual. The largest village probably was Wales with an estimated five hundred persons (Ray, 1964, 79). Since the historic Kodiak Island group population was about 6,000, larger settlements may have existed among the Koniag, but no village census exists from this area for the early period of Russian occupation (Petroff, 1884, 33).

Representative Community Patterns

NUNAMIUT

Drawing mainly on the study by Gubser (1965), we find Nunamiut social integration strongest at the nuclear family level and the emotional attachments to this unit lifelong. The nuclear family households, or the rarer small extended family dwelling units, were clustered in local groups or bands. A band was composed of those families living together in one settlement whenever possible and ranging over a defined area, usually a river valley, in the central Brooks Range. The tribe's integration was based on ties of blood and marriage, a common way of life, a tribal designation, and an occupancy of the same geographical region. The people did not consider the band to be the most efficient subsistence unit; on the contrary, the nuclear family was considered the most effective exploitative unit. The reason for banding together was to have the companionship of others.

Certain men exerted sustained influence on the lives of individuals who were not members of their nuclear or extended families. These were leaders with charisma, although they did not necessarily depend on supernatural aid. Such a man was a careful observer of the natural world and made logical predictions about animals, climate, weather, and other men. If such a person was additionally a shaman, his potential for leadership seemingly was increased. An individual with these characteristics was called an umialik, one who owns an umiak, but the word did not carry the same force of meaning as among the northern coastal Eskimos. To the Nunamiut an umialik was above all else an excellent hunter, or a great trader, or a combination of the two. An umialik influenced the decisions of the local group to which he belonged, and through his skills he accumulated more material property than most men. He supervised collective caribou hunts, and the people listened to his advice about hunting caribou because experience had taught them that he was wise. Thus an umialik was the focal point for economic cohesion. Such a man retained his position of influence only so long as he was correct in his predictions and effective in his supervisory capacity; if he failed repeatedly, he was replaced informally. It was unlikely that his ability would pass on to a son, and there was no formal training for the role.

Not only was there a leader to provide social unity, but also there was a physical structure, the karigi, that brought the group together. The Nunamiut karigi was a dome-shaped tent erected when a band or other large aggregate of people clustered, usually during the spring and fall caribou migrations. Each family, as it was able, contributed skins to cover the karigi. In it men ate communal meals after large numbers of caribou had been killed, and here also spontaneous or prearranged dances were held. A shaman might hold a seance in the structure, and it served as a workshop as well as a place for men to lounge. The karigi was neutral ground where disputes were settled, hopefully without violence.

Differences between individuals most often, but not always, were settled amicably. The common causes for disputes were accusations of property theft, adultery, murder, and general anti-social behavior. If a dispute began to assume some magnitude and a settlement between the antagonists could not be reached, the contesting parties would confront each other in the karigi. The older, wise men of the community spoke of such differences in the past and how they had been resolved. The umialik discussed the problem, and probably his voice carried the most weight in the final settlement. In a case of theft the umialik, as the man with the most material goods, was likely to have been the victim. If he had more than one wife, his ties of blood and marriage were greater than those of others, and he could depend on many persons for support. Furthermore, by being an umialik he was a person whose opinion the others respected. If an individual was a social nonconformist, the men of the karigi would decide collectively what action should be taken against him. The sanctions ranged from ostracizing the offender by not speaking to him, to driving him from the settlement or, much more rarely, killing him. In instances of nonconformity, however, every effort was made to settle the matter without having the dispute reach the karigi. When the community was forced to act, it meant that the people had not settled their differences as honest men with the interest of the community at heart.

As has been noted, trade among northern Eskimos added significantly to their range of foods, raw materials, and manufactured goods. While the trade itself was very important, of almost equal significance was the amiable relationship an inland Eskimo had with his coastal trading partner. Partnerships with Eskimos of other tribes assured one of a friendly reception when visiting other areas as well as a fair exchange in trading ventures. Both men and women had such partners and traded with these individuals alone. A partnership was bound with an exchange of gifts by the individuals involved, and a rich man might have several partners. Partners did not haggle over exchanges; in fact, they were more generous than they would be with people of their own band. If there was something in particular which one partner sought, he "asked" for it, meaning he desired it in trade. A man such as an umialik built a reputation as a great trader by being generous in his exchanges and by accumulating an inordinate amount of material for trading. Reciprocal trade relationships were lifelong unless one of the partners negated the arrangement; the basis for termination usually was the feeling that one had been cheated. In times when caribou were scarce or absent and starvation threatened, a hunter and his family might be forced to move to the coast. Here they would live temporarily with his trading partner. Coastal Eskimos other than trading partners, however, were treated with reserve and perhaps a tinge of fear.

Accepting Nunamiut traditions, their first contacts with the Kutchin Indians took place in the vicinity of the Kobuk and Noatak river headwaters, near Walker Lake. According to the Nunamiut account, the Kutchin had ranged into this country before 1800, and the Kobuk Eskimos had fought them to retain possession of the area, which had been Eskimo for generations. The Indians withdrew under this pressure toward Howard Pass, where the Nunamiut were living. Again there was conflict, and the Kutchin drifted eastward to areas surrounding Anaktuvuk Pass. Here the Indians followed a way of life very much like that of the Nunamiut. In some instances both Indians and Eskimos learned the language of the other, and they entertained each other with songs and dances. Conflicts which developed stemmed from disputes over women, and there are tales of raids and reprisals. Attacks were made by Nunamiut bands as units, preferably against unsuspecting groups, although battles between armed and prepared parties were known.

Relations were amicable between the Koyukon tribe of Athapaskans from the river of the same name and the Nunamiut, but the two people did not reach the point of intermarrying. It is interesting that the Nunamiut regarded the Kobuk Eskimos as almost like Indians because of their close relationship with the Koyukon. Conflict between the Nunamiut and other Eskimos was with the Tareumiut, particularly those of Point Barrow. According to both groups, trouble usually stemmed from the seizure of women or less often from some other real or imagined wrong. In violent battle only a single man reportedly would be spared in order that he could convey word of the defeat to his allies. Disputes between two tribes were at the band or family level, but they were uncommon.

TAREUMIUT

Drawing primarily on the accounts by Rainey (1947) and Spencer (1959) for the fabric of Tareumiut community life, we find residence units of small extended families. Brothers, their wives, and children lived together, or parents lived with their children and the in-marrying spouses. If all the persons of these social groups could not be accommodated in a single dwelling, some built houses nearby. Clearly recognized economic obligations fell on the nuclear family, but there was an overall dependence on other members of the residence unit, house group, or one's personal kindred. Such economic reciprocity did not extend to the community as a whole, however.

A man's most important social and economic bond beyond his household was with an umialik, an individual who not only owned a large skin boat but also led a whaling crew. A whaling crew usually consisted of relatives of the umialik, and their economic welfare depended to a great extent on him. A distinct tendency existed for the role of umialik to pass down a family line; nonetheless, with the support of his kindred any man owning an umiak could aspire to lead a whaling crew. In order to compete with the existing umialiks an aspirant was obliged to contribute substantial aid in terms of food and material property to potential crew members. Furthermore, he sought to convince them that he could provide for their welfare better than their present whaling captain could. Because of their abilities as leaders and as the owners of large quantities of material property, umialiks had the greatest authority within a community. As Spencer (1959, 179) has written, an umialik "was marked by dignity, modesty, popularity, circumspection, and great wealth." In attracting and holding a crew an umialik depended on the goodwill of his followers and could not coerce individuals into a dependency relationship. An umialik was a man with charisma, wealth, and the ability to lead his crew in successful whale hunts year after year. The crew, which played the most important part in a whale's capture, was awarded most of the meat; the umialik received the flukes, which were the delicacy. Thus, the more whales taken by a crew the more meat the boat owner could distribute to them and the greater the likelihood that he could retain their cooperation. If a whaling season was poor for a particular crew, the umialik sought aid from his kindred to support his men and hoped that they would remain loyal to him until the next whaling season.

The six Tareumiut karigis at Point Hope were constructed in the same manner as large houses. Two or three karigis were built in large Point Barrow area villages. Point Barrow karigis had permanent foundations and walls but were roofed temporarily with skins, snowblocks, or wood without sod covering. At Point Barrow a karigi was named and in a loose sense owned by the umialiks whose crews operated out of it. The whaling captains contributed materials for karigi construction, and whenever the role of umialik passed down a family line, identification with the same karigi continued over a number of generations. An individual changed karigi ties, however, if he joined the whaling crew of an umialik identified with another karigi. Although the structure was not used during the summer, at other times the men and boys socialized here most often and intensively. Men might sleep in the karigi on occasion, and their meals, which had been prepared by the women at home, were eaten there. The karigi was where games often were played, ceremonies usually performed, and social functions held. Here the whaling equipment was readied for the next season and the ceremonial obligations performed by the umialiks.

Relationships between community members sometimes were marred by personal animosities, which might erupt as family feuds. The most common cause of a feud was the unjust murder of an individual. If a habitual thief or ruffian was killed, it usually was considered for the common good and no counteraction would be taken. A woman was the most likely cause of a murder. Any number of types of sexual involvement with females might lead to violent death. If the victim's kindred felt that the murder was just, they would not seek revenge although they would make a token show of force. If they felt that the killing was unjust, a feud between the families involved would follow. Violence between families within a community was settled quickly, but it was likely to linger if the families lived in different villages. A means for correcting less errant behavior was for a man to compose a song about the faults of another and to sing it in the karigi to shame and ridicule the victim into conformity.

The blood ties of kinship were strong and identification with an umialik extremely important, but there were also other social institutions which encompassed the average individual. A voluntary partnership established with a Nunamiut insured a steady supply of caribou skins for clothing and other inland products. Furthermore, a coastal man might on occasion travel inland with his Nunamiut trading partner who would vouch for him; the same guarantee applied when a Nunamiut lingered at a coastal settlement. A Tareumiut might have as many as six trading partners, some of whom were at coastal villages other than his own. Partnerships, often developing into strong friendships, formed the only nonkin ties apart from those between a man and an umialik who was not a relative. A joking partner might be an unrelated member of one's whaling crew, or a trading partner might secondarily be a joking partner. Extracommunity joking partners were expected to compose songs about each other which were humorous and mildly insulting. The songs were carried by others to the joking partner, to be heard and enjoyed by all the community.

Beyond the feuds which erupted between Tareumiut families, physical violence was uncommon. There is one story of an unsuccessful inland Eskimo attack on Point Hope and another about a late prehistoric battle with the Noatagmiut (Rainey, 1947, 240; VanStone, 1962, 19). Although Nunamiut conflicts with coastal Eskimos were known, they appear to have been unusual (Gubser, 1965, 43). The coastal and inland peoples in arctic Alaska were far too dependent on each other to permit long-term mutual hostilities to disrupt their critical economic ties.

NUNIWAGAMIUT

From the monograph by Lantis (1946) we learn that a large Nuniwagamiut village included about one hundred ten persons, two kashgees, and about fourteen houses. Each house was occupied by from two to four nuclear families. Although economic cooperation within a household was important, familial well-being seems to have focused on the larger kin groups, the patrilineages, of which there appear to have been five. The right to use tangible designs, including property marks, and objects associated with a particular animal passed along patrilineal lines. The animal associations represented spiritual aids which, along with secret hunting songs, were important to members of that patrilineage for success in hunting seals. The animals from whom one obtained power could not be hunted intentionally, nor could the power be alienated. However, the animal name was not assumed by the family nor was descent calculated from the animal. Leadership in a patrilineage was controlled by a man who knew all of its sacred songs, possessed many amulets, directed the group's ceremonial life, and was a successful hunter as well as a generous person. Among the Nuniwagamiut extrafamilial cooperation in hunting was not the norm, and the role of the umialik was unknown. Outstanding Nunivak Eskimo hunters did attract a following of less capable persons but had no positive control over them.

Beyond the physical household and the ties within a patrilineage were a man's bonds with a kashgee. Each kashgee was named, and although the membership changed often, it was the physical unit with which a man was associated closely. After reaching the age of five, a male moved into the kashgee nearest his home. A kashgee served as the center for community ceremonies, as the bathhouse, as a workshop for men, and as the place where men lived. It was here that youths observed and copied the craft skills of adult men. The description of kashgee life indicates that membership was not tightly integrated. Nonetheless, the men of a kashgee formed two groups, based on the side of the kashgee they occupied, and competed with each other in dancing and gift-giving. The division is stated explicitly to have been on a nonkinship basis.

Antisocial behavior which led to some form of overt action seems to have been rare and was confined largely to theft and murder. To steal a material item was somewhat futile, since personal property could be identified easily by the property mark each item bore. If a theft did occur, the thief was considered a pathological individual, and he would be scorned rather than formally punished. If a killing occurred, it was the duty of the offended family to settle the matter; this was not a subject for community-wide concern. Revenge was most often the responsibility of the eldest son of the victim. Children were always taught that it was the duty of the eldest son to rectify the killing of a family member, and no other recourse was known. Before retribution was exacted, the murderer was shunned, and the community members simply waited until the matter was settled finally with his murder.

Two different forms of partnership relations, both of which were inherited through the paternal line, were reported for Nunivak Eskimos. Joking partners appear to have been the children of half cross-cousins. Such individuals composed songs, to be sung at dances, which poked fun at their joking partners. Verbal jokes likewise were exchanged, and under no circumstances could one take offense at the manner in which he was ridiculed by a joking partner. In serious partnerships all of the children of partners were partners in turn. The children of a man had several sets of such partners since their father had a number of serious partners. This partnership association was carried down the male line only, and while a man had a number of partners, he was most likely close to only a small number of such individuals. An original partnership was an agreement between two unrelated men or a man and a woman of the same generation to extend mutual aid. While partners of the opposite sex were not prohibited from marrying, no such marriages were recorded. Serious partners extended economic aid to each other and offered moral support when necessary. In addition, a man might have sexual intercourse with a partner's wife.

Formal hostilities between Nuniwagamiut communities did not exist; neither did the Nuniwagamiut fight the adjacent Eskimos of Hooper Bay or Nelson Island, among whom they had relatives and friends. Collectively, these groups were allied against the Ikogmiut, whom they fought only during the summer. Offensive warfare was to avenge the death of a relative or to surmount a previous defeat in battle, not to capture women. An attacking party was accompanied by a shaman who sang songs to bring favorable weather and later would remove arrowpoints from the wounded if necessary. A war party was without a formal leader; it traveled in secret and sent out scouts to reconnoiter the enemy settlement. Ideally a surprise attack was begun at daybreak by men who first had stripped to the waist and sometimes had removed their boots for greater freedom of action. Arrows were shot through the skylights of the enemy's houses, and as the survivors emerged, the men engaged in close combat. Neither slat nor leather armor was worn, but shields made of wooden slats might be carried by attackers. Not only the men but also the women and children might be killed, although young girls sometimes were spared and carried off. Defense of their island homeland was difficult, for when an enemy party appeared there was no time to summon their allies. Defensive measures included having secret household compartments in which children could be concealed, hidden tunnel exits from houses and kashgees, and secret passages connecting these structures. Before one battle the Nunivakers are said to have erected a breastwork and scattered broken caribou bones on the ground to cut the boots and feet of the invaders.

CHUGACH

Among the Chugach the nuclear family as described by Birket-Smith (1953) was the most important social unit, and a household might at times consist of brothers who had married sisters. Little is known about household life or the economic responsibilities within a household, but it is clear that the male occupants of a house cooperated in hunting activities. Leadership among the Chugach was more formalized than that found in any tribes described previously, and a single community or adjacent communities had a chief aided by an assistant chief. These two leaders were unrelated, although the role of each passed down a paternal line. If a chief had no son, one of his brothers or one of his brothers' sons replaced him. In the event that these individuals did not exist, a sister's son might become chief. If none of these persons existed, the assistant chief assumed the role, and a replacement for him was selected. A chief was a man of wealth; he and his family wore clothing made of more valuable furs than those used by ordinary persons. A chief guided the subsistence activities of his community in addition to leading hunting and war parties. Although such an individual had no formal power over other villagers, he obtained their cooperation through his position of authority and respect. He did not work himself but was supported by the labors of others. As a chief aged, he was replaced on hunts by an appointed leader, and if at any time he was considered incapable of leadership, he could be replaced by common agreement. At the opposite end of the community scale were chattels, who were either Koniag war captives or individuals purchased from adjacent Eyak or Tlingit Indians. These males or females performed menial tasks for their owners. They were not abused and might marry either another chattel or a free person.

The Chugach differed from the other Eskimos discussed in not having a men's house or kashgee. It is possible that the house of a chief served at least some of the functions of a kashgee elsewhere. Furthermore, although the Chugach had trading relationships with persons of adjacent Indian and Eskimo tribes, no formal trading centers existed and trading partnerships are not reported.

The most disruptive antisocial actions were thefts, murders, and wife abductions. If the thief was discovered after an object was stolen, the object was returned to the original owner and the matter dropped. A song might be composed to ridicule a habitual thief, and this action usually was sufficient to effect his reform. If a married woman was raped, the offender was killed. When one person killed another without provocation, it was the obligation of the brothers of the dead man to avenge his death by killing the murderer. To accomplish this end they might enlist the aid of relatives. The chief seems to have had little responsibility in settling differences between families, and here, as among other Alaskan Eskimos, revenge was a family affair.

Contrary to the predominant Eskimo pattern, warfare was more formalized, with frequent feuds between Chugach villages and lasting hostilities with adjacent Indians and other Eskimos. The decision to launch an attack against an enemy was made by a community chief, and the volunteers painted their faces black for the venture. An attacking party traveled by umiak and raided a settlement early in the morning. Offensive weapons included bows and arrows, daggers, spears, slings, wooden clubs, and braining stones attached to a thong or thrown at an enemy. Each community had one or more "strong men" who went into battle armed only with a club to knock down flying arrows. Enemy men were killed, but women and children were made captives. The houses were plundered and then set afire. Heads of slain enemies appear to have been taken to the victors' village, exhibited, and then buried. After killing an enemy, a Chugach warrior observed food and sexual taboos for five days, but he was not obligated to follow these rules if he had eaten his victim's heart. The most important defensive equipment was armor made from wooden slats. As many as thirty men might also protect themselves behind a long screen. If an attack was anticipated, refuge was taken on an inaccessible rock where houses had previously been built and provisions stocked.

Comparison of Community Life

In general, Alaskan Eskimo nuclear family membership was quite unstable. The high mortality rate of infants and young children, the short life expectancy of adults, and the frequency of divorce all were contributing factors. A nuclear family was small and consisted of a couple and two to three children who would survive into adult life. Under these conditions there must have been a wide variety of individuals attached to the core nuclear families for household units to be composed of up to twenty individuals. These units might include one or more parents or siblings of the couple, stepchildren, more distantly related persons, adopted children, orphans, and nonrelatives. In a household which consisted of a nuclear family plus others of the above categories, there would be comparatively few males to support the members. While households sought to maintain their economic independence, it appears unlikely that any particular household could be self-sufficient for a long period of time. The cushion against economic privation was mutual aid provided within kinship groups. Households whose members did not have close kinship bonds with others in a community had a precarious economic existence. This dependence on mutual economic aid deterred individual families from casually leaving one community and seeking membership in another, where they would be unlikely to have as many relatives as in their home village.

Among communities of caribou hunters mutual aid beyond the household was offered whenever possible, but due to the nature of the subsistence efforts a household with poor productive potential probably could not perpetuate itself. The same general conditions probably prevailed among the arctic hunters and fishermen. For the coastal whalers the situation was different because of the greater productive potential of the environment and more adequate knowledge of exploitative methods. Here comparatively large numbers of persons lived in one community, and kindred could function effectively in offering mutual aid. Attachment to an umialik offered still greater security. For the Bering Sea area we know little of community life except for reports concerning the Nunivak Eskimos. Here the emphasis was on the patrilineage to provide economic security. The Pacific whalers and fishermen appear to have been integrated more fully on a community-wide basis.

The implications of extracommunity partnerships were considered previously, and the other important contacts beyond one's settlement resulted in either warfare or some measure of acculturation. It is almost impossible to be certain of the nature of Indian-Eskimo relations at the time of earliest historic contact except in select cases. At one extreme was the late prehistoric take-over of Eskimo country by Tanaina Indians in the Cook Inlet region (de Laguna, 1934, 13–15) and the stunning defeat of Chugach Eskimos by the Eyak Indians (Birket-Smith and de Laguna, 1938, 147). The Pacific Eskimo tribes were unable to stabilize their relationship with Indians and were withdrawing before Indian pressures. At the other extreme, an area of joint occupancy by the Georgetown Ingalik subtribe and the Eskimos was reported for the central Kuskokwim in early historic times (Oswalt, 1962, 1–4). Here, judging from historic trends, the Indians were being assimilated by Eskimos. The detailed ethnography for the Anvik subtribe of Ingalik (Osgood, 1940, 1958, 1959) indicates that these Indians also had absorbed many Eskimo characteristics and were acculturated by the Ikogmiut Eskimos. Zagoskin (1967, 136–37) and Allen (1900, 465) mentioned that although the settlement of Ulukuk on the upper Unalakleet River was inhabited by what would today be termed Koyukon Indians, the persons living along the lower river were Eskimos. This arrangement is contrary to the usual patterning in which Eskimos held only short rivers leading to the sea. Another boundary in a state of flux was reported by Stoney (1900, 828). He noted that the oldest Kobuk people, although he probably meant only those of the upper river, still spoke an Athapaskan language in 1885–1886 and "say that their fathers knew no other." This statement suggests that Athapaskan Indians were assimilated quite recently by Eskimos in the area of the upper Kobuk River. Thus, in western Alaska the Eskimos were moving eastward and absorbing Indians, whereas the Pacific Eskimos of Cook Inlet were losing territory because of Tanaina Indian pressures.

Chapter 8

The Individual

Probably the most vivid means of conveying the operation of a sociocultural system is to plot a composite life cycle of an individual. Any amalgamated view of a person from womb to tomb is removed from actuality since no two persons respond in the same manner to sociocultural stimuli, and yet such a view reveals the general cast to life. Furthermore, persons making up a society form the basis for kinship systems, social structures, and social organizations. Also included in the life-cycle description are cultural behaviors which are individually focused, meaning mainly forms of bodily adornment. The earlier ethnographic chapters have been presented in terms of representative tribes and the variations from these. In this chapter, however, a single, composite Alaskan Eskimo life cycle is offered with certain elaborations for particular tribes. The reason for this organizational shift is to avoid descriptions which would be largely repetitive because of the overall similarities.

The life cycle of an Eskimo in Alaska, if he lived long enough, passed through three distinct phases. First, a person was by birth a member of a family of orientation. Throughout his infancy and childhood he had a dependency relationship in his family which decreased rapidly during adolescence. Within a family of orientation a great deal of wastage resulted from the high rate of infant mortality. Emotional ties within the family were not well developed due to the deaths of members, the frequency of divorce, and the fact that men often did not live in the household in which small children were raised. As a child grew up it was, by American standards, treated leniently, and there were few discontinuities in child-rearing practices. Restrictions were placed on a girl at her menarche, and ceremonial recognition was given to adolescents of both sexes when they first contributed to the subsistence welfare of their families.

Girls married soon after puberty, but males married in early adulthood. The couple had children and began a new cycle in which they were the persons heading a family of procreation, which was in turn the family of orientation for their children. At this stage the energy, luck, and skill of the couple were most required. An adult Eskimo man was neither a romantic nor a philosopher concerned with detached abstractions. He was an empiricist whose daily thoughts centered about economic security, and he involved himself with such practical problems as attempting to think like the animals he hunted so that he could take them efficiently, or varying the time, place, or depth at which a fish net was set so that its yield would improve. His economic plans were short-range, usually encompassing a single year. The struggle to stay alive was a focus of his waking hours, and yet it was not an unrelenting, oppressive concern. He was aided by a stoic attitude and an acceptance of reality; still, his thinking about how to survive remained flexible. He was willing to try new ideas of his own or of others in order to make a better living. While his cooperation with other persons was sometimes essential in order to make a living, he was by temperament and inclination an individualist who depended most on his own skills and abilities.

In the third and final phase of an individual's life, he was ideally attached to his family of procreation as a secondary member. In old age he was as active as his physical abilities permitted, but his time was increasingly spent in reflection. As is also true among old people in other societies, while awaiting death he lamented the decline of vitality in the younger generation.

Pregnancy, Birth, and Infanticide

Among Alaskan Eskimos more specific patterns for behavior were established for pregnant women than for any other category of individuals. These patterns were designed to insure a safe delivery as well as to be a positive influence on the maturation of the fetus. Irrespective of the prevailing weather a birth usually took place in isolation and away from the ordinary family residence. While in isolation the mother was prohibited from eating fresh foods and used only her own containers. At the end of the prescribed time, she bathed, put on new clothing, and returned to her former place in the household. As Lantis (1947, 1–2) has observed, community-wide recognition of a birth was rare; it occurred only among the Yuit, and even here it was sporadic. A Nuniwagamiut man gave a sweatbath for the men of his kashgee when his first child was born (Lantis, 1946, 224). Among the adjacent coastal Eskimos, a feast was given at the birth of a child, and people from the surrounding area were invited. As a part of the celebration, gifts were distributed to the old men and women who attended (Lantis, 1947, 2; Rasmussen, 1927, 350). The Chugach celebrated the return of a mother with her new infant by having a community feast and distributing gifts (Birket-Smith, 1953, 85).

Infanticide was practiced everywhere, and the justifications offered by the Eskimos were that the parents could not support the offspring and no one was willing to adopt it, or that the neonate was diseased or malformed (Simpson, 1875, 250). Among the Chugach, however, it apparently was common only among unwed mothers (Birket-Smith, 1953, 85). The murder of an offspring of either sex usually took place within a few days of the birth. If it was necessary to abandon an older child for want of food, a girl was left in preference to a boy. The Nunamiut practiced infanticide on occasion (Ingstad, 1954, 54; Simpson, 1875, 250), and it was reported as common among the Ikogmiut in 1890–1891 (Edmonds, ms. 15). Missionaries among the Kuskowagamiut noted its high frequency, although killing a male offspring was almost unheard of (Oswalt, 1963a, 133–34). The usual method for killing everywhere seems to have been by exposure to subzero temperatures, although smothering and drowning also occurred. In addition, an infant might be buried alive with its dead mother (Edmonds, ms. 15; Oswalt, 1963a, 137, 144). The importance of infanticide among aboriginal Alaskan Eskimos is not clear, but it seems to have been uncommon. Possibly it became more prevalent in early historic times when the people were exposed to new fatal and debilitating diseases which made it more difficult for a nuclear family to maintain its stability.

Naming the Child

Naming an offspring was accompanied with a minimum of ritual if any was observed at all. The selection of a name was simplest among the Inuit, where an individual most often received the name of a deceased relative. He acquired at least some protection from the relative's spirit, and he might be expected to reflect some behavioral characteristics or perhaps the appearance of the person (Gubser, 1965, 206; Spencer, 1959, 286–91). The naming process among the Yuit, as indicated by the Nunivak and Chugach customs, was more complex. Among the former an infant was named either after a living or dead relative, usually a grandparent, of the appropriate sex since names were either male or female. The idea that an individual was protected by the spirit of the person after whom he was named did not exist. Still, names had a supernatural quality and were not normally used by adults.

Teknonymy was practiced, and nicknames which described some characteristic of the person were used. Some names memorialized an accomplishment and other names were derived from kin terms of reference (Lantis, 1946, 236–38). The Chugach husband of a pregnant woman selected a name for the offspring before the birth, and since names were associated with one sex, two names were chosen. The name was from a close but deceased relative; however, the child was not expected to resemble the person after whom he was named, nor did he perpetuate that person's spirit. In addition, a living person might bestow his own name on a favorite child, and a nickname might be given by an old person so that the child would have a long life. An alternative name might be taken to note some outstanding individual accomplishment, and close friends might use secret nicknames (Birket-Smith, 1953, 85–87).

Among the lower-river Kuskowagamiut a name was taken from the most recently deceased person in the locality with no regard to kinship ties, and spiritual qualities plus the physical and behavioral characteristics of the dead person were absorbed by the namesake. The names usually were not identified with a particular sex. A child's name would be changed if he often were ill so that a new name might bring a better future (Oswalt, 1963a, 134).

Childhood

Eskimo parents are described as being highly indulgent toward their children, but as Lantis (1960, 167) has commented, this characteristic of familial life possibly has been overplayed. It is nonetheless true that Eskimo children were affectionately regarded by parents and physical punishments were not a normal part of discipline. An infant spent most of its time in the back of its mother's parka, except among the Pacific Eskimos where cradles were used, and it was common for an offspring to nurse as long as three years. Small children of either sex were provided with a variety of toys, which often had counterparts in the adult technologies. As a rule children played at adult activities or at games which would increase their physical prowess. Among the Nunamiut, for example, were balls made from caribou skin, caribou femur heads for juggling, ropes or sinews out of which to make cat's cradles, the moss-stuffed skins of squirrels for boys to shoot with small bows and arrows, toy umiaks and kayaks, dolls of caribou skin stuffed with hair, toboggans from moose-leg skins, and spinning tops of wood (Gubser, 1965, 102–03). Children of both sexes played together when quite young, but as they grew older, they separated into male and female groups. Among the Yuit tribes, boys between the ages of five and ten usually went to live in a kashgee with other males, whereas girls remained in the natal homes with their mothers. Even among the Inuit, where the karigi was not the usual sleeping place for males, it was frequented often by men and boys. Thus, there was a clear line dividing males from females as they developed physically and socially.

Both Inuit and Yuit females were tattooed, either around the time of puberty or less often during childhood. The most com-

Figure 12. Kotzebue Sound Eskimos (after Choris, 1822).

Figure 13. Koniag man (after Sauer, 1802).

Figure 14. Chugach man (after Cook and King, 1785).

mon pattern was a series of lines from the lower lip to the chin (Lantis, 1946, 225; Nelson, 1899, 50; Simpson, 1875, 241; Zagos-kin, 1967, 211). In addition, the left wrists of Nunivak women, the breasts and wrists of Chugach women, and the breasts and backs of Koniag women were tattooed (Birket-Smith, 1953, 69; Lantis, 1946, 225; Lisiansky, 1814, 195). Tattooing of males was quite rare. The ears of women were pierced to receive large earrings. These were worn by the Tareumiut (Simpson, 1875, 240–41) and probably by the Kovagmiut (Cantwell, 1889b, 88). Nelson (1899, 52–53) noted that in western Alaska the lower pinna of a woman's ear might be pierced to receive ornaments. Presumably this was limited to the Yuit since it is not mentioned for the north; the edges of men's and women's ears were pierced and ornamented among the Koniag (Lisiansky, 1814, 194–95) and Chugach (Birket-Smith, 1953, 69). Large earrings were worn by the central Bering Sea Yuit males (Lantis, 1946, 226; Nelson, 1899, 53). Throughout the Alaska mainland, the nasal septum of a girl was pierced and one or more beads suspended from the hole, according to Nelson (1899, 52); he states further that adult females did not wear such ornaments. However, Kuskowagamiut women reportedly wore beads from a hole in the nasal septum (Oswalt, 1963a, 27–28), and on Nunivak Island adults of both sexes had similar ornaments (Lantis, 1946, 225).

Labrets were worn only by men among the Inuit and the Unaligmiut, but among the Yuit tribes apart from the Unalig-miut, labrets might be worn by women as well as by men. The holes might be made in infancy, but they were more often pierced during childhood or at the time of puberty. Rarely, however, was the operation ritualized. Labret styles varied widely; a Tareumiut male wore two lateral labrets at the lower border of the lip, although an earlier style here was reportedly a single medial form. Central Bering Sea coast women wore one or two sickle-shaped labrets, either one at the center of the face just beneath the lower lip or one on either side. The Koniag men had labrets as long as four inches, which they wore beneath the lower lip, and the women had a series of from two to six small labrets beneath the lower lip (Hrdlička, 1944, 45; Lisiansky, 1814, 195, 200–01; Murdoch, 1890, 143; Nelson, 1899, 45).

The transition between childhood and young adult status was marked by a series of "first" ceremonies, and as Lantis (1947, 4–8) has recorded, these were more elaborate among the Yuit tribes. In the north, when a boy killed his first animal or bird, there might be ceremonial recognition by holding a small feast in his honor and distributing presents. The same ceremony might be repeated for other species killed, but this was not mandatory nor widespread in occurrence. Among the Yuit tribes the pattern was much more fully developed. On Nunivak Island, for which the descriptions are best, we find that when a young boy killed his first bird the event was noted by presenting food and gifts to the men of the kashgee. The bird was skinned by the boy's mother, and at the next Bladder Feast its skin, along with the skins of birds taken by other boys, was hung at the back of the kashgee in a place of honor. Once again presents were given by the father to honor the event, and apparently this was done for the first of each species of bird and animal which a boy killed. The big "first" in the hunting activities of a youth was the killing of his first seal. From the time of this kill to the end of the next Bladder Feast, neither the boy nor his mother could eat seal meat or consume seal oil. The first of each seal species a boy killed was distributed to the men of his kashgee; the boy's family kept none of it. Only after killing a bearded seal was the young male expected to behave socially as a man; he was about twenty at this time. He could not eat any meat from the first walrus he killed, but he was given other walrus meat as the men of his kashgee ate some of his kill in celebration of the event. The walrus head was kept in his kashgee for five days, and then the hunter and the men of his kashgee took a sweatbath there. Afterwards the hunter and other men and women danced. The hunter composed and sang a new song for the occasion, and food was distributed to the guests. The first caribou an individual killed placed no food restrictions on him, nor were there significant behavioral prohibitions connected with the kill (Lantis, 1946, 226–27).

The pattern of the "first" observances for the Nuniwagamiut finds partial parallels among the Kuskowagamiut (Oswalt, 1963a, 137–38) and the Chugach (Birket-Smith, 1953, 87). They occurred elsewhere among the Yuit, but the variations have not been established. The "first" for girls usually meant the first berries picked by a small girl, but this was far less important than the achievements of males. The most important ceremony for a girl took place when she menstruated for the first time. The menarche meant physical isolation and restrictions on her behavior, clothing, and food. Again the restrictions and ritual were more complex among the Yuit than the Inuit. After this time a girl was free to marry, although on Nunivak and probably elsewhere in the adjacent coastal region she might already be a wife. Marriage rituals were rare, and even if there was an exchange of gifts, there was no community-wide recognition of the event except rarely among some Yuit.

THE POSITION OF ORPHANS

A child born into a family at a propitious time was the center of the fond and considerate attention of older siblings and adults. The same was true of an infant if adopted by relatives, and it was generally the case if a nonrelative adopted a child (Gubser, 1965, 146–47; Lantis, 1946, 241). The fate of an orphan, however, might be quite different. Such an individual usually was an older child with no near relatives or with relatives who were unwilling to adopt him. Under these circumstances an orphan might be taken into a household and maintained for the services he could render, but he was not integrated into the kinship structure of the family. The orphan who was able to succeed in life was a folk hero among both the Inuit and Yuit tribes (Lantis, 1946, 314; Oswalt, 1963a, 137; Spencer, 1959, 90).

Marriage, Kinship, and Descent

A child bride on Nunivak had sexual intercourse before she reached puberty; among the Kuskowagamiut a shaman was the first to have intercourse with a girl (Lantis, 1946, 225, 233–34; Von Wrangell, 1839). Sexual intercourse between unmarried adolescents or adults was accepted as normal and a matter of little concern. Adultery, unless it led to a prolonged disruption of a family, was accepted, and divorces were usually effected with a minimum of social disruption. Homosexuality among the Tareumiut and Nunamiut was apparently unknown (Gubser, 1965, 110–11; Spencer, 1959, 246), but father-daughter incest was reported (Gubser, 1965, 64; Rainey, 1947, 243). Among the Tareumiut intercourse between a man and a female dog was reported, but such behavior does not appear to have been common (Rainey, 1947, 243). Sexual deviations thus were rare among the Inuit; they were more common among some Yuit tribes. Transvestites, raised from infancy as females, "married" males among the Koniag, a practice that seems to have been rather common (Lisiansky, 1814, 199). Chugach transvestites were individuals manifesting physical characteristics of both sexes who likewise performed the labors of both men and women. Such persons, however, did not marry (Birket-Smith, 1953, 94).

An individual calculated descent on both sides of his family in a bilateral or nonunilineal manner. However, among all Alaskan Eskimos some stress was placed on the male line, particularly among the Nuniwagamiut (Lantis, 1946, 239–44). In the classification of social organization by Murdock (1949) descent and cousin terminologies are regarded as critical factors. Among Alaskan Eskimos the cousin terms reported are of two forms, either Eskimo or Iroquois. The former is the same form as found currently in the United States, with "cousins" lumped together but separate from siblings. The Iroquois type combines siblings and parallel cousins (father's brother's children and mother's sister's children), but distinguishes them from cross-cousins. (father's sister's children and mother's brother's children). In Murdock's typology of primary social organization forms, the Nunamiut exhibit the Eskimo type (bilateral descent and Eskimo cousin terms), and all the others for whom the data are reasonably complete (Chugach, Kuskowagamiut, Nuniwagamiut, and Tareumiut) are the Yuman type (bilateral descent and Iroquois cousin terms). None of the Alaskan Eskimos fit neatly into the classic Eskimo type. The Nunamiut approached it but did not have the "normal Eskimo" pattern of neolocal residence (for a married couple to establish a household independent of the husband's or wife's family). Instead the Nunamiut couple became matrilocal (lived with or near the wife's family), and thus matri-Eskimo is a more precise accounting.

The primary Yuman type of social organization is typical for Alaskan Eskimos. Murdock (1949, 231–32) regarded the Yuman type as unstable with descent in a state of flux and little internal consistency. In Alaska the unstable quality is reflected in the varying forms of marriage residence. The Tareumiut tended to be bilocal (as many married couples lived with or near the wife's family as lived with or near the groom's family); the Nuniwagamiut and Kuskowagamiut were matrilocal; the Chugach were matri-patrilocal (the married couple lived temporarily in association with the wife's family and later shifted to live permanently with or near the husband's family). The variations in residence forms suggest that the social organization was not stabilized nor was it moving in one specific direction. For an evolutionary reconstruction of the changes in Alaskan Eskimo social structure the recent analysis by Whitten (1964) should be consulted.

An individual was prohibited from marrying close relatives on either side of his family except among the Chugach, whose customs are not entirely clear. Apparently in this tribe a man might marry his mother's sister or a cross-cousin (Birket-Smith, 1953, 80–83). Among the Nuniwagamiut a male might be permitted to marry a cross-cousin (Lantis, 1946, 234). Marriages were monogamous as a rule, although polygyny was practiced by a few males everywhere.

Marriages among the Nunamiut, to cite one pattern, often grew out of teenage love affairs, in which sexual intercourse was permitted and lovers exchanged small gifts. By the time a male was in his early twenties he was expected to marry; during previous sexual affairs, he had often begun to fix his attention on a particular girl. She was most likely from the same band but younger than the male; less often a lover was from another band, and in rare cases, from a coastal Eskimo settlement. If an affair was serious enough to lead to permanence, there were marital arrangements. However, the parents of the courting couple might disapprove of a marriage and intercede to terminate the affair. A young man was regarded as a desirable son-in-law if he was a good hunter and was an honest man. The only restriction in selecting a mate pertained to blood relationship. A marriage partner should not be a first, second, or third cousin, although marriages between second and third cousins were known. The expected residence pattern was for the couple to live in the household of the wife's family for at least the first year, although the couple often remained permanently associated with this unit. After a year they might join the husband's parents if his aid was needed at home (Gubser, 1965, 63–67, 114, 179).

As an example of the Yuit marriage customs, the Nunivak Eskimos once again may be cited. After a young Nunivak man had killed his first bearded seal and then observed the associated prohibitions until the next Bladder Feast, he was ready to marry. A girl married for the first time before reaching puberty, and her husband was about twenty years old. Because of the small number of persons on the island everyone was at least distantly related; still, they preferred to marry among themselves. If a man wanted to marry a girl, he might give her a modest gift and enlist some older person to approach her family. If they were agreeable to the match, the potential husband gave the bride-to-be a parka made of skins he had obtained directly or indirectly. When the girl went to her suitor's kashgee and presented him with select food served in a new dish, the marriage was consummated. If the man was from another settlement, which often was the case, he took up residence in his wife's village. If he lived in the same village as his spouse, he took his clothing and dishes to her parents' house. A young married couple was expected to be in love, and marriages took place most frequently in the summer when the couple could camp out or sometimes have the house to themselves. If a marriage took place in the winter, the couple had to begin their married life in a crowded household, and this they were reluctant to do. A girl was a functioning wife before she began to menstruate, and her husband was obligated to observe taboos associated with her menarche. During her first period her husband could not go to the beach, walk on the ice, or use a kayak, and he kept his parka hood up, especially when out-of-doors. Like the girl he wore mittens outside during the summer, and he observed her food restrictions. During subsequent menstrual periods he followed her restrictions, although probably with less care as the years passed (Lantis, 1946, 225, 233–34).

Adult Life

An adult was expected to fit unobtrusively into his community except among the Nunamiut where a man openly boasted of his accomplishments (Gubser, 1965, 125). Elsewhere, when an individual excelled through his abilities or luck, he would disparage his success or at least not boast of it. Since his success decreased as he became less physically capable, an older man could seldom stand out significantly from the others in his community. The best-known Eskimo who departed from this norm was Attungowrah, who lived at Point Hope during the early historic period. He terrified other villagers because of his great physical strength and his reputation as a shaman. He had five wives, murdered six persons, was an umialik, and controlled all of the trading at Point Hope. He eventually became embroiled in a feud and was shot, although not fatally wounded. As he was recuperating, he was knifed to death by one of his wives

(Brower, 1942, 34–60, 149–50; Rainey, 1947, 243; Wells, 1890, 10–11).

In spite of the facts that great men were rare and that the potential for achievement was uniform for most individuals, in some areas there were advantages to being a member of a particular family. Among arctic whalers an umialik might pass on his whaling equipment to a son and thereby give him the opportunity to excel beyond others at his generational level. Such a son had to enlist and keep a hunting crew together on the basis of his own abilities, however. Thus, status was largely achieved among the Inuit; the same was true but to a lesser extent among the Yuit tribes. The most radical departure was among the Pacific whalers and fishermen. The Chugach, with their chiefs, commoners, and slaves, had created three distinct but somewhat flexible social categories. Furthermore, only certain individuals among them possessed the esoteric knowledge necessary for successful whaling. The same combination existed among the Koniag; here, however, a slave might be killed at the death of his owner, an occurrence which is unreported for the Chugach and suggests a more rigid structure (Birket-Smith, 1953, 92–94; Hrdlička, 1944, 73–74). A role which passed along family lines and was reported sporadically among the Yuit was that of "dance leader"; among the Koniag, the dance leader taught children the dances and supervised public ceremonies. The word used on Kodiak for such a person was applied also to a Russian Orthodox priest, suggesting that supernatural control as well as secular responsibility was vested in the office (Lisiansky, 1814, 208). Among the Kuskowagamiut the position of dance leader was passed from father to son but does not appear to have been as important an office as among the Koniag (Oswalt, 1963a, 71, 87).

Death and Burial

Death, as birth and puberty, was a family affair among the Inuit. A body was prepared for burial and most often removed through the house skylight soon after death. The amount of goods to be left with the body was minimal for an ordinary person but more abundant for a person of wealth. The grave goods usually were broken and deposited next to the extended corpse, which was placed on the ground surface or in a shallow grave. After the burial, it was necessary for those associated with the ceremony to restrict their activities for four or five days. Variations from the burial forms cited for the Inuit include the Kovagmiut practice of placing a man's body in a canoe and covering it with spruce poles arranged in a cone shape. Among these people, too, a body might be placed in a tepee-shaped frame of logs, with the branches of a nearby tree removed to mark the area. The Kovagmiut also practiced platform burial, although the platform might simply be two log tripods on which was placed a beam to which the body was lashed. Platform burials also are reported for the adjacent coastal region (Cantwell, 1889b, 83; Giddings, 1961a, 50, 154; Grinnell, 1901, 33; Gubser, 1965, 217–18; Porter, 1893, 138).

Among the Yuit, burial practices were more varied. The bodies usually were flexed and wrapped in either skins or grass matting or both. The grave goods were often broken, and the body usually was placed directly on the ground, in a coffin at ground level, or raised above the ground on four corner posts. Along the central Bering Sea coast paintings of hunting activities or of family "totems" were executed on the coffin or on boards set next to it. In the same region posts adorned with sculptured figures of animals or of people often were erected near a burial. A body was not removed through a doorway for burial, and it was prepared for interment very soon after death, or in some cases before the death occurred. The most radical departure from these practices was the mummification practiced among the Koniag and Chugach, but this custom does not appear to have been common among members of either tribe (Birket-Smith, 1953, 89–91; Lantis, 1947, 9–20; Nelson, 1899, 310–22; Zagoskin, 1967, 229).

In the life cycle of Alaskan Eskimos the major transitions

were family matters in spite of the fact that communities were quite small and most people within a settlement were at least distantly related to one another. From this circumstance it is evident that villages were loosely integrated social units. Only the Chugach and possibly some of the other Pacific Eskimos had more complexity in their social lives. Although the same pattern of events in a life cycle is recorded everywhere, there is more uniformity in the patterning among the Inuit than among the Yuit.

Chapter 9

Religious Patterns

Exploitation of the land versus that of the sea has played a major role in the ethnological interpretation of Eskimo adaptations. Eskimos also made this dichotomy, but their conception of it was largely in supernatural terms. According to their system, the spirits of terrestrial and marine creatures were opposed to and repelled by each other. This distinction found daily expression in the handling of land and sea mammals. For example, as long as a Point Barrow woman was preparing caribou-skin clothing, she was prohibited from touching seals. Also, before hunting whales in the spring, the people burned all bones of the land animals taken since the previous spring; prior to a spring caribou hunt, the men washed their bodies free of seal oil. It was possible at Point Barrow to hunt sea and land animals at the same time of the year, however, and they could be eaten at the same meal if the participants washed their hands between servings (Spencer, 1959, 264–66, 272). Among the Nunamiut, seal and caribou meat could not be cooked together in the same vessel (Gubser, 1965, 200), but the Kobuk Eskimos drew a different distinction. Here the

division was between river fish and land animals. Thus, the skins
of caribou and sheep could not be processed when salmon were
ascending the river (Giddings, 1961a, 20). At Point Hope one of
the few general taboos was against throwing caribou hair into the
sea during the winter. To do so was displeasing to whales and
blocked the breathing holes of seals (Rainey, 1947, 274). Even the
most southeasterly Alaskan Eskimos, the Chugach, could not
cook land and sea mammals in the same container, and the skins of
such animals could not be combined in a single garment (Birket-
Smith, 1953, 117–18). On the other hand, a certain dependency
between land and sea mammals occurred. The Point Hope people
rubbed blubber from a sea mammal on the nose of each caribou
killed (Rainey, 1947, 267), and it was a widespread practice to
offer a sea mammal a drink of fresh water soon after its death.

Origins

Many Eskimos, including both Inuit and Yuit, did not attempt to explain their creation. This acceptance of the status quo
was true of the Tareumiut of Point Hope (Rainey, 1947, 269),
the Nuniwagamiut (Lantis, 1946, 313), the Chugach (Birket-
Smith, 1953, 119), and probably others, were the record more
complete. Some tribes, however, had origin beliefs, and many of
these followed the same general pattern. The most atypical was
that of the Nunamiut. Their beginnings were traced to a primeval
time when a giant man named Aiyagomahala created their ancestors, in a form smaller than himself, somewhere at the head of the
Alatna River. Here they all lived a long time, and the giant taught
the people many of the skills essential for survival. In the environment were the animal species found living in the area today;
perhaps these had also been created by Aiyagomahala. At one
point he told the people to collect skins and other products of the
inland animals so that they might trade, although the people did
not know the meaning of trade. The creator traveled to Point
Barrow, and although he was a stranger, the Eskimos there
invited him into their karigi, where he told of the inland people

he had made. In order to repay the Point Barrow people for the *muktuk* (whale skin with blubber attached) which they gave him, Aiyagomahala caused animals of two of the species which he had created to appear. First, a great herd of caribou passed so near that the people could kill many with their bows and arrows. The caribou were followed by wolves, some of which also were killed. After telling the people of Point Barrow how to reach the Nunamiut country, Aiyagomahala left, carrying a gift of blubber in a large container. On returning to his people, the creator taught them how to construct a karigi and how to use a stone lamp for burning oil. He later instructed the Point Barrow people, who had traveled inland to trade, to invite the Nunamiut the next year by sending two messengers to announce the time of trading. Thus the important pattern of coastal and inland Eskimo exchanges of feasts and goods became established, and later, trade relations were opened with other nearby Eskimos. Soon the institution of trading partnerships was begun, with every man having such a partner in each Eskimo group with which he traded. Aiyagomahala prepared to leave permanently, but before his departure he instructed the people to aid and care for one another. It was speculated by some Nunamiut that perhaps he went elsewhere to create other Eskimo groups (Gubser, 1965, 29–32). The Nunamiut seem to have created an origin myth in an effort to establish their individuality. The fact that this complex myth has been developed by a group which only recently moved into the area of its mythological origin illustrates how rapidly such myths may become established.

To most Alaskan Eskimos who sought to explain their origins, Raven was the most likely creator. Accounts of his creation of the Eskimos were told in western Alaska from the arctic coast southward to the Kuskokwim River, according to Nelson. The following is a résumé of an origin myth recorded from an old Unaligmiut man who had learned it as a boy from an old man living in the Bering Strait region.

According to this myth, Raven created beach peas which grew on the naked earth, and from one pod a full-grown man burst forth. Raven approached, pushed up his beak, and also became a man. He told the first man that while he had created the peas, it was without knowing that a man would emerge from them. From clay Raven formed various pairs of animals at different times and gave life to them. Mountain sheep were created first, followed by reindeer and then caribou; a woman was formed next, to become the wife of the first man. Raven went on to create certain fish as well as other creatures and to teach the human couple how to live in their emerging environment. The woman bore a son and then a daughter, who were to marry. Raven turned back to the original pea pod from which the first man had been born and found that three other men had emerged from the same pod. Raven led the first man inland, but the other three were taken to the coast—again the coastal and inland division—where they were taught to exploit the resources of the sea (Nelson, 1899, 452–56).

According to the Koniag, Raven brought light to the world, and at the same time a bladder containing a man and a woman dropped from the sky. The size of the container was increased by their blowing, and mountains were made "by stretching their hands and feet." The man scratched his head on the mountains to create forests, from which animals emerged. The woman urinated to produce the sea, and spat to form other waters (Lisiansky, 1814, 197–98). Among other accounts of human origins is a Point Barrow myth which recorded that a tall tube sticking in the ground was broken by a "man," and both men and women emerged (Murdoch, 1886, 595). Another tale from the same area records that a spirit made a clay image of a man, and after it dried the spirit breathed on it, whereupon the image became alive (Ray, 1885, 47).

Sun and Moon

Tales concerning the creation of the sun and moon are never identical, but they fall into two distinctive groups. Either Raven obtained the sun by deception, with the moon being created coincidentally or as another part of the story, or else the sun represents a girl who fled from a covetous male relative, who then became the moon.

In the Nunamiut account, which involves Raven, there once was an umialik with a marriageable daughter who rejected all suitors. The umialik kept in his house two balls of light, one dull and one bright. Only when the umialik went abroad with one or the other light could people see to hunt, and he refused to part with either light. Raven lived among the people in the form of a human being, and he wanted to obtain light for all the villagers. With his great power Raven became a small feather which the umialik's daughter unknowingly drank in water dipped from a lake. Within a very short period of time she bore an offspring that was Raven but that appeared to be an ordinary infant except for a lump on his forehead. He learned to talk quickly and grew at an inordinate rate. He wanted a light for a toy, and the umialik finally gave him the smaller one. Raven was still unhappy and cried for the larger light, which in desperation was finally given him. He played with the bright light, and when unnoticed, he fled with it. He broke the ball with his beak, which had developed from the lump on his forehead, and after that there was continuous light. Once again Raven became a bird and flew off. The daughter wished that the light were divided into a large light for day and a smaller one for night so that the people could rest in darkness. Her desire was fulfilled, and thus the sun and moon came into being. In his disappointment the umialik destroyed his smaller light (Gubser, 1965, 35–39). Variations of this myth, in which the differences may be considerable, have been reported for the Tareumiut (Rainey, 1947, 269; Spencer, 1959, 385), Kovagmiut (Giddings, 1961a, 69–71), Noatagmiut (Lucier, 1958, 92), and Ikogmiut (Nelson, 1899, 483–85). A Chugach myth also records that Raven brought the sun, but the story is quite different from the ones cited above, and the moon had a separate origin (Birket-Smith, 1953, 163–64, 175).

The other primary form of the sun and moon myth involved an earthly male and female and is described for the Kovagmiut with a brother and sister as the principals (Giddings, 1961a, 65–66). While the girl was isolated during her menarche, she was visited by a man who fondled her breasts. When he returned, she marked his face with charcoal. Later she peered through the skylight of the men's house to identify the marked man and discovered that he was her brother. She was so humiliated that she cut off one breast, which she placed on a platter and served to him in the karigi. Afterwards she ran outside and rose running into the sky, which reddened with her blood. She was followed by her brother, who also was lifted into the sky. The girl became the sun and her brother the moon. This episode in the creation of the natural world is known with variations among the Tareumiut of Point Hope (Gubser, 1965, 194–95; Rainey, 1947, 270), Noatagmiut (Lucier, 1958, 91), Nuniwagamiut (Lantis, 1946, 268–69), Unaligmiut (Nelson, 1899, 481), Ikogmiut (Nelson, 1899, 482), and Koniag (Lantis, 1938b, 136).

Ordinarily the sun was much less important in Eskimo thoughts than the moon. The moon was the place to which shamans frequently journeyed in their search for supernatural aid, and moon-man was the keeper of the souls of men and animals among the Point Hope Tareumiut (Gubser, 1965, 171; Lantis, 1947, 36; Oswalt, 1963a, 88; Rainey, 1947, 270–71). There was, however, a daily sunrise ritual on Kodiak Island during which people sat on the tops of their houses or on some other high point and looked to the east until the sun rose. At Point Hope the Tareumiut women held their children up to the east as the sun rose (Lantis, 1947, 35; Rainey, 1947, 240).

The Land and Its Occupants

If the land was thought to have been created, it usually was by Raven, and the accounts embody the Earth-Diver theme. In variations of this myth Raven speared from his kayak and retrieved floating bunch grass, an animallike creature, or a piece of ground from which to create land large and firm enough to dwell on. This idea of the earth's origin is found among the Tareumiut (Rainey, 1947, 269–70; Spencer, 1959, 384–85) and Kovagmiut (Giddings, 1961a, 69). Among the Nunivak Eskimos no account was offered for the creation of the earth (Lantis, 1946, 313), and neither was one known to the Nunamiut (Gubser, 1965, 32). Once again origins seem to have mattered very little to most Eskimos; when a myth to account for the earth was present at all, it was most likely found in northwestern Alaska. The earth itself was considered flat, and the sky above was a turning hemisphere supported on four posts, each marking a cardinal direction, according to combined Tareumiut accounts (Rainey, 1947, 270; Spencer, 1959, 257). Its flatness is agreed to by the Nunamiut and the Koniag; the idea of support posts seems to occur also among the Koniag (Gubser, 1965, 193; Lantis, 1938b, 137).

In the formation of the natural world a giant man has already been mentioned, the Nunamiut creator Aiyagomahala. He did more than originate things, for he taught his people practical skills and slew prehistoric "people-killers." Aiyagomahala was a giant and a supernatural, but another individual was in part responsible for perfecting the order of nature among the Nunamiut. This man, Kayaktuaguniktuu, was a giant child of ordinary-sized Eskimo parents who lived along the Kobuk River. He left home after his father attempted to kill him, and his first adventure was to kill another giant, one who had been killing people. After slaying other people-killers, he lived among various animals who had human qualities. It was he who taught women to bear offspring without the operation which previously had killed the mother. He also cut an extra joint in the leg of the caribou to increase its fleetness and taught animals how to defecate. The marvelous teachings and deeds of the Kobuk giant made it possible for various species to begin functioning as they do today (Gubser, 1965, 39–42). Among the Nunamiut, Kayaktuaguniktuu was a borrowed mythological figure, but to the Eskimos of his Kobuk

River homeland he was a local hero (Giddings, 1961a, 94–98). The Kobuk accounts of him, when they parallel those of the Nunamiut, have greater detail. He was known to the Noatagmiut but apparently not as a performer of great deeds for the benefit of men (Lucier, 1958, 106–08).

Many other giants were thought to be present in the environment and were more feared than respected. Human giants were uncommon on Nunivak, although they occasionally served shamans (Lantis, 1946, 198). Among the Chugach they lived mainly in Ahtena Indian country and were capable of changing their form by magical means (Birket-Smith, 1953, 125). At Point Barrow the giants were shy, solitary individuals who do not appear to have harmed people. They arose from normal persons who had become lost and then grew to giant stature (Spencer, 1959, 261). Giant supernaturals conceived in human form thus were known to exist, but they were significant only in the lives of the Nunamiut and Kobuk River people.

Dwarfs in human form were more diverse creatures. The Nuniwagamiut knew of harmless dwarfs who had many of the characteristics of Eskimos. Although only about a foot in height, they were both quick and strong. If one were to seize a man, the captive could be held until the dwarf chose to release him. One variety of this dwarf form lived on the land, and another stayed in the ocean (Lantis, 1946, 198). Strong dwarfs a foot high were associated with the sea among the Chugach, and while they could aid men, they seldom were seen and seldom offered their supernatural help (Birket-Smith, 1953, 125). Again, sea-oriented dwarfs existed at Point Barrow, and as on Nunivak, they had many of the same characteristics as Eskimos and were harmless (Spencer, 1959, 260–61). Another specific kind of dwarf was one with a pointed cap and round, protruding mouth. These beings were known from Nunivak, and although they might aid a shaman, they were potentially dangerous for ordinary men (Lantis, 1946, 198; 1960, 113–27). Perhaps these dwarfs were related to the creatures with pointed heads but seemingly normal-sized bodies who were seen only by shamans among the Chugach (Birket-Smith, 1953, 124). The dwarfs were reportedly the makers of the small, delicate flint tools of the Arctic Small Tool tradition at Cape Denbigh. The local Eskimos apparently knew of these artifacts, and because of their smallness they could not conceive of a normal-sized person making and using them (Giddings, 1964, 4–6). The same reasoning prevailed among the Nunamiut (Gubser, 1965, 210) with reference to the finds of small artifacts. In summary, the idea of supernaturals who varied from the norm in size by being either giants or dwarfs was present in certain areas, but it was not common or of great importance anywhere.

Comparatively little imagination is required to conceive of beings larger or smaller than man, but to originate and perpetuate ideas about nonhuman species involved thinking of a different order. Such creatures were reported among Alaskan Eskimos and were more important than either giants or dwarfs. The Tareumiut of Point Barrow knew of a seal form with a human face and hair, polar bears with ten legs, and a doglike creature who protected walrus (Spencer, 1959, 261–63). The walrus dog, as described in detail among the Unaligmiut, had four legs, a doglike head, and a long scaly tail which could kill a man with a blow (Nelson, 1899, 442–43). The Unaligmiut had also conceived of a shrew that lived on the ice and was capable of quickly entering a man's clothing through the toe of a boot. If the victim did not move, the shrew crawled over his body and left through the same hole. Such a person would have good hunting in the future. However, if the person moved when the shrew was running about, it would burrow into his heart and kill him (Nelson, 1899, 442). Half-people with one arm and one leg were known among the Chugach (Birket-Smith, 1953, 125), and the Nuniwagamiut reported persons who were half-animal (Lantis, 1946, 198). The idea of the presence of these creatures was important, since many of them posed nonnatural hazards in exploiting the environment.

Their existence also provided a meaningful explanation if something unnatural was seen fleetingly in the distance, in a fog, or at other times when normal vision was impossible.

These descriptions have been offered as the supernatural background of the Eskimo world. Statements about origins, environmental relationships, and nonnatural creatures are drawn largely from the mythologies and serve as a partial background for religious behavior.

Spirits

The approach to the supernatural forces was primarily animistic, with shamans as part-time specialists, and the amount of ritual ranged from very little to a great deal. In a discussion of Eskimo and Aleut religion, Marsh (1954) set forth a comparative framework of basic beliefs which generally will be followed. The initial category is that of charms, which were tangible objects, formulas, or songs. An individual acquired them through purchase, transfer, inheritance, or a personal supernatural contact. Among the Point Hope Tareumiut the concepts surrounding charms were the cornerstone of the supernatural system (Rainey, 1947, 272–74), and this relationship was also true elsewhere. The Tareumiut charms were separated into two classes in a system which encompassed about half of the Point Hope community. A person participating in the system was associated either with "things of dead people" or with "things of women in childbirth and menstruating women." Membership in the system was effected through transfer, not inheritance. The charms were associated with certain animals, but how the connection came into being is not known. It is recorded that the animals aided and protected their human associates on a personal basis. Tangible representations of them included items such as a wolverine's tail or a polar bear's nose; these were sewn to garments. Many children received their charms from an adult relative beyond the nuclear family on either the paternal or maternal side. The transfer, including a personal name of the transferrer, occurred when the giver spat into the child's mouth. He or she instructed the child's mother in the necessary behavior patterns accompanying the charm, and these the child was taught when he grew older. In addition, males learned secret hunting songs appropriate for their charms. A means for acquiring a charm without the namesake involvement was by the choice of the child's parents. An individual activated a charm by making contact with items associated either with dead people or with childbirth and menstruation, depending on its general class. What was essential for one class was diametrically opposite to that of the other class. An individual could be immunized against opposite dangers, however, if his mother ate something of this class before the child received a charm but after it had been decided in which group he would belong. The complexities of this system were elaborate, and similar associations with charms played an extremely important part in the lives of other Alaskan Eskimos. The Nuniwagamiut pattern has been described in detail (Lantis, 1946, 204–05, 239–40). Here diverse charms, each with specific attributes and usually represented by an animal carving, were worn by the possessor. They were acquired most often through inheritance from one's father. Charms, including songs, could not be alienated and were the primary source of individual supernatural power. Lantis (1946, 205) summarized their importance: "The concepts of *spirit powers* and *objects containing those powers* and of *amuletic songs* form the core of Nunivak religion."

A second spiritual category was composed of "persons," a word whose form varied dialectically but was *inua* among the Inuit. Since inua is well established in the literature, it will be the designation used to mean "owner" or "generic spirit." Marsh (1954, 23) regarded the inua as "a psychic projection of the object's existence." It was an abstract manifestation of the physical form and controlled its concrete counterparts. This was then a guardian spirit of a species, and ceremonies might be performed to maintain rapport with it. Among the Nunamiut all animals and some inanimate objects such as lakes, mountains, directions of the wind, and atmosphere had inuas. The inuas have always existed and have the potential for continuous existence either as a quality associated with an inanimate object or as the force of life in an animate object. An inua associated with something inanimate might originally have belonged to a living object. For example, some Eskimos suggested that the inua of a lake was originally the spirit of a man who had drowned there. Innumerable beliefs existed about the abilities of an inua. Thus the inua of a grizzly bear resented a dead person's touching a bearskin, and for this reason, if an ill person were placed on such a skin, the inua would drive the malady from his body. Ordinary persons attempted to pacify the various inuas by observing certain taboos. For example, they did not cook seal and caribou meat in the same vessel, since to do so angered the respective inuas and resulted in poor hunting (Gubser, 1965, 199–200). Of all the common animals important to the Nunamiut only dogs had no inua (Gubser, 1965, 293), an idea found also among the Tareumiut (Spencer, 1959, 289) but not among the Unaligmiut (Nelson, 1899, 435).

The third cluster of supernaturals included the souls of men and animals. Considerable diversity occurred in the beliefs surrounding these, or at least there is little uniformity in the literature. One soul form might be termed "life," another "immortal," and a third the "name" soul. Their physical form of expression was variable, but they probably were most often in the image of their living counterpart. At Point Hope the lifetime soul ceased to exist at death, but the immortal soul could remain associated with the place of death or burial. Additionally—and this I assume—a name soul might be transferred with an individual's name to a child (Rainey, 1947, 271–72). On Nunivak the name soul did not exist, the life soul left the body at death, and the immortal soul continued its existence forever (Lantis, 1946, 197–98).

The fourth category of spirits, termed "demonic" by Marsh (1954, 27), has already been described in part as the supernatural giants, dwarfs, and half-beings. They had human qualities, often lived in the manner of Eskimos, but usually were unapproachable by ordinary persons. To these creatures could be added innumerable other exotic beings, often quasi-representations of animals with strange anatomical configurations. A widespread term for such a being was *tunerak*, and whatever its form, it was a major source of shamanistic power.

The fifth and final category consisted of the inuas of the universe. On Nunivak Island this inua was the "spirit of the world." Here too, another separate but similar force was the "eye of the world," suggested by Marsh (1954, 29) as being the moon-man. At Point Hope a moon-man termed Alignuk controlled men and animals in the world, and an apparently similar concept was known among the Unaligmiut. The Chugach, on the other hand, conceived of a "spirit owner of the air" associated with the sun and weather (Birket-Smith, 1953, 120–21; Lantis, 1946, 197; Nelson, 1899, 430; Rainey, 1947, 270–71).

Shamans

Each of the five forces was a source of power used by humans in maintaining the natural world. They might be dealt with by ordinary individuals, by the community collectively, or largely by shamans. Ordinary persons depended primarily on individual charms but could and did employ the other spirit categories at times. The inuas were dealt with by shamans or by the community in rituals, whereas sorcerers and shamans handled malignant spirits. Shamanistic power came largely from the "demonic" class of spirits, which might better be viewed as nonnatural humans or nonnatural animals. It should be stressed that just as no clear line divided the natural from the supernatural sphere, so also no clear boundary separated shamans from ordinary persons. Shamans simply were better versed and more competent in extrasensory matters than the average person. From the diversity in recorded shamanistic concepts it is apparent that Eskimo thinking about such matters was highly variable in its details.

Alaskan Eskimo shamans participated in rituals and performed independently on other occasions. Their principal duties
were to cure the sick, influence the weather, predict the future,
and promote the general welfare by helping to make animals
amenable to capture. During his performance, a shaman usually
sang songs which he had composed, obtained from another shaman, or acquired by supernatural means. The tambourine-type
drum which furnished accompaniment was played by the shaman
or an assistant. When a shaman danced, his face might be covered
by a mask which had been made by him or by someone else under
his direction. A performance often included sleight-of-hand,
trances, and spirit flights. Most powerful shamans were male, but
females did on occasion become shamans. The most successful
shamans controlled diverse categories of spirits and were able to
convince villagers of their powers over the years. A shaman
suspected of employing his abilities to harm people in his own
community might be killed by common consent. An individual
became a shaman after first seeing spirit beings in dreams or when
alone. He sought informal instruction from a practicing shaman
and was likely to serve as a shaman's assistant before performing
independently.

The activities of shamans among the Kovagmiut will serve to
illustrate features of the complex among one Inuit tribe. To
become a shaman it was necessary to dream of spirits. Later the
dreamer spat blood, which might be a way of expressing that he
became ill or wasted away under the stress. When alone and away
from others, he saw a tunerak, which looked human but was in
reality an animal spirit. This tunerak one day took possession of
the individual, causing him to wander about without clothing.
After his recovery, indicating control of the spirit, the man made
a drum and began to perform as a shaman. One particular shaman
controlled "little people" as his source of power. In a performance, which might be held to establish the location of caribou, he
had himself bound thoroughly so that it was impossible for him to
move. Members of the audience drummed and sang; as the little

people began to control the shaman the only light, that in a stone lamp, was extinguished. At this time, too, members of the audience closed their eyes and kept them closed for the remainder of the performance. In the dark the shaman seemingly untied himself, and using the bow and arrows that had been placed beside him, he shot an arrow each time the bow string tanged. The arrows were thought to pass through the walls of the ceremonial structure, travel to different distant places, turn about, and return. When all the arrows were back, the lamp was relighted, and the shaman was seen still tied, with the bow beneath the rope on his back and the arrows stuck in his body. The ropes were untied and the arrows removed out of sight of the observers. Afterwards the arrows were inspected for caribou blood and hair to establish whether they had met caribou on their magic flight (Giddings, 1961a, 15–16).

A shaman served his community and might in the process accumulate greater wealth than most persons. He was an individual with real authority and supernatural powers. He also was capable of turning his powers against other persons, leading to their illness or death. Often a rival shaman was his victim. Witchcraft was not, however, a constant danger in the daily lives of ordinary persons. A powerful killer of men at Point Hope was a *kikituk*, a supernatural animal represented in wood. It had four short legs, an elongated body, a flat head, and sharp bone teeth. The lower jaw was hinged and could be moved by pulling a sinew cord. The power of a kikituk was likened by Rainey (1947, 277–79) to a short-range shotgun blast. A shaman who possessed such a spirit ordinarily kept it in his body. When he needed aid, he grew "pregnant," as does a woman, and gave birth to his kikituk as a woman would bear an offspring. In one recorded instance a shaman sent his kikituk to kill a rival shaman. After the victim's death the successful shaman coaxed the kikituk back from the dead man's body and swallowed it. Within his body the kikituk remained dormant until its services were required again.

According to Lantis, a shaman's spirit aids would be summoned to the site of the performance or else the spirit of the shaman would go abroad. In the former instance a spirit either possessed the shaman, resulting in frenzied behavior followed by exhaustion, or the presence of the spirit was made known by ventriloquism on the shaman's part. In instances of spirit flight a shaman, through his familiar spirit, was most likely to visit the moon, but a trip could be to other locations such as to the land of the dead. Most often the purpose of communicating with an amenable spirit was to foretell the future or diagnose illness. Additionally, in order to impress others with his powers, a shaman performed before audiences. A repertoire might include diverse sleight-of-hand feats, being tied and then managing to free himself, or being burnt alive, strangled, or stabbed. In his role as a curer a shaman first summoned spirit helpers and through them expelled the disease from the patient. He might seem to remove a disease substance, sometimes by sucking (Lantis, 1947, 85–90; see also Birket-Smith, 1953, 126–28; Gubser, 1965, 171, 207; Oswalt, 1963a, 86–101; Rainey, 1947, 274–79).

In Eskimo theory anyone could become a shaman after the proper dream experience, but in fact the role often passed from father to son or from a man to some other close relative in the next generation (Birket-Smith, 1953, 126; Gubser, 1965, 156; Oswalt, 1963a, 86–87). Biographical information about shamans is rare, and the best information of this nature is from Nunivak Island. In a summary statement about a male shaman and a female shaman there, Lantis (1960, 168) wrote: "Although the sample is small, our two cases of shamans agree well in showing lonely children who felt rejected, who thus were powerfully motivated to escape into a dream existence, but who also were deliberately taught shamanism. Both said, moreover, that they were urged on by the community." These individuals each feared the spirits initially but became confident after developing the ability to control them.

A Kovagmiut man, Mauneluk, is fascinating because he was an antishaman, an iconoclast, and a nonbeliever in supernatural powers. He seems to have had indirect knowledge of whites but was not in direct contact with them. He dared to drink from the water bucket of a menstruating girl, ate products of the land mixed with foods from the sea, and challenged shamans to harm him. In spite of all his contrary ways, he was reputed never to have suffered harm because of his activities. He encouraged women to bear offspring in the village rather than in isolation, and he was able to persuade people to follow at least some of his examples (Giddings, 1961a, 31–34).

Rites, Rituals, and Ceremonies

Eskimo relations with supernatural forces emphasized the potency of charms possessed by individuals and the helpfulness of particular spirits to individuals. This focus of spirit control in the hands of individuals, with varying restrictions for each type of spirit, has come to be regarded as the core of Eskimo religion. In Alaska, however, supernatural matters involved a great deal more, and this elaboration was expressed not only in rites but also in rituals and elaborate ceremonies. In the discussion of these I have followed the comparative analysis of Lantis (1947) and occasionally supplemented it with more recent sources.

"First-fruits" rites were simple but widespread among the Inuit and Yuit tribes. The usual pattern was for the first of certain species taken during a year to be handled in an extraordinary manner. When a Nunamiut man, for example, took his first fox, wolf, or wolverine during the year, he hung the skin up for one day. He was obligated not to drink from the family water container for four days if the animal was a male, or for five days if he had killed a female. Furthermore, he related to his family the circumstances surrounding the kill in order to encourage further success. On Nunivak Island rites were observed by the hunter's family for the first bearded seal taken each year. The returning hunter followed a particular pattern of behavior and sang secret songs when coming ashore in his kayak. When he arrived home, his hair was washed in urine by his wife, and he fastened his charm belt about her. The seal was skinned in an unusual manner, and the remains were handled differently than usual. The Nuniwagamiut likewise had specific rites for the year's first take of walrus, polar bear, and caribou. A first-salmon or first-fish rite among the Chugach involved eating the entire fish save for the gall and gills. Among the Kuskowagamiut the head of the first salmon was removed and was probably handled in a special manner; none of the remainder of the fish was wasted (Birket-Smith, 1953, 42; Gubser, 1965, 208–09; Lantis, 1947, 43–44; Oswalt, 1963a, 90).

Probably the most widespread ceremony in which entire communities participated was the Messenger Feast. Although it was most elaborate among the Bering Sea Eskimos, it was also important among the Tareumiut of Point Barrow and possibly occurred among the Chugach (Birket-Smith, 1953, 110; Nelson, 1899, 361–63; Oswalt, 1963a, 62–64; Spencer, 1959, 210–28). The feast derived its name from the fact that the host community sent messengers to the guest community with an invitation to the event. The messengers bore sticks with a pictorial or mnemonic record of what were desired as "gifts" by the hosts. The hosts performed masked dances often depicting the activities of animals or hunting scenes, and the guests likewise performed. The primary purpose of the event was the exchange of gifts, but because the performance was pleasing to the spirits of animals, there were supernatural implications (Lantis, 1947, 67–73). The feast was most elaborate in the Yuk-Cux area, where trading centers were unusual, and served as a significant means for obtaining nonlocal products.

Other hunting ceremonies, which tended to be less widespread, placed greater stress on supernatural matters, although there might be gift exchanges and purely social dimensions to the celebrations. Among the Yuit tribes, especially those of the Bering Sea area, the Bladder Feast was an extremely complex ceremony. The bladders of game animals were saved by each hunter, for it was in the bladder that an animal's inua dwelled. The inflated bladders were painted and hung in the kashgees, to be honored during the Bladder Feast by rituals and offerings of food and water. The human participants purified themselves with smoke from wild celery stalks and by taking sweatbaths. The climax came when the bladders were taken down, deflated, and pushed through a hole in the ice so that the inuas could be perpetuated. This feast was the most elaborate means for honoring animals killed. It was also common and widespread to return animal skulls to the sea or throw animal bones in water to prevent their being chewed by dogs. Lantis (1947, 52–53) summarized the contents of hunting rituals as follows: "(1) elaboration of the paraphernalia used in the ceremony, such as mechanical contrivances rigged up to be moved by strings, (2) use of ceremonial paddles, (3) mimic portrayals of hunting scenes and of animal behavior, often with the use of masks, (4) the concept of honoring the animals, doing as the animal spirits have instructed in some great mythic encounter between them and a human hero, and (5) an exchange of real goods."

Memorial feasts honoring dead human beings probably were held everywhere except on Nunivak Island, and once again they were more elaborate among the Yuit tribes. A minor memorial feast was held once, twice, or three times a year to honor those persons who had died during the previous year. Among the Bering Sea Yuit, except for the Nuniwagamiut, a second memorial feast, the Great Feast to the Dead, was held each four to ten years. People with the latter complex were obligated to honor their dead with the minor feasts to pacify their souls until the great feast was held. The day before a feast to the dead a relative of the deceased placed by the grave a wooden stake on which was attached a model seal spear or model paddle for a man and a dish for a woman. This gesture notified the soul that the time for the feast was at hand. Lamps were lighted in the kashgee to guide the spirits, and songs of invitation were sung to them. The souls, which gathered in the kashgee fire pit first, then entered the bodies of their namesakes, and through these living persons, they received offerings of food and water. Additionally, water was poured beneath the cracks in the kashgee floor for the souls. The spirits of the dead were sent back to their graves by stamping on the floor, and when the remaining food had been consumed by the audience, the ceremony was ended (Hawkes, 1914, 31–32; Nelson, 1899, 363–65; Zagoskin, 1967, 112). Yearly offerings to the dead were made among the Inuit as well; for example, at Point Hope at the end of the whaling season each deceased person received on his grave a small piece of muktuk (Rainey, 1947, 262–63).

A Great Feast to the Dead was held in order to free the souls of the deceased from the earth forever. The nearest male relative of the deceased with the aid of relatives and friends began to accumulate material property and great stores of food. They did so for a number of years, until it was informally agreed that a great memorial feast could be held. When the time arrived, guests came from surrounding villages and often from great distances in order to participate. The dead souls were summoned much as before and honored as in a lesser feast for the dead, but rather than occupying a single day the Great Feast to the Dead lasted four to five days. The most important added feature was the distribution of great quantities of property and food to the guests in the name of the dead. On the lower Kuskokwim each day of gift distribution was devoted to a different product; frozen fish were given on the first day, dried fish the next, miscellaneous articles the third day, and seal oil on the final day. At one such event in 1887 nearly six hundred guests arrived at Napaskiak, which had a population of about one hundred twenty-five. The first day nearly 3,000 pounds of frozen fish were distributed along with about eighty gallons of *agutuk*, Eskimo ice cream made of berries mixed with oil and congealed with snow. On the third day one old woman distributed about two dozen of each of the following manufactures: fish-skin boots, grass socks, fish-skin rain parkas, woven-grass bags for fish, grass baskets, and small wooden buckets, as well as forty tin dippers. At the gift distributions the namesakes of the deceased persons received the most valuable gifts, including a set of clothing for each (Hawkes, 1914, 33–39; Nelson, 1899, 365–79; Oswalt, 1963a, 64–67; Zagoskin, 1967, 229–30). Memorial feasts for the dead of great and lesser importance were held among the Chugach. The great feast was held in a large settlement on alternate years and lasted up to two weeks. Here, too, the emphasis was on distributing gifts (Birket-Smith, 1953, 112–13).

Ceremonial Equipment

Face masks were the most important artifacts which set ceremonial performers apart from the audience. The masks usually were carved from spruce wood and painted. Masks of the Inuit tribes were small wooden face covers with human features represented either stylistically or in a manner approaching naturalism. At Point Barrow they were used in dances, but their association with supernaturals was vague if not absent. On the other hand, animal heads stuffed and worn by dancers were most likely associated with specific inuas and had supernatural associations (Murdoch, 1892, 266–70; Spencer, 1959, 293–94). Members of Yuit tribes along the Bering Sea coasts and in the adjacent interior had masks which were worn during the performance of social dances and others which were clearly supernatural in their associations. The wooden masks worn in social dances often were designed to make the audience laugh, not because of the mask itself but because of the gestures of the dancer. Comic masks often were caricatures of Indians (Hawkes, 1913, 12–14; Himmelheber, 1953, 54–55; Zagoskin, 1967, 226–27).

The masks of Bering Sea Eskimos which were used during religious events were made most frequently by shamans or perhaps by skilled woodworkers under the direction of an inspired shaman. Himmelheber (1953, 47–60) divided such masks into two categories, those designed to influence the inuas of animals important in the subsistence welfare and others which represented the spirit aids of shamans. The masks representing specific inuas might have an animal or a bird head on half the mask and a human head represented on the other half, the division being down the center of the mask. Another form was essentially an animal head but with a human head in a small portrayal somewhere on the mask. Another means for conveying the same idea was a hinged mask with an outer representation of an animal or a bird, and an inner portion, revealed by pulling a cord, that depicted the inua. These combinations conveyed the meaning that animals were capable of assuming human forms. Further variations included masks representing entire animals, animal heads without visible inuas, complete bodies with movable limbs, and diverse mask appendages. A shaman's spirit aid, his tunerak, was represented on a mask which the shaman or someone else might wear. The physical mask forms were much the same as for the animal inuas, with the additional category of distorted human faces. Very little is known about the employment of masks by the Chugach. They were used in association with hunting rituals as well as by shamans and in comic performances (Birket-Smith, 1953, 109–13).

The most important musical instrument was the tambou-rine-type drum. It consisted of a round frame of spruce over which was stretched and tied a split seal or walrus bladder. At one point along the frame a short handle was attached. The Inuit struck the rim of a drum with a stick, whereas the central Bering Sea coast Yuit hit the membrane itself with the stick. In the north drums were about a foot in diameter; southern drumheads were as much as three feet in diameter and often were painted with assorted scenes. For a dance large and small drums might be employed together to produce different tones; additionally, in the north a piece of wood might be beaten with an ivory stick for added effect. The male drummers might sing as they drummed, or others might provide an accompanying song. Male dance per-formers might strip entirely or partially, and women performers might strip to the waist. Social dance performances, which were frequent and popular, usually could be given either by men or by women. They did not follow strict routines but tended to be varied and often were spontaneous.

A folktale attempted to explain the difference between Inuit and Yuit dancing as well as sewing styles. The story relates that originally there was one woman but there were two men, one living in the north and another in the south. During their quarrel over the woman she was split at the waist, with the lower half going to the southern man and the upper portion to the man of the north. Each man replaced his missing half with a wooden part which grew together with the real section. For this reason the northern women danced as though they were still of wood but they were good seamstresses, whereas southern women were poorer sewers but good dancers (Hawkes, 1913, 11). Northern dances tended to be angular and vigorous, and women did not often perform in them. In the south women danced often but did not move their feet. They swayed gracefully and gestured with their hands keeping time with the music. In their hands they often held wands of wood with feather attachments, and in religious dances they grasped small wooden finger masks (Hawkes, 1913, 11; Himmelheber, 1953, 59–60; Lantis, 1947, 90–104; Nelson, 1899, 350–57; Spencer, 1959, 191).

Chapter 10

Alaskan Eskimos:
Interpretations

In spite of all that has been written about Alaskan Eskimos, they are just beginning to find their place in the ethnographic sun. They have long been in the shadow of Canadian and Greenlandic Eskimos in a total understanding of Eskimos. There are good historical reasons for this situation, and, admittedly, most Alaskan Eskimos did not face the rigors associated with the far, far north and thus are slightly mundane. By and large the source materials on Alaskan Eskimos are neither as balanced nor as complete as for some more easterly population segments. The accounts of explorations in Alaska, with the notable exception of Zagoskin's, are disappointing. The works of Nelson and Murdoch have great merit but serious limitations. The only thorough ethnographic study is by Lantis for the Nunivak Island Eskimos. This work covers many topics which are weak in other Eskimo ethnographies, and the rich descriptions are of a culture which was fully viable when the study was made. It contains a better account of social life and nonmaterial culture than any other study of Alaskan Eskimos. Insofar as literary style, breadth of coverage, and insight are concerned, the Nunamiut study by Gubser is outstanding. It is for a reconstituted society, however: one which had ceased to exist by 1920 but was consolidated again nearly a generation later. Why certain Nunamiut returned and others did not might be significant; the returnees seem to have been traditionalists who had kept their old ways while dispersed. In the studies of the Nunamiut the name of one informant, Simon Paneak, occurs constantly; other Eskimos and whites alike have clustered about him (Gubser, 1965, xi–xv; Ingstad, 1954, 41–42; L. Irving, 1953, 37). Paneak has been described by diverse people as a remarkably intelligent man, and I cannot but wonder whether his views are not an honest but somewhat unreal ethnographic reconstruction.

The ethnographic studies available for other areas of Alaska have serious limitations of one form or another. The sources on the Tareumiut are restricted in coverage. For material culture and some aspects of social life the studies by Simpson and Murdoch are quite satisfactory, but details about the nonmaterial culture are few. Thus it has been necessary to jump in time from accounts for the 1850's and 1880's to Rainey's Point Hope study made in 1940. This source is excellent but limited in scope. The only other Tareumiut study, that by Spencer, was made in 1952–1953, and, although rich in detail, it is even further removed in time from the aboriginal scene. Spencer's study is primarily a reconstruction of the whale-hunting Point Barrow Eskimos, but the people he studied probably were not the Barrow people of Simpson's and Murdoch's time. Ford (in Stewart, 1959, 246) makes this quite clear: "Charley Brower [a long-term white resident of Point Barrow] told me several times that the original Barrow population, which comprised the Barrow community when he first went there, about 1890, had almost all died in the course of various epidemics, and that the population of the early

1930's was almost completely inland Eskimo who had come from the interior—from the drainage of the Colville, and other rivers to the east." Diamond Jenness (1927, 168), on the basis of his studies in the region from 1913 to 1916, made the same assertion that disease had killed most of the original Barrow area residents at the end of the nineteenth century and that the majority of those there during the time of his fieldwork were from inland areas. Thus when Spencer (1959, 1) writes that "in the contemporary culture there is much to suggest the undisrupted native past" I cannot but wonder; Spencer's work was used only with reservations.

The other ethnographic monographs are more limited in scope. Of these I relied most heavily on the Chugach presentation by Birket-Smith. The Kovagmiut description by Giddings and my study of the Kuskowagamiut served primarily to balance the comparisons. Furthermore, supplementary information from diverse articles added greater perspective. Still there are areal gaps in the source materials. We know virtually nothing about the Noatagmiut or the Selawikmiut, but these gaps are not too serious since there is the Kobuk study by Giddings. There are no ethnographies for all of the Seward Peninsula people, the Eskimos of the Bering Sea coast, or the Koniag. Future reconstructions for any people from Bristol Bay southward are unlikely because of the long exposure of these Eskimos to rather intensive Anglo-American influences, but this is not true of some villages on or near the central Bering Sea coast. Intensive contact in some of this area has begun only within the last twenty years. In all likelihood the tribe with the greatest salvage potential is the Kaialigamiut. Fortunately, Jonathan Jenness recently made a study of the nearby Magemiut, and when his work appears, an obvious gap for this sector of Alaska will be filled. The Yukon River Ikogmiut are another people who seem from my casual contacts with them to be quite conservative and worthy of attention.

Insofar as integrative studies of the Alaskan Eskimo data are concerned, only Lantis has made major contributions. Her publications of 1938, 1947, and 1954 are outstanding. The comparative statements on kinship systems by Giddings (1952b) and Whitten (1964) are also important in the interpretation of ethnographic data. The monographs by Birket-Smith (1929, 1953) and Birket-Smith with de Laguna (1938) provide a further comparative view of trait distributions.

Origins

Eskimo culture arose first in the Bering Sea area, and although its background is traceable to eastern Siberia, its emergence as a cultural entity was in western Alaska. The Siberian taproots are clear. It is here that the remote linguistic relatives of Eskimos, representatives of the Chukotan phylum, are found today. The closest bonds in blood type and bone morphology likewise point to eastern Siberia. By contrast Eskimos stand apart from American Indian populations in all of these characteristics. Archaeological evidence for close typological similarities with eastern Siberian sites is absent, an expected situation if Eskimo culture arose as distinct in Alaska. The linguistic evidence leaves little doubt that Alaska was the area in which Eskimos flourished. The Eskimoan linguistic phylum stands essentially alone in the New World. The major division within Eskimoan, into the Eskimo and the Aleut stocks, occurred in Alaska. The Aleut stock remained limited to Alaska, and in western Alaska the Eskimo stock became more diversified than in any other region of Eskimo occupancy.

To verify that Eskimo culture arose in Alaska it is necessary first to show that the Eskimo way of life, meaning an economy adapted to the exploitation of the arctic seas, has its greatest time depth in Alaska. The earliest Alaskan mainland culture of unquestioned sea-mammal hunters is Old Whaling, dating 1800 b.c. In the historic Aleut area the earliest levels of the Chaluka site on Umnak Island, which were occupied at about the same time, suggest a well-developed technology for sea-mammal hunting more clearly than does Old Whaling. Farther back in time is the Arctic Small Tool tradition of 3000 B.C., associated with some coastal and a few inland sites in the Eskimo area. There is not enough organic preservation for this horizon to be certain that the people were sea-mammal hunters, but the lithic forms blend into those later forms which clearly are Eskimo. The Arctic Small Tool tradition is the best candidate for elemental Aleut and Eskimo. In eastern Siberia there are no remains of developed sea-mammal economies at 1800 B.C. or earlier.

A major problem in interpreting Eskimoan developments is to explain why the Eskimos and Aleuts, who had a common historic border, emerged as so distinct. The cultural break might be explained by an alien-wedge hypothesis. According to this theory, the Eskimoan linguistic phylum is visualized as splitting into the Aleut and Eskimo stocks after an Indian group from southwestern Alaska moved into the area and divided the people into two segments. An Indian wedge driving to the coast has precedent in the historic Pacific Eskimo area. The Tanaina intruded onto southern Cook Inlet to separate Eskimos, but the division was only partially complete at contact. To identify an Indian intrusion in the distant past, however, would be difficult, especially if the Indians borrowed heavily from the local people's technology, as did the Tanaina. In the Naknek River drainage sequence at the Brooks River Falls phase, dating around A.D. 1000, are new forms which do not appear to have spread from an Aleutian or north Pacific center and must at present be regarded as coming from inland Indians of southwestern Alaska. If such an inference is valid, then there is some evidence for Indian intrusion into the Aleut-Eskimo boundary area.

At historic contact we might logically expect to find a speech community in the Aleut-Eskimo boundary area, the Alaska Peninsula, with evidence of intergradation between the two stocks. As pointed out in the opening chapter, the Alaska Peninsula has in the past been viewed as the homeland of the Aglegmiut, but since this interpretation is no longer tenable, earlier border-area occupants must be sought to prove or disprove linguistic intergradation. Such evidence appears at present to be unobtainable from field studies, although it might exist in historical records.

Cultural Developments

The widespread and somewhat variable Arctic Small Tool tradition stands as the technological base for Eskimo culture. Its developments crystallized in Alaska from a Siberian, not a New World, background and spread across the arctic from Alaska to Greenland. The small-tool tradition did not penetrate the Pacific drainages, and by the time it had reached Bristol Bay it was modified drastically. Because of wide flexibility in exploitative devices, its bearers could hunt on the land or sea and could remain inland or move out along the coasts. The geography of western Alaska from the arctic coasts to Bristol Bay has no sharp breaks to impede the tradition's spread. The coast of the Eskimoan biotic province is continuous except along northern Norton Bay where the Hudsonian forests reach the sea, but in all likelihood they did not do so at the time period being considered. Coastal resources included the same land animals, seals, and fish but in different local concentrations. Thus in this coastal zone and out of the Arctic Small Tool tradition Eskimo culture began to assume distinct subcultural forms.

The rise of whale hunting in the north was matched with the development of salmon-based economies along Bristol Bay, and both took place before 1800 B.C. Economic specializations of small groups occurred repeatedly; those who became caribou hunters, committed to an inland way of life, generally flourished temporarily and then failed. Over the area as a whole, however, the general pattern was one of land and sea exploitation as represented by Choris and Ipiutak, or of a stronger attachment to the coast as in Norton and Birnirk. Continuities between the economies at these archaeological periods and the tribes at historic contact are obvious, except for the division of hunters and fishermen into Bering Sea and arctic branches. The Denbigh Flint complex site at Iyatayet and other coastal sites with the same type of stonework were occupied by hunters and fishermen; the inland representatives of the Denbigh Flint complex were caribou hunters; the Old Whaling remains were of arctic whalers; the Norton, Ipiutak, and Birnirk people were all hunters and fishermen. The continuity between these archaeological periods and tribes at historic contact is best for the diversified hunters and fishermen; it does not exist for the arctic whalers or the caribou hunters.

In the historic Eskimo area of Alaska the major geographical break occurred at the Alaska Peninsula. Near here the Eskimoan and Hudsonian biotic province gave way to the Aleutian, and to the east was the Sitkan biotic province. The Aleutian biotic province of the Alaska Peninsula was divided along its length by the Aleutian Range, a north-south separation between the Pacific and Bering Sea drainages. This mountain range was an effective barrier to cultural exchanges between the two regions. Although the mountains could be crossed physically, the ecological separation which they represented rarely was bridged. According to Dumond's reconstruction of the Naknek River drainage sequence, extending from 2000 to 1000 B.C. and again from A.D. 1 to 1850, the Aleutian Range was a barrier to the spread of cultural ideas except for a period around A.D. 1200 when the path led south. The Naknek area ties through time were predominantly with the north, and perhaps Eskimos did not occupy the Pacific area until after A.D. 1200. The year A.D. 1200 was almost a magical point in Eskimo time, but given the accuracy of the chronology, this critical moment may have been somewhat earlier or later. No radical change in traits appears suddenly, but it is possible to speak of their coalescence in the Thule culture appearing in the west around this time. The technological inventory had greater functional utility than before, and no major changes were to take place in it again until historic contact. About A.D. 1200 Thule culture spread rapidly and widely in the north; the Pacific area, in turn, was influenced strongly from the north, and somewhat later Kodiak Island felt the effect of alien ideas.

Inuit and Yuit Separation

The Eskimo language stock diverged to form the Inuit and Yuit languages as the people separated into two groups throughout the first Christian millennium. The divergence occurred as Eskimos bearing the Norton culture moved out from Norton Bay and encompassed all the coastal area from the Alaska Peninsula northward. From this base arose the arctic Inuit people, as represented best by Near Ipiutak Eskimo remains. The Yuit still centered along the Bering Sea coast, but they extended into eastern Siberia. On Seward Peninsula the Inuit and Yuit were intermingled, although the Yuit dominated all of the southern portion. Along the arctic coasts of Alaska at a few centers such as Point Hope the Inuit emerged as distinct and strong. By A.D. 1500 they were able to push southward and control western Seward Peninsula, thereby separating the Siberian from the Alaskan Yuit. In the early historic period the Unaligmiut tribe of Yuit gave clear evidence of having borrowed numerous ideas from their Inuit neighbors. Linguistic borrowings between the Yuit and Inuit were suggested by Diamond Jenness, although the evidence was not accepted by Swadesh. Summarily, the Yuit and Inuit emerged from Bering Sea coast and arctic coast centers as two distinct Eskimo groups. A shatter zone existed on Seward Peninsula, and new ideas from Siberia influenced both Alaskan Eskimo segments. The northern Inuit formed the smaller of the two groups, but for some unknown reason they were able to push southward and replace the Yuit on western Seward Peninsula and were beginning to control the Norton Sound area at the beginning of history.

Population Shifts

Just before historic contact the major direction for striking population shifts was to the south. The Malemiut moved south across Seward Peninsula, the Aglegmiut traveled from the Kuskokwim area into the Bristol Bay region, and the Kuskowagamiut went across a mountain divide to the western Nushagak River drainage. Furthermore, in recent but prehistoric times the Kauwerak had moved to southern Seward Peninsula, and the Suk had crossed the Alaska Peninsula to reach the Pacific drainage area. The implication is that changes occurred in diverse northern localities which were of sufficient magnitude to give the bearers advantages over the occupants of the environmentally richer areas to the south. Each of these moves was one of a people and not of the diffusion of ideas from one tribe to the next. No single factor or combination of factors can be marshaled to explain the shifts. It is clear that the Malemiut expansion was one of traders; on the other hand, the Kuskowagamiut may have been successful raiders.

Eskimos also were extending their control inland along major rivers flowing into the Bering Sea and the western Arctic Ocean. Here the process was one of acculturating and assimilating Indians. This was true of the Kobuk Eskimos in their relations with the Koyukon Indians and also characterized the Ikogmiut and Kuskowagamiut contacts with the Anvik and Georgetown Ingalik subtribes. On the Yukon River in the early contact period some Anvik Ingalik spoke Eskimo (Osgood, 1959, 60; Zagoskin, 1967, 190). Where the Georgetown Ingalik and Kuskowagamiut mingled along the banks of the central Kuskokwim, some Eskimos and Indians were bilingual, but more often it seems the Indians learned to speak Eskimo.

Eskimos did not always gain control over foreign groups, a fact that was most noticeable along their southern fringe. The Aleuts were encroaching successfully from the west upon the Peninsular Eskimos during the early historic period. Apparently at the time of contact Aleuts held the Shumagin Islands and were moving eastward along the northern shore of the Alaska Peninsula. It is possible that their expansion was under Russian protection and was not prehistoric. Likewise the Tanaina pushed the Unixkugmiut from Cook Inlet, and the Eyak separated one Chugach subtribe from the others. Beyond Alaska, Eskimo expansions into northern temperate environments succeeded temporarily, but Eskimos came to be replaced by Indians. This was true at the mouth of the St. Lawrence River and perhaps for the Caribou Eskimos at the Churchill River mouth. The statement that Eskimos adapt well to diverse environmental conditions is applicable only to diversities within arctic and subarctic settings.

Land versus Sea Exploitation

A recurrent theme in the analysis of Eskimo culture has been to stress the division between exploitation of inland and that of coastal resources. Expectedly, a reaction has developed against the utility of this division as a conceptual tool (W. Taylor, 1966). From the present study I would conclude that there was no basic coastal-inland division of Eskimos but rather an essential unity among them regardless of differences in ecological zones. This unity between coastal and inland groups was vital in arctic Alaska, less forceful along the Bering Sea, and not applicable along the Pacific. Neither way of life was sufficient unto itself beyond the north Pacific; there was, rather, a dependence on resources from both areas. If a people could not hunt both sea mammals and caribou, they relied on trade for a balance of products. People who primarily hunted caribou required fat from sea mammals in their diet, and coastal people with adequate fat supplies required caribou skins for clothing.

In spite of all that has been written about an inland caribou-hunting base for Eskimo culture, an inland origin is most unlikely. Too much of the basis of Eskimo culture is sea-oriented, and both antiquity and continuity are found at coastal localities. The earliest Alaskan Eskimos, the bearers of the Arctic Small Tool tradition, were coastal more often than inland residents. The inland caribou hunters who were Eskimos lived on the margins of survival and failed repeatedly, as in the Barren Grounds of Canada and the Brooks Range of Alaska. Even more important, when inland caribou hunters disappeared, their area was sooner or later reoccupied by a new group of caribou hunters who moved inland from the coast. In the 10,000-year archaeological record for the central Brooks Range, Campbell (1962) sees each caribou-based economy replaced by another in a nondevelopmental pattern.

Regional Comparison

In the three sections to follow, a comparative summary is developed for the three major clusters of tribes, the Pacific Eskimos, the Bering Sea Eskimos or Yuit who include both the Nunivak and Mainland peoples, and finally the arctic Eskimos or Inuit. The purpose of these sections is to draw conclusions within each of the three groups, which represent the major geographical and linguistic segments of Alaskan Eskimos.

PACIFIC ESKIMOS

At the time of historic contact there were 8,700 Pacific Eskimos, all of whom spoke the Suk dialect of Yupik. They were divided into three tribes with an average population density of twenty-four persons per one hundred square kilometers. This combined density is approximate since the Unixkugmiut population figure is a pure guess. The density is high because the island Koniag density approached one hundred per hundred square kilometers of utilized land. The average density of the Pacific Eskimos is far higher than that of the other clusters of Eskimo tribes but is not dissimilar to other densities along the coast of western North America southward to California (Kroeber, 1939, Map 18). This area had the greatest overall density for any continuous region north of Mexico. The Pacific Eskimos participated in a developed maritime economy in an area with rich and diverse resources.

The Koniag were the most successful in terms of maintaining the greatest number of people. The population of the Kodiak Island group was high in part because of the local abundance of resources, although there were periodic, if not annual, food scarcities. Resources on the adjacent mainland were much more limited, and only 500 of the 6,500 Koniag lived there even though the mainland was about the same size as the island. A superficial survey of mainland archaeological sites did not reveal any vast and deep kitchen middens like those found on the island group (Oswalt, 1955, 53–54), nor was this a region of major salmon-spawning streams. The mainland Koniag were a struggling parent population of the more successful islanders. The islands comprising the Kodiak group were at least twenty or more miles from the adjacent mainland, a fact that made frequent raids by other peoples unlikely and offered a certain degree of physical security. Another factor which made the islands a desirable home was that diverse species of salmon spawned in great numbers in the streams. Then, too, the coastline was deeply indented with headlands and bays that offered ideal conditions for sea-mammal hunting. Perhaps equally important was the fact that the Koniag were situated at a north Pacific crossroads where they received ideas from Aleuts, Indians, and other Eskimos. The combination of these factors, and doubtless others, led to a clear Eskimo cultural climax among the island Koniag.

It is possible to say very little about the Unixkugmiut of the Sitkan biotic province. Although they occupied a province with great resource potential, their particular niche, like that of the mainland Koniag, does not appear to have been very productive and their numbers were few. Their not-too-distant ancestors had occupied at least the lower portion of Cook Inlet, but they were raided successfully by the Koniag and eventually displaced by the Tanaina. They were Suk-speaking Eskimos whose roots were shallow and whose success was moderate.

Concerning the other tribe in the Sitkan biotic province, the Chugach of Prince William Sound, it is possible to conclude considerably more. Both de Laguna (1956, 256–57) and Birket-Smith (1953, 8) stressed the fact that despite an environment which offered so much, the population of Prince William Sound was unexpectedly low. Admittedly the Chugach were subject to raids by the Eyak, Koniag, and Tlingit, with the Eyak soundly defeating one group of Chugach (Birket-Smith and de Laguna, 1938, 147), but this fact alone does not adequately explain the small Chugach population. They were no more numerous in the recent past, as is evident from the small and scattered sites with shallow kitchen middens. It is possible that these people had not lived in the area for more than five hundred years before historic contact. Since few Eyak words were borrowed from the Chugach and nearly half of these came through the Russians, it may be concluded that the contacts with the Eyak were both late and not intensive. Eyak word borrowings from Tlingit, on the other hand, were somewhat more numerous. If Krauss (1965, 185–86) is correct in suggesting that the Eyak lived in the area of their historic occupancy even before the Christian era, then the paucity of Chugach borrowings is a strong indication of a late arrival in the area by the Chugach.

The Chugach population density of fifteen persons per hundred square kilometers is the most reliable for Eskimos in the north Pacific hygrophytic forest and bears comparison with the densities for Northwest Coast maritime Indians in the same general ecological zone. The Tlingit density was ten persons, the Tsimshian density was thirty-two, and the island-dwelling Haida, ninety-five (Kroeber, 1939, 135). Comparing these densities, the Chugach maintained a proportionally larger population than the Tlingit but a smaller one than the other two tribes. In this context it might be mentioned that the Tlingit may also have been recent arrivals in their area of historic occupancy.

The oldest archaeological remains reported to date in the area occupied by the Pacific whalers and fishermen of historic times are on the islands of the Kodiak group and date 3500 B.C. From this time to some point between A.D. 900 and 1500 there is continuity in the archaeological record, but during that time an abrupt change in artifact forms occurred (Clark, 1966). The change possibly represents the arrival of the proto-Suk from the shores of Bristol Bay (Dumond, 1964, 37–38; 1965, 1242–43). It seems

likely that the Eskimos to become Suk crossed the Alaska Peninsula around A.D. 1200 and soon moved to the Pacific shores and to
Kodiak. They introduced many new cultural elements and assimilated the existing population. Prior to A.D. 1200 the Pacific Eskimo
area had been occupied not by Suk speakers but by persons
representing a north Pacific sea-hunting tradition. They were
maritime hunters with a flint-working technology which had
given way around 2000 B.C. to a greater stress on ground slate.
The development was not local but was derived from the same
base which gave rise to the Marpole and Locarno Beach inventories found near the Fraser River mouth in southwestern British
Columbia.

In certain respects the Pacific Eskimos stand apart from other
Alaskan Eskimos, a separation that becomes evident in a comparison of trait inventories for the period of historic contact. Among
the traits which were absent among the Chugach but were found
widely from the Alaska Peninsula northward were the use of
blunt arrows for birds, multipronged bird darts and bird arrows,
bolas, gill nets for fish, and seal nets. The Koniag were the only
Pacific Eskimos among whom seal nets and bird arrows were
found. A more exhaustive list of absences might be compiled, but
these examples show that some of the typical Bering Strait area
hunting devices faded away in the south. Among the traits and
trait complexes present among the Pacific Eskimos but absent
among other Alaskan Eskimos were the following: a well-
developed warfare complex including fortified and habitable posi-
tions, whaling with poisoned slate-lance blades and secret rituals
for whale hunters, separate sleeping rooms in the houses, transvestites common particularly among the Koniag, "slavery" and the
killing of a slave at the death of his owner, differential forms of
burial for persons of different statuses, breast tattoos on women,
halibut hooks, and cylindrical wooden quivers. Again this list
could be expanded, but enough characteristics in diverse categories have been cited to point up the significance of the differences.

In some ways the Pacific Eskimo sea-hunting complex differs

from that found among other Eskimos. A wide variety of darts were used with throwing boards, and there was an emphasis on barbed harpoon heads rather than the toggling form. This latter characteristic was shared, however, by Bering Sea coast tribes. Unique to the Pacific Eskimos was their type of complex kayak. The Pacific Eskimos had the standard form but in addition had a two-holed variety which was the most sophisticated small ocean-going vessel found anywhere. It must be pointed out, too, that the whaling practices of the Pacific Eskimos, as seen particularly among the Koniag since knowledge of them is best, shared specific and unusual characteristics with only the southern Northwest Coast Indians, either the Nootka or Quinault, or both tribes. Examples of such characteristics include the initiation of youthful whalers, the use of ceremonially bathed human corpses, and the carrying of human remains in a whaling vessel during a hunt (Lantis, 1938a, 440, 443, 451–52). Thus as Borden (1962, 18) was the most recent to point out, this is a link between the southern Northwest Coast and the Pacific Eskimo area. It must be added, too, that according to Pinart (1873, 674) the Koniag said that when they arrived on Kodiak Island they found the Tlingit already present. That the prior occupants were Tlingit is an open question, but the earlier people had a maritime-adapted culture not unlike the modern Tlingit. A myth, this time concerning Koniag origins, identifies their earlier homeland as north of the Alaska Peninsula (Lisiansky, 1814, 196–97). From her thorough analysis of Alaskan Eskimo ceremonial life, Lantis (1947, 118) concluded that the Koniag were tied most closely to southwestern Alaskan Eskimos and did not come from beyond the Nushagak-Kuskokwim region to intrude into the Pacific area.

BERING SEA COAST AND NUNIVAK ESKIMOS

At the time of historic contact nearly 9,000 Yuk speakers lived along the Bering Sea coast and in adjacent interior regions. In addition to these people, who composed seven different tribes, the region was populated by 1,600 Peninsular Eskimos who were possibly Yuk speakers and 400 Cux speakers, all of one tribe on Nunivak Island. The average population density (persons per hundred square kilometers) was ten for the Cux and four for the Yuk, including the Peninsular Eskimos. The Cux lived exclusively in the Eskimoan biotic province, and the Peninsular Eskimos were occupants of a segment of the Aleutian province. About one fourth of the Yuk area was in the Hudsonian biotic province and nearly all the rest in the Eskimoan province. In terms of population about 2,800 lived in the Hudsonian province, and of these, over two thirds were Kuskowagamiut. Thus, the inland penetration of the latter tribe was the deepest and the most successful. One reason for the Kuskowagamiut success was the friendly relationship they had with the adjacent Ingalik of the Georgetown subtribe, although why this relationship was amicable is not known.

The Bering Sea coast was the Alaskan region of greatest Eskimo antiquity and continuity. In a physical sense it was the core area from which daughter populations spread north and south. The linguistic evidence for considering this as the area of dispersal already has been cited. In addition, the Yuk speakers here had developed the greatest diversity of tribes per square kilometer to be found anywhere in Alaska and had the largest absolute population of any linguistic segment. The Yuk had diversified into many contrasting subsistence types and likewise were the most successful in penetrating an alien environment, the Hudsonian biotic province. Finally, the Yuk tribes which faced Athapaskans in the latter's homeland were successful in assimilating the Indians, whereas the reverse was not the case. In combination, the vitality, diversity, and size of the Yuk population plus the cited linguistic evidence suggest that along the Alaskan Bering Sea coast Eskimo culture was very old and perhaps older than anywhere else.

Lacking a detailed ethnography for any particular Yuk tribe or the details of Cux material culture, it is unwise to attempt a discussion of traits except in a general way. Neither the Yuk, except perhaps those on Besboro Island, nor the Cux hunted great whales, but both had a broad inventory of weapons and equipment for open-water sea-mammal hunting from kayaks. In this area the barbed harpoon dart was favored over the toggle-headed harpoon. Here "totemism" was notable, matrilocal residence was common, in the bilateral-descent system a distinct stress was placed on the male line, and Iroquois cousin terms were prevalent. This was the region of the great permanent kashgees which housed the men and boys of a community and served as the structure in which males took dry heat baths. The Bladder Feast and the Great Feast of the Dead were both elaborate and key ceremonies. Additional characteristics included pottery with line-dot surface treatment, the harpoon line board, wooden face and finger masks which were complex and diverse, elaborate ivory carvings, and notable woodworking ability. The Cux and many Yuk were Bering Sea hunters and fishermen whose rich and flexible technology, coupled with a comparative abundance of resources, anticipated their moderate success.

The caribou-hunting Togiagamiut subtribe was a remnant of a once larger population and possibly represented the survival of an Ipiutak-related culture with remains in the Cape Newenham area (Larsen, 1950). Clear links with the northern manifestations of Ipiutak will be discovered along the central coast, but no Yuit caribou hunters other than the Togiagamiut group survived into historic times. Intensive salmon fishing was an economic activity of early Bering Sea Eskimos, but deep penetration by the Yuk of the great rivers in southwestern Alaska was recent. Both the lower Kuskokwim River Yuk and the Ikogmiut near the present-day Yukon settlement of St. Marys had settled some eighty miles from the sea by historic times. On the adjacent seacoast the Bladder Feast to perpetuate sea mammals was the key ritual, but in these inland riverine areas only an occasional beluga whale or hair seal was killed. The Ikogmiut near St. Marys retained the bladder ceremonials, but wild celery stalks (probably *Angelica lucida*) were placed on the surface of the ice as a substitute for pushing the bladders of sea mammals through a hole cut in the ice (Nelson, 1899, 392). The lower Kuskokwim Eskimos performed the Bladder Feast, but the brief accounts of it given by observers who described other ceremonies in some detail indicate that it was unimportant (Oswalt, 1963a, 67–68). Thus the riverine Yuk were losing their ties with coastal Eskimo ceremonies but had not replaced them yet with any rituals based on salmon, their major source of food. The inland penetration of the Kuskowagamiut and Ikogmiut was successful economically, and to a lesser degree so was that of the Kiatagmiut (VanStone, ms. 2).

The Nunivak Yupik language diverged from Yuk sufficiently to be classed as a separate dialect, but it was not nearly as different from Yuk as was Suk. On the basis of their degree of linguistic divergence from Yuk, the Nunivakers probably had not occupied the island for long, certainly for less than a thousand years. No archaeological remains found on the island suggest even this much antiquity. The only argument advanced for an old occupation of Nunivak is based on the presence there of check-stamped pottery. No form of this ware, except for isolated sherds, is considered by Dumond (1965, 1244) to date much later than A.D. 900. This interpretation, however, ignores the complete check-stamped vessel with iron staples reported for an unknown location in Alaska (de Laguna, 1947, 229) and the sherds from a house at Deering which was abandoned in A.D. 1902 (Oswalt, 1952, 28).

ARCTIC ESKIMOS

The 6,350 Inuit were divided into eight tribes with a population density (persons per hundred square kilometers) of two. They lived mainly in the Eskimoan biotic province; populations concentrated in the Hudsonian province were much smaller than the coastal ones. They were less successful in their inland penetration than were the Yuit, partially because the resources were not as great. One fact about Inuit population distribution does not appear in the statistics. The Inuit settlement pattern was such that villages, where the populations were sizeable by Eskimo standards, often were concentrated at favored points of coastal land; however, such communities were separated much more widely than were Yuit settlements. Given the distance between these major coastal settlements, we might expect more variation within a tribe than within the Yuit tribes. Such was not the case, however, due to the mobility of the people and to the relative recency of Inuit tribal separations.

The one cultural complex which made some of the coastal Inuit stand out and apart from all other Alaskan Eskimos was their whaling method. The hunting of great whales from an open skin boat with a well-organized crew whose harpooner used a large toggle-headed harpoon was not present elsewhere. It was also among the coastal Inuit that the maupok and utok seal-hunting methods were most often reported, the plank or log house roof was gabled and supported by one or more crossbeams, the variety in toggle harpoons was greatest, and the tailor-made skin clothing was most complex. In most other respects the Inuit sociocultural system was like that of the Yuit, especially the Cux and Yuk. The Messenger Feast, the relations with the world of spirits, the importance of personal charms, the position of a shaman in a community, and the tools and household equipment were all much the same. Inuit culture was less complex than that of the Yuit, however, and numerous Yuit traits were not present among the Inuit.

The most stable and successful Inuit communities were those of arctic whale hunters and were found from Point Barrow to Sledge Island and perhaps to Besboro Island in the northern Bering Sea. Near the center of this area whale hunting extended back to around 2000 B.C. in the whale-based economy at Cape Krusenstern. Apart from the Kobuk River region, little is known about these Inuit who are described as arctic hunters and fishermen. Their inland penetration of the Kobuk and adjacent river systems was earlier than the Yuk intrusions inland along the Yukon and Kuskokwim rivers. As has been mentioned repeatedly, the inland caribou-hunting Inuit are a recent and perhaps even a historic population in the central Brooks Range. Given the inland environmental conditions of the area north of Bering Strait, we would expect in prehistoric times, as well as in early historic times, to find subcultural radiations more unsuccessful here than in the south. In this area slight changes in ecological patterning, such as the development of a shallow off-shore area or a decline in caribou numbers, could be disastrous and lead to the coalescence of a people or to their extinction.

Tribal Densities Compared

Now that the three major population segments, the Pacific, Bering Sea, and arctic Eskimos, have been compared with each other, it is possible to turn to other comparisons. First, however, the distorted nature of the data for certain tribes must be recognized so that these groups may be eliminated from broad comparisons. The *Aglegmiut* were a displaced tribe who entered their historic homeland during late prehistoric times. Their population density of four persons per hundred square kilometers is below what we would expect for a population in an area with such rich resources, resources that the Aglegmiut were fully capable of exploiting with their existing technology. Were it not for the Russian entry into the area, they would have become extinct sooner than they did. Their population was small and scattered, and their social life was disorganized. Therefore, they may in no way be considered as typical Bering Sea Eskimos at contact. The *Magemiut* density of three clearly is out of line with that of adjacent tribes, lending support to the assertion by J. Jenness that my population estimate for the Magemiut is too low; however, no revision in this density is possible until more information on this tribe is available. The *Kuskowagamiut* density of four probably is too low but for another reason. I suspect that some of the hinterland away from the river was not exploited; it was, however, calculated in determining the density. A more realistic Kuskowagamiut density might be six, comparable to that of the Ikogmiut.

The *Kingikmiut* density of sixteen stands far above that of other tribes north of the Alaska Peninsula and is understandable only in terms of their position as the New World people with the closest trading ties in the Old World. The importance of Wales as a market center and transshipment point probably was greater than the existing literature would suggest. The tribal density of two for the *Kiatagmiut* is unquestionably valid, but it is much lower than what would be expected for the area. An explanation might be that Aglegmiut and Kuskowagamiut intrusions in late prehistoric times had forced the Kiatagmiut to withdraw up the Nushagak River to settings less favorable than those they had frequented earlier. It is with the least confidence that I set aside the Kiatagmiut density as being unrealistic. The *Unixkugmiut* must be dropped because their population for the contact period is unknown. The tribal density which reflects the most glaring departure from areal similarity is that of the *Peninsular Eskimos.* Their density of three must be compared with the conservative Koniag density of thirty and Kroeber's (1939, Table 7) Aleut calculation of sixty-four. These figures reinforce the deduction that at the time of contact the Peninsular Eskimos were in the process of some major adjustment.

Language Group	Area	Densities*	Tribes
Inupik	northern	1–2	Kovagmiut, Noatagmiut, Nunamiut, Selawikmiut, Tareumiut
	southern	4	Kauwerak, Malemiut
Yupik	northern	3	Unaligmiut
	central	5–10	Ikogmiut, Kaialigamiut, Nuniwagamiut, Togiagamiut
	southern	15–30	Chugach, Koniag

* Persons per hundred square kilometers.

If the abnormalities cited above are set aside, the population densities among Alaskan Eskimos show a rather steady increase from north to south. The clusters are shown in the table. The best evidence for pending internal splits at the contact period is for two tribes with very low densities, the Kovagmiut and the Noa-tagmiut. The two reasons for projecting that such splits soon would have occurred are that first, the densities were low, which made it comparatively difficult to maintain meaningful ties within the tribe, and second, the two different subsistence foci of each of these tribes, caribou hunting and arctic hunting and fishing, served to separate them internally on an economic basis.

Social Developments

The Old Whaling houses dating 1800 B.C. are the earliest known Western Eskimo dwellings. Each had a large room, with one to three smaller rooms adjoining it. In all likelihood a dwelling was occupied by a small family group. If, as Giddings has suggested, the Old Whalers hunted whales in organized crews from large boats, their way of life had the same economic base and the same household composition as the arctic whalers at the time of contact. The possibility should be entertained that the arctic whaling economy began nearly four thousand years ago and continued within a single tradition without a major change in emphasis until historic times. By 700 B.C. at the Choris type site there is the suggestion of "communal" houses. The largest pit measured some forty by twenty feet and contained such a wide variety of artifacts that Giddings could not regard it as a ceremonial structure. Apart from the prehistoric Choris and the historic Koniag household units, the norm in both prehistory and at contact was that one to three nuclear families lived together in one house, suggesting that the close association of small nuclear family groups is an old and stable form of Western Eskimo social structure.

In Eskimo culture, with the overwhelming emphasis on subsistence activities of men for economic survival, a patrilocal or
neolocal marriage residence pattern might be expected. However,
the Tareumiut were bilocal with a preference for patrilocal
(Spencer, 1959, 64, 74, 78), the Nunamiut matrilocal with bilocal
as an alternative (Gubser, 1965, 65–66), and the Chugach matri-
patrilocal (Birket-Smith, 1953, 81). The Koniag, Nuniwagamiut,
and Kuskowagamiut all were matrilocal (Lantis, 1946, 234; Lisiansky, 1814, 198; Oswalt, 1963a, 139). Recent analyses of
marriage-residence patterns have stressed that a simple statement
of the ideal and its alternatives rarely is adequate, and this seems
true of Alaskan Eskimos, particularly the Yuit.

Social life was indisputably built on the nuclear family as the
primary unit. Still this fact should not obscure the importance of
an individual's obligations to his household, to his kindred, to a
voluntary association, to siblings who were either biological or
classificatory, and at times to a paternal line. There was less
cohesion in Yuit nuclear families than in Inuit. The primary
difference in their patterns of living was the importance of the
men's or ceremonial house among all Yuit except the Chugach.
Nunivak and Mainland Yuit boys went to live in a kashgee when
they were quite young and remained closely associated with this
or another ceremonial structure throughout their lives. As a result, the kashgees were patricentric, and the households were
matricentric. This development may explain why matrilocality
emerged among Yuit as the dominant form of marriage residence.
Most marriages were within a community, and it would be logical
for the bride to remain at home after marriage since her husband
remained in his kashgee. There would be little reason for the
bride to move into the house of her husband's mother and sisters.
In instances of the male marrying out of his natal community, he
would associate himself with a new kashgee, and again it would
be logical for his bride to remain in the house of her mother. This
residence pattern does not fit neatly into a normal type since

typically husbands were residents of a kashgee and were visitors in their wives' households. The occurrence of a "matrilocal" residence pattern among the Yuit is interpreted as an effect of the development of the kashgee as a social institution and was not brought about by economic factors.

The Yuit residence pattern had a direct bearing on the social distance dividing males from females. Close-knit nuclear family ties could not be expected since boys and their fathers lived separately from mothers, daughters, and young children. The boys were taught adult male skills in a kashgee, whereas girls learned from their mothers. A male freely visited his wife's house, but she and her daughters frequented the kashgee of the husband or sons only to take them food or to participate in some special kashgee event.

Eskimos often are described as a people who worked diligently, like the proverbial squirrel, gathering acorns for the long winter of forced inactivity. According to Lantis's presentation of the Nunivak seasonal round, these people were indeed very active in subsistence pursuits whenever possible. This may be an accurate view for Nunivak, but comparable diligence was not the norm elsewhere. A certain degree of perseverance was necessary and was found during the productive seasons; nonetheless, it was not considered essential to accumulate enough surplus food to last through a single year, even when it was entirely possible to do so. Fish went uncaught even though they were still running heavily; caribou went unhunted as feasts were held to consume great kills already made. Furthermore, food products might be allowed to spoil and then go unconsumed. The extreme was reached among the Koniag, where the resources were more than adequate for the heavy population, and yet the people depleted their supplies and were forced to resort to shellfish, a second-class but readily available food, before spring. Even when a surplus had been accumulated, it might be depleted rapidly by unanticipated guests or ceremonial feasts, leading to scarcities before winter was over. Thus, there was no Protestant ethic among Alaskan Eskimos.

Religious Developments

In each of the six major subsistence patterns, physical survival depended on a man's ability to take game and fish. It would be expected, therefore, that the major subsistence items would have a significant place in tribal religions. Previously it was noted that Eskimo supernaturalism was based mainly on charms which aided individuals. More complex, but still individually based, were the family charms passed down a patrilineal line among the Nunivak Eskimos or the esoteric knowledge required before hunting great whales among the Pacific Eskimos. Beyond these involvements were those of a largely negative character, such as the taboos against combining land and sea products. In addition, we might expect animal or fish cults which required community-wide participation. It would be anticipated that those tribes whose economies were based largely on very few species were most likely to have an intensive religious focus on the species involved. Furthermore, the greater the antiquity and continuity for such specialized economies, the more likely the supernatural involvements were to be well integrated into tribal life.

The Bering Sea hunting and fishing economy has been represented as the oldest subsistence type and the one with the greatest continuity. Early historic representatives of this type on the central Bering Sea coast, such as the Nuniwagamiut and Unaligmiut, would be expected to have a well-integrated involvement with the species taken. This is precisely the case. The Bladder Feast was the most complex of the cults, and its main focus was on seals. Next in importance was the involvement of whaling peoples in the cult of great whales, but this cult centered in activities of the umialiks and did not include most community members as participants. Pacific whaling again was in the hands of a few individuals who possessed highly specialized knowledge, and rituals did not embrace entire communities. The arctic hunters and fishermen did not have rituals comparable in either scope or intensity to those of the Bering Sea peoples or whalers. As has already been demonstrated, the peoples with salmon-based economies did not have community-wide rituals to honor salmon, and the same may be said of the caribou hunters if Gubser's analysis of the Nunamiut is taken as the norm and Spencer's data ignored. Summarily, animal cults were well integrated into community life only among the Yuit; lesser integration centering about certain individuals existed for the whalers in both the north and south. Salmon and caribou were not the foci of ritual attention among those tribes where these species were key to survival. This situation is contrary to the normal expectation and may have a significant correlation with the fact that these were the economies with the least time depth.

Difficulties in Defining Eskimo Culture

The mental set which is Eskimo culture to anthropologists is clear, concise, and wrong. There is no Eskimo culture any more than there is an Athapaskan or a Pueblo culture. True enough, there is a cluster of traits found among most Eskimos, but it is not an identical cluster among diverse populations. Among the Eskimos in Alaska many characteristics considered to be typically Eskimo are found only intermittently. For example, the toggle harpoon was not used by the Nunamiut; tailor-made clothing was not worn by the Pacific Eskimos and footwear was not always used; Eskimo cousin terms were rare; the multipronged bird spear, bolas, and kashgee were unknown to the Chugach; and the Nunivak Eskimos usually did not hunt seals either at their breathing holes in the winter or as they rested on the ice in the spring. Alaskan Eskimos did not appeal to Sedna, the goddess of the sea, for game, and so on. A list of Alaskan Eskimo traits would include the kayak and umiak, the bow and arrow, the lamp, the use of bilateral descent, the importance of personal charms, the practice of blood revenge, and so on. Most of these traits not only are found among all Eskimos but also are so general and widespread among other peoples that they mean comparatively little as definitive characteristics. I do not suggest abandoning the term *Eskimo*, for it is a useful label to recognize gross linguistic, social, cultural, and racial similarities in one widespread population, but it must be recognized that this single word *Eskimo* masks a great deal of subcultural diversity. Above all else, the purpose of this book has been to describe and analyze the subcultural diversity for a more precise view of what it meant to be an Alaskan Eskimo.

Bibliography

ABBREVIATIONS

AA   *American Antiquity*
AAL   *Arctic Aeromedical Laboratory* (Ladd Air Force Base, Alaska; later, Fort Wainwright, Alaska)
APUA   *Anthropological Papers of the University of Alaska*
CA   *Current Anthropology*
IJAL   *International Journal of American Linguistics*
MG   *Meddelelser om Grønland* (Copenhagen)
321CA   *Proceedings of the Thirty-second International Congress of Americanists* (Copenhagen: Munksgaard, 1958)

ADAMS, THOMAS, AND BENJAMIN G. COVINO
1958   Racial variations to a standardized cold stress. *Journal of Applied Physiology*, v. 12, 9–12.

ALLEN, HENRY T.
1900   A military reconnoissance of the Copper River valley, 1855. In *Compilation of Narratives of Explorations in Alaska*, 411–88. Washington, D.C.: Government Printing Office.

ARONSON, JOSEPH D.
1941   The history of disease among the natives of Alaska. *Transactions and Studies of the College of Physicians of Philadelphia*, series 4, v. 8, 27–34.

ATKINSON, C. E., ET AL.
ms.   Salmon of the north Pacific Ocean IV. Spawning populations of Pacific salmon in the United States.

BAILEY, GEORGE W.

1880   Report upon Alaska and its people. In *Executive Document No. 132, 46th Congress, 2nd Session*, 2–27. Washington, D.C.: Government Printing Office.

BASELINE AND SERVICE STATISTICS—BETHEL TRANSMITTAL #1

1962   Bethel Service Unit Field Health Study, Alaska Department of Health and Welfare and U.S. Public Health Service.

BEARDSLEY, RICHARD K., ET AL.

1956   Functional and evolutionary implications of community patterning. In *Seminars in Archaeology: 1955, Society for American Archaeology Memoir*, no. 11, 129–57.

BERGSLAND, KNUT

1951   Aleut demonstratives and the Aleut-Eskimo relationship. *IJAL*, v. 17, 167–79.

1958a   Aleut and proto-Eskimo. *32ICA*, 624–31.

1958b   Is lexico-statistic dating valid? *32ICA*, 654–57.

BERGSLAND, KNUT, AND HANS VOGT

1962   On the validity of glottochronology. *CA*, v. 3, 115–53.

BIRKET-SMITH, KAJ

1929   The Caribou Eskimos. *Report of the Fifth Thule Expedition 1921–24*, v. 5, pt. 2. Copenhagen.

1941   Early collections from the Pacific Eskimo. *Ethnographical Studies. Nationalmuseets Skrifter, Etnografisk Raekke*, 1, 121–63. Copenhagen.

1953   The Chugach Eskimo. *Nationalmuseets Skrifter, Etnografisk Raekke*, 6. Copenhagen.

BIRKET-SMITH, KAJ, AND FREDERICA DE LAGUNA

1938   *Eyak Indians of the Copper River Delta, Alaska.* Copenhagen: Levin & Munksgaard.

BLUMBERG, BARUCH S., ET AL.

1961   A study of the prevalence of arthritis in Alaskan Eskimos. *Arthritis and Rheumatism*, v. 4, 325–41.

BOAS, FRANZ

1888   The Eskimo. *Proceedings and Transactions of the Royal Society of Canada for the Year 1887*, v. 5, sec. 2, 35–39.

1905   The Jesup North Pacific Expedition. *Thirteenth International Congress of Americanists*, 91–100. Easton, Pa.: Eschenbach Printing Co.

1933   Relationships between north-west America and north-east Asia. In *American Aborigines*, edited by Diamond Jenness, 355–70. [Toronto:] University of Toronto Press.

BOGORAS, WALDEMAR G.

1902   The folklore of northeastern Asia, as compared with that of northwestern America. *American Anthropologist*, n.s., v. 4, 577–683.

1924   New problems of ethnographical research in polar countries. *Proceedings of the Twenty-first International Congress of Americanists*, pt. 1, 226–46. The Hague.

1931   Elements of the culture of the circumpolar zone. *Smithsonian Report for 1930*, 465–82. Washington, D.C.: Government Printing Office.

BORDEN, CHARLES E.

1962   West coast crossties with Alaska. In *Arctic Institute of North America, Technical Paper*, no. 11, edited by John M. Campbell, 9–19.

BROOKS, ALFRED HULSE

1953   *Blazing Alaska's Trails*. Caldwell, Idaho: Caxton Printers.

BROWER, CHARLES D.

1942   *Fifty Years below Zero*. New York: Dodd, Mead & Co.

CAMPBELL, BERNARD

1963   Quantitative taxonomy and human evolution. In Classification and human evolution, *Viking Fund Publications in Anthropology*, no. 37, 50–74.

CAMPBELL, JOHN M.

1962   Cultural succession at Anaktuvuk Pass, arctic Alaska. In *Arctic Institute of North America, Technical Paper*, no. 11, edited by John M. Campbell, 39–54.

CANTWELL, JOHN C.

1889a   A narrative account of the exploration of the Kowak River, Alaska. In *Report of the Cruise of the Revenue Marine Steamer Corwin in the Arctic Ocean in the Year 1884*, 47–74. Washington, D.C.: Government Printing Office.

1889b   Exploration of the Kowak River, Alaska, Ethnological Notes. In *Report of the Cruise of the Revenue Marine Steamer Corwin in the Arctic Ocean in the Year 1884*, 75–98. Washington, D.C.: Government Printing Office.

CAPPS, STEPHEN R.
1937   Kodiak and adjacent islands, Alaska. *United States Geological Survey, Bulletin* 880-C, 111–84. Washington, D.C.: Government Printing Office.

CHANG, KWANG-CHIH
1962a New evidence of fossil man in China. *Science*, v. 136, no. 3518, 749–60.
1962b A typology of settlement and community patterns in some circumpolar societies. *Arctic Anthropology*, v. 1, no. 1, 28–41.

CHARD, CHESTER S.
1955   Eskimo archaeology in Siberia. *Southwestern Journal of Anthropology*, v. 11, 150–77.
1959   The western roots of Eskimo culture. *Proceedings of the Thirty-third International Congress of Americanists*, v. 2, 81–87. San Jose, Costa Rica: Lehmann.

CHORIS, L.
1822   *Voyage pittoresque autour du monde.* Paris: Firmin Didot.

CHOWNING, ANN
1962   Raven myths in northwestern North America and northeastern Asia. *Arctic Anthropology*, v. 1, no. 1, 1–5.

CLARK, DONALD W.
1956   Upper Station site. In Archaeology of the Uyak Site, Kodiak Island, Alaska, by Robert F. Heizer, *University of California Anthropological Records*, v. 17, 94–97.
1966   Perspectives in the prehistory of Kodiak Island, Alaska. *AA*, v. 31, 358–71.

COLLINS, HENRY B.
1937   Archeology of St. Lawrence Island, Alaska. *Smithsonian Institution Miscellaneous Collections*, v. 96, no. 1. Washington, D.C.: Government Printing Office.
1951   The origin and antiquity of the Eskimo. *Smithsonian Report for 1950*, 423–67. Washington, D.C.: Government Printing Office.
1954   Comments on: Time depths of American linguistic groupings. *American Anthropologist*, n.s., v. 56, 364–72.

COLLINS, HENRY B., ET AL.
1945   The Aleutian Islands: Their people and natural history.

Smithsonian Institution War Background Studies, no. 21. Washington, D.C.: Government Printing Office.

COOK, JAMES, AND JAMES KING

1785   *A Voyage to the Pacific Ocean.* 3 v. and atlas, 2d ed. London: G. Nicol and T. Cadell.

CORCORAN, PATRICIA A., ET AL.

1959   Blood groups of Alaskan Eskimos and Indians. *American Journal of Physical Anthropology,* v. 17, 187–93.

CRANTZ, DAVID

1767   *History of Greenland.* 2 v. London: Brethren's Society for the Furtherance of the Gospel among the Heathen.

DAVIS, THOMAS R. A.

1957   An outbreak of infectious hepatitis in two arctic villages. *New England Journal of Medicine,* v. 256, 881–84.

DAWKINS, WILLIAM B.

1874   *Cave Hunting.* London: Macmillan and Co.

DEBETZ, G.

1959   The skeletal remains of the Ipiutak cemetery [sic]. *Proceedings of the Thirty-third International Congress of Americanists,* v. 2, 57–64. San Jose, Costa Rica: Lehmann.

DICE, LEE R.

1943   *Biotic Provinces of North America.* Ann Arbor: University of Michigan Press.

DIKOV, N. N.

1965   The Stone Age of Kamchatka and the Chukchi Peninsula in the light of new archaeological data. *Arctic Anthropology,* v. 3, no. 1, 10–25.

DUMOND, DONALD E.

1962   Prehistory in the Naknek drainage: A preliminary statement. In *Research on Northwest Prehistory,* 7–54. Department of Anthropology, University of Oregon.

1964   A note on the prehistory of southwestern Alaska. *APUA,* v. 12, 33–45.

1965   On Eskaleutian linguistics, archaeology, and prehistory. *American Anthropologist,* n.s., v. 67, 1231–57.

EAGAN, CHARLES J.

1966   The responses to finger cooling of Alaskan Eskimos after nine months of urban life in a temperate climate. *Biometeorology* II, 822–30. Proceedings of the Third International Biometeorological Congress, Pau, S. France.

EDMONDS, H. M. W.

ms.   Report on the Eskimos of the Yukon Delta. Copy in University of Washington Library, Seattle, Washington.

EICHENWALD, HEINZ F., AND JAMES W. MOSLEY

1959   *Viral Hepatitis.* Washington, D.C.: U.S. Department of Health, Education and Welfare.

ELLIOTT, HENRY W.

1886   *Our Arctic Province.* New York: Charles Scribner's Sons.

FAY, FRANCIS H.

1957   History and present status of the Pacific walrus population. *Transactions of the Twenty-second North American Wildlife Conference*, 431–45.

FISCUS, CLIFFORD

1965   Correspondence.

FORD, JAMES A.

1959   Eskimo prehistory in the vicinity of Point Barrow, Alaska. *Anthropological Papers of the American Museum of Natural History*, v. 47, pt. 1.

FOURNELLE, H. J., ET AL.

1958   A bacteriological and parasitological survey of enteric infections in an Alaskan Eskimo area. *American Journal of Public Health*, v. 48, 1489–97.

1959   Seasonal study of enteric infections in Alaskan Eskimos. *Public Health Reports*, v. 74, 55–59.

GABRIELSON, IRA N., AND FREDERICK C. LINCOLN

1959   *Birds of Alaska.* Harrisburg: The Stackpole Company.

GIDDINGS, JAMES L.

1952a The Arctic Woodland Culture of the Kobuk River. *University of Pennsylvania Museum, Museum Monographs.*

1952b Observations on the "Eskimo Type" of kinship and social structure. *APUA*, v. 1, no. 1, 5–10.

1957   Round houses in the western Arctic. *AA*, v. 23, 121–35.

1961a Kobuk River people. *University of Alaska Studies of Northern Peoples*, no. 1.

1961b Cultural continuities of Eskimos. *AA*, v. 27, 155–73.
1962 Alaska aboriginal culture. *The National Survey of Historic Sites and Buildings*, theme 16. [Washington, D.C.:] National Park Service.
1964 *Archeology of Cape Denbigh*. Providence: Brown University Press.

GJESSING, GUTORM
1944 Circumpolar stone age. *Acta Arctica*, v. 2.
1960 Circumpolar social systems. *Acta Arctica*, v. 12, 75–81.

GORDON, JOHN E., AND FRANK L. BABBOTT
1959 Acute intestinal infection in Alaska. *Public Health Reports*, v. 74, 49–54.

GRIGGS, ROBERT F.
1922 *Valley of Ten Thousand Smokes*. Washington, D.C.: The National Geographic Society.

GRINNELL, JOSEPH
1901 *Gold Hunting in Alaska*. Chicago: David C. Cook Publishing Company.

GUBSER, NICHOLAS J.
1965 *Nunamiut Eskimos: Hunters of Caribou*. New Haven and London: Yale University Press.

HAMMEL, H. T.
1964 Terrestrial animals in cold: Recent studies of primitive man. In *Handbook of Physiology*, 413–34, edited by C. G. Wilber. Washington, D.C.: American Physiological Society.

HAMMERICH, LOUIS L.
1951 Can Eskimo be related to Indo-European? *IJAL*, v. 17, 217–23.
1958a The Western Eskimo dialects. *32ICA*, 632–39.
1958b The origin of the Eskimo. *32ICA*, 640–44.
1960 Some linguistic problems in the arctic. In The Circumpolar Conference in Copenhagen, 1958, *Acta Arctica*, v. 12, 83–89.

HATT, GUDMUND
1916a Kyst- og inlandskultur i det arktiske. *Geografisk Tidsskrift*, v. 23, 284–90.
1916b Moccasins and their relation to arctic footwear. *American Anthropological Association Memoir*, no. 15. Lancaster, Pa.: The New Era Printing Co.

HAWKES, ERNEST WILLIAM

1913   The "Inviting-In" feast of the Alaska Eskimo. *Canada Department of Mines, Anthropological Series*, no. 3.

1914   The dance festivals of the Alaskan Eskimo. *University of Pennsylvania, The University Museum, Anthropological Publications*, v. 6, no. 2.

HELLER, CHRISTINE A.

1953   *Wild Edible and Poisonous Plants of Alaska.* [College, Alaska:] University of Alaska, Extension Service.

HEWES, GORDON W., ET AL.

1960   More on Lexicostatistics. *CA*, v. 1, 338–45.

HIMMELHEBER, HANS

1953   *Eskimokünstler.* Eisenach: Erich Röth Verlag.

HINZ, JOHN

1944   *Grammar and Vocabulary of the Eskimo Language.* Bethlehem, Pa.: The Society for Propagating the Gospel.

HIRSCH, DAVID I.

1954   Glottochronology and Eskimo and Eskimo-Aleut prehistory. *American Anthropologist*, n.s., v. 56, 825–38.

HITCHCOCK, DOROTHY J.

1950   Parasitological study on the Eskimos in the Bethel area of Alaska. *Journal of Parasitology*, v. 36, 232–34.

1951   Parasitological study on the Eskimos in the Kotzebue area of Alaska. *Journal of Parasitology*, v. 37, 309–11.

HOSLEY, EDWARD HOWARD

ms.   Factionalism and acculturation in an Alaskan Athapaskan community.

HRDLIČKA, ALEŠ

1930   Anthropological survey in Alaska. *Bureau of American Ethnology, 46th Annual Report*, 19–374. Washington, D.C.: Government Printing Office.

1936a Fecundity of Eskimo women. *American Journal of Physical Anthropology*, v. 22, 91–95.

1936b Puberty in Eskimo girls. *Proceedings of the National Academy of Sciences*, v. 22, 355–57.

1944   *Anthropology of Kodiak Island.* Philadelphia: Wistar Institute of Anatomy and Biology.

HUSTICH, ILMARI

1953   The boreal limits of conifers. *Arctic*, v. 6, 149–62.

HYMES, D. H.

1960   Lexicostatistics so far. *CA*, v. 1, 3–44.

INGSTAD, HELGE

1954   *Nunamiut*. New York: W. W. Norton & Company.

IRVING, LAURENCE

1953   The naming of birds by Nunamiut Eskimo. *Arctic*, v. 6, 35–43.

IRVING, WILLIAM N.

1953   Evidence of early tundra cultures in northern Alaska. *APUA*, v. 1, no. 2, 55–85.

1962   A provisional comparison of some Alaskan and Asian stone industries. In *Arctic Institute of North America, Technical Paper*, no. 11, edited by John M. Campbell, 55–68.

JENNESS, DIAMOND

1927   Notes on the phonology of the Eskimo dialect of Cape Prince of Wales, Alaska. *IJAL*, v. 4, 168–80.

1928a Comparative vocabulary of the Western Eskimo dialects. *Report of the Canadian Arctic Expedition, 1913–18*, v. 15, pt. A. Ottawa: King's Printer.

1928b Ethnological problems of arctic America. In Problems of Polar Research, *American Geographical Society, Special Publication*, no. 7, 167–75. Worcester, Mass.: Commonwealth Press.

1933   The problem of the Eskimo. In *American Aborigines*, edited by Diamond Jenness, 371–96. [Toronto:] University of Toronto Press.

JOCHELSON, WALDEMAR

1908   Koryak. *Jesup North Pacific Expedition, Memoir of the American Museum of Natural History*, v. 6.

KOWTA, MARKOTO

ms.   Old Togiak in prehistory.

KRAUSS, MICHAEL E.

1965   Eyak: A preliminary report. *The Canadian Journal of Linguistics*, v. 10, 167–86.

KROEBER, ALFRED L.

1939   Cultural and natural areas of native North America. *University of California Publications in American Archaeology and Ethnology*, v. 38. Berkeley: University of California Press.

DE LAGUNA, FREDERICA

1932   A comparison of Eskimo and Palaeolithic art. *American Journal of Archaeology*, v. 36, 477–511, PL. 19–23.

1933   A comparison of Eskimo and Palaeolithic art, part II. *American Journal of Archaeology*, v. 37, 77–107, PL. 18–24.

1934   *Archaeology of Cook Inlet, Alaska*. Philadelphia: University of Pennsylvania Press.

1947   Prehistory of northern North America as seen from the Yukon. *AA*, memoir no. 3.

1956   *Chugach Prehistory*. Seattle: University of Washington Press.

LANTIS, MARGARET

1938a   The Alaskan whale cult and its affinities. *American Anthropologist*, n.s., v. 40, 438–64.

1938b   The mythology of Kodiak Island, Alaska. *Journal of American Folk-Lore*. v. 51, 123–72.

1946   The social culture of the Nunivak Eskimo. *Transactions of the American Philosophical Society*, n.s., v. 35, pt. 3, 153–323.

1947   *Alaskan Eskimo Ceremonialism*. New York: J. J. Augustin.

1954   Research on human ecology of the American arctic. Mimeographed, Arctic-Desert-Tropic Information Center, Maxwell Air Force Base, Alabama.

1960   *Eskimo Childhood and Interpersonal Relationships*. Seattle: University of Washington Press.

LARSEN, HELGE

1950   Archaeological investigations in southwestern Alaska. *AA*, v. 15, 177–86.

1951   De dansk-amerikanske Alaska-ekspeditioner 1949–50. *Saertryk af Geografisk Tidsskrift*, v. 51, 63–93.

1952   The Ipiutak culture: Its origin and relationships. In *Indian Tribes of Aboriginal America*, edited by Sol Tax, 22–30. Chicago: University of Chicago Press.

1958   The material culture of the Nunamiut and its relation to other forms of Eskimo culture in northern Alaska. *32ICA*, 574–82.

LARSEN, HELGE, AND FROELICH G. RAINEY

1948   Ipiutak and the arctic whale hunting culture. *Anthropological Papers of the American Museum of Natural History*, v. 42.

LASKER, GABRIEL W.

1961   *Evolution of Man*. New York: Holt, Rinehart and Winston, Inc.

LAUGHLIN, WILLIAM S.

1950 Blood groups, morphology and population size of the Eskimos. *Cold Spring Harbor Symposia on Quantitative Biology*, v. 15, 165–73.

1957 Blood groups of the Anaktuvuk Eskimos, Alaska. *APUA*, v. 6, 5–15.

1963 Eskimos and Aleuts: Their origins and evolution. *Science*, v. 142, no. 3593, 633–45.

LAUGHLIN, WILLIAM S., AND JEAN S. AIGNER

1966 Preliminary analysis of the Anangula unifacial core and blade industry. *Arctic Anthropology*, v. 3, no. 2, 41–56.

LEES, ROBERT B.

1953 The basis of glottochronology. *Language*, v. 29, 113–27.

LEVIN, M. G.

1959 Ancient Eskimo cemetery in Uellen (Chukotka). *Proceedings of the Thirty-third International Congress of Americanists*, v. 2, 65–71. San Jose, Costa Rica: Lehmann.

LISIANSKY, UREY

1814 *A Voyage Round the World in the Years 1803, 4, 5, & 6.* London: John Booth.

LUCIER, CHARLES

1954 Buckland Eskimo myths. *APUA*, v. 2, 215–33.

1958 Noatagmiut Eskimo myths. *APUA*, v. 6, 89–117.

1965 Correspondence.

MCCARTNEY, A. P., AND C. G. TURNER II

1966 Stratigraphy of the Anangula unifacial core and blade site. *Arctic Anthropology*, v. 3, no. 2, 28–40.

MCCLELLAN, CATHARINE

1964 Culture contacts in the early historic period in northwest North America. *Arctic Anthropology*, v. 2, no. 2, 3–15.

MACHATTIE, LORNE, ET AL.

1961 Eskimo metabolism as measured by the technique of 24-hour indirect calorimetry and graphic analysis. *AAL*.

MCLENEGAN, S. B.

1887 Exploration of the Noatak River, Alaska. In *Report of the Cruise of the Revenue Marine Steamer Corwin in the Arctic Ocean in the Year 1885*, 53–80. Washington, D.C.: Government Printing Office.

MANVILLE, RICHARD H., AND STANLEY P. YOUNG

1965   Distribution of Alaskan mammals. *Bureau of Sport Fisheries and Wildlife Circular 211,* United States Department of the Interior.

MARSH, GORDON H.

1954   A comparative survey of Eskimo-Aleut religion. *APUA,* v. 3, 21–36.

MARSH, GORDON H., AND MORRIS SWADESH

1951   Eskimo-Aleut correspondences. *IJAL,* v. 17, 209–16.

MATHIASSEN, THERKEL

1927   Archaeology of the Central Eskimos. *Report of the Fifth Thule Expedition 1921–24,* v. 4, pt. 2.

MATTSON, CHESTER R.

1962   Chum salmon resources of Alaska from Bristol Bay to Point Hope. *United States Fish and Wildlife Service Special Scientific Report—Fisheries* no. 425. Washington, D.C.

MEEHAN, J. P., ET AL.

1954   Cutaneous pain threshold in the native Alaskan Indian and Eskimo. *Journal of Applied Physiology,* v. 6, 397–400.

MILAN, FREDERICK A., ET AL.

1963   Temperature regulation of Eskimos, Indians, and Caucasians in a bath calorimeter. *Journal of Applied Physiology,* v. 18, 378–82.

MOBERG, CARL-AXEL

1960   On some circumpolar arctic problems in north European archeology. *Acta Arctica,* v. 12, 67–74.

MONTAGU, ASHLEY

1946   *Adolescent Sterility.* Springfield: Charles C Thomas.

MOONEY, JAMES

1928   The aboriginal population of America north of Mexico. *Smithsonian Miscellaneous Collections,* v. 80, no. 7. Washington, D.C.: Government Printing Office.

MURDOCH, JOHN

1886   A few legendary fragments from the Point Barrow Eskimos. *American Naturalist,* v. 20, 593–99.

1888   Review of: *Eskimo Tribes* by Henry Rink. *American Anthropologist,* v. 1, 125–33.

1892   Ethnological results of the Point Barrow expedition. *Bureau of Ethnology, 9th Annual Report,* 3–441. Washington, D.C.: Government Printing Office.

MURDOCK, GEORGE P.

1949   *Social Structure.* New York: Macmillan Company.

NELSON, EDWARD W.

1899   Eskimo about Bering Strait. *Bureau of American Ethnology, 18th Annual Report,* pt. 1.

OSGOOD, CORNELIUS

1937   Ethnography of the Tanaina. *Yale University Publications in Anthropology,* no. 16.

1940   Ingalik material culture. *Yale University Publications in Anthropology,* no. 22.

1958   Ingalik social culture. *Yale University Publications in Anthropology,* no. 53.

1959   Ingalik mental culture. *Yale University Publications in Anthropology,* no. 56.

OSWALT, WENDELL H.

1949   Dated houses at Squirrel River, Alaska. *Tree-Ring Bulletin,* v. 16, 7–8.

1952   Pottery from Hooper Bay Village, Alaska. *AA,* v. 18, 18–29.

1955   Prehistoric sea mammal hunters at Kaflia, Alaska. *APUA,* v. 4, 23–61.

1957   A Western Eskimo ethnobotany. *APUA,* v. 6, 16–36.

1960   Eskimos and Indians of western Alaska, 1861–1868. *APUA,* v. 8, 100–18.

1962   Historical populations in western Alaska and migration theory. *APUA,* v. 11, 1–14.

1963a *Mission of Change in Alaska.* San Marino: The Huntington Library.

1963b *Napaskiak, An Alaskan Eskimo Community.* Tucson: University of Arizona Press.

1964   Traditional storyknife tales of Yuk girls. *Proceedings of the American Philosophical Society,* v. 108, 310–36.

OSWALT, WENDELL H., AND JAMES W. VANSTONE

1967   Ethnoarcheology of Crow Village, Alaska. *Bureau of American Ethnology,* Bulletin 199.

PARRAN, THOMAS (PROJECT LEADER)

1954   *Alaska's Health.* [Pittsburgh, Pa.:] The Graduate School of
       Public Health. University of Pittsburgh.

PAULS, FRANK P., ET AL.

1953   Distribution of blood groups among the Eskimos, Indians,
       and whites of western Alaska. *American Journal of Human
Genetics*, v. 5, 252–56.

PENNOYER, STEVEN, ET AL.

1965   Arctic-Yukon-Kuskokwim area salmon fishing history. *De-
       partment of Fish and Game, Information Leaflet* 70. Juneau.

PETROFF, IVAN

1884   *Report on the Population, Industries, and Resources of Alaska.*
       Census Office, Department of the Interior. Washington, D.C.:
Government Printing Office.

PINART, ALPHONSE

1873   Eskimaux et Koloches. *Revue d'Anthropologie*, v. 2, 673–80.

PORTER, ROBERT P. (COMPILATOR)

1893   *Report on Population and Resources of Alaska at the Eleventh
       Census: 1890.* Census Office, Department of the Interior.
Washington, D.C.: Government Printing Office.

RAINEY, FROELICH G.

1941   Eskimo prehistory: The Okvik site on the Punuk Islands.
       *Anthropological Papers of the American Museum of Natural
History*, v. 37, pt. 4.

1947   The whale hunters of Tigara. *Anthropological Papers of the
       American Museum of Natural History*, v. 41, pt. 2.

RASMUSSEN, KNUD

1927   *Across Arctic America.* New York and London: G. P.
       Putnam's Sons.

RAUSCH, ROBERT

1952   Hydatid disease in boreal regions. *Arctic*, v. 5, 157–74.

RAUSCH, ROBERT, ET AL.

1956   Studies on the helminth fauna of Alaska, XXVII, The oc-
       currence of larvae of *Trichinella spiralis* in Alaskan mammals.
Journal of Parasitology, v. 42, 259–71.

RAY, DOROTHY J.

1964 Nineteenth century settlement and subsistence patterns in Bering Strait. *Arctic Anthropology*, v. 2, no. 2, 61–94.

RAY, P. H.

1885 Ethnographic sketch of the natives of Point Barrow. In *Report of the International Polar Expedition to Point Barrow, Alaska*, 35–87, Plates I–V. Washington, D.C.: Government Printing Office.

RHODE, CLARENCE J., AND WILL BARKER

1953 Alaska's Fish and Wildlife. *Fish and Wildlife Service, United States Department of the Interior, Circular 17.*

RINK, HENRY

1875a On the descent of the Eskimo. In *A Selection of Papers on Arctic Geography and Ethnology*, 230–32. London: John Murray.

1875b *Tales and Traditions of the Eskimo*. Edinburgh and London: William Blackwood and Sons.

1891 The Eskimo tribes. *MG*, v. 11.

RODAHL, KAARE

1952 Basal metabolism of the Eskimo. *AAL.*

1954 Diet and cardiovascular disease in the Eskimos. *Transactions of the American College of Cardiology*, v. 4, 192–97.

RODAHL, KAARE, AND JAMES EDWARDS

1952 The body surface area of Eskimos as determined by the linear and the height-weight formulas. *AAL.*

ROMANOWSKY AND FRANKENHAUSER

1962 Five years of medical observations in the colonies of the Russian-American Company, pts. 1, 2. *Alaska Medicine*, v. 4, 33–37, 62–64 (translation from *The Medical Newspaper of Russia*, in German, 1849, v. 6, 153–61).

ROSSE, IRVING C.

1883 Medical and anthropological notes on Alaska. In *Cruise of the Revenue-Steamer Corwin in Alaska and the N.W. Arctic Ocean in 1881*, 5–43. Washington, D.C.: Government Printing Office.

RUDENKO, S. I.

1961 Ancient culture of the Bering Sea and the Eskimo problem. *Arctic Institute of North America, Anthropology of the*

North: Translations from Russian Sources, no. 1, edited by Henry N. Michael.

RUSSIAN-AMERICAN COMPANY
Communications Sent and Communications Received. Documents in the United States National Archives.

SAPIR, EDWARD
1916   Time perspective in aboriginal American culture. *Canada Department of Mines, Anthropological Series,* no. 13.

SAUER, MARTIN
1802   *An Account of a Geographical and Astronomical Expedition into the Northern Parts of Russia.* London: Cadell and Davies.

SCOTT, EDWARD M., ET AL.
1955   Anemia in Alaskan Eskimos. *Journal of Nutrition,* v. 55, 137–49.
1958   Serum-cholesterol levels and blood-pressure of Alaskan Eskimo men. *Lancet,* v. 2, 667–68.
1959   Lack of abnormal hemoglobins in Alaskan Eskimos, Indians, and Aleuts. *Science,* v. 129, no. 3350, 719–20.

SHAPIRO, HARRY L.
1931   The Alaskan Eskimo. *Anthropological Papers of the American Museum of Natural History,* v. 31, pt. 4, 347–84.

SIMPSON, JOHN
1875   Observations on the Western Eskimo, and the country they inhabit. In *A Selection of Papers on Arctic Geography and Ethnology,* 233–75. London: John Murray.

SMITH, PHILIP E. L.
1962   Solutrean origins and the question of eastern diffusion. *Arctic Anthropology,* v. 1, no. 1, 58–67.

SOLLAS, WILLIAM J.
1924   *Ancient Hunters.* New York: Macmillan Company.

SPENCER, ROBERT F.
1959   North Alaskan Eskimo. *Bureau of American Ethnology, Bulletin 171.*

STEENSBY, H. P.
1917   An anthropogeographical study of the origin of the Eskimo culture. *MG,* v. 53, 39–228.

STEFANSSON, VILHJALMUR

1914a The Stefansson-Anderson Arctic Expedition of the American Museum. *Anthropological Papers of the American Museum of Natural History*, v. 14, pt. 1.

1914b Prehistoric and present commerce among the arctic coast Eskimo. *Canada Department of Mines, Anthropological Series*, no. 3.

STEWART, T. D.

1959 Skeletal remains from the vicinity of Point Barrow, Alaska. In Eskimo prehistory in the vicinity of Point Barrow, Alaska, by James A. Ford. *Anthropological Papers of the American Museum of Natural History*, v. 47, pt. 1, 245–55.

STONEY, GEORGE M.

1900 Explorations in Alaska. *Proceedings of the United States Naval Institute*, v. 25, 533–84, 799–849.

SWADESH, MORRIS

1951a Unaaliq and proto Eskimo. *IJAL*, v. 17, 66–70.

1951b Unaaliq and proto Eskimo II: Phonemes and morphophonemes. *IJAL*, v. 18, 25–34.

1952a Unaaliq and proto Eskimo III: Synchronic notes. *IJAL*, v. 18, 69–76.

1952b Unaaliq and proto Eskimo IV: Diachronic notes. *IJAL*, v. 18, 166–71.

1952c Unaaliq and proto Eskimo V: Comparative vocabulary. *IJAL*, v. 18, 241–56.

1952d Lexico-statistic dating of prehistoric ethnic contacts. *Proceedings of the American Philosophical Society*, v. 96, 452–63.

1954 Time depths of American linguistic groupings. *American Anthropologist*, n.s., v. 56, 361–64.

1955 Towards greater accuracy in lexicostatistic dating. *IJAL*, v. 21, 121–37.

1958 Some new glottochronologic dates for Amerindian linguistic groups. *32ICA*, 671–74.

1962 Linguistic relations across Bering Strait. *American Anthropologist*, n.s., v. 64, 1262–91.

SWINEFORD, ALFRED P.

1898 *Alaska, Its History, Climate and Natural Resources.* Chicago and New York: Rand.

TAYLOR, KENNETH I.

1966   A demographic study of Karluk, Kodiak Island, Alaska, 1962–1964. *Arctic Anthropology*, v. 3, no. 2, 211–39, plus charts.

TAYLOR, RAYMOND F., AND ELBERT L. LITTLE

1950   Pocket Guide to Alaska Trees. United States Department of Agricultural Forest Service. *Agricultural Handbook*, no. 5.

TAYLOR, WILLIAM E.

1966   An archaeological perspective on Eskimo economy. *Antiquity*, v. 40, 114–20.

THALBITZER, WILLIAM

1904   A phonetical study of the Eskimo language. *MG*, v. 31, 1–406.

1945   Uhlenbeck's Eskimo-Indo-European hypothesis, a critical revision. *Travaux de Cercle Linguistique de Copenhague*, v. 1, 66–96.

1952   Possible early contacts between Eskimo and Old World languages. In *Indian Tribes of Aboriginal America*, 50–54, edited by Sol Tax. Chicago: University of Chicago Press.

TIKHMENEV, PETR A.

1861   *Historical Review of Foundation of the Russian-American Company*, Part 1. St. Petersburg: Edward Veimar (translated title, unpublished Dimitri Krenov translation).

1863   *Historical Review of Foundation of the Russian-American Company*, Part 2. St. Petersburg: Edward Veimar (translated title, unpublished Dimitri Krenov translation).

TRAGER, GEORGE L., AND FELICIA E. HARBEN

1958   North American Indian languages: Classification and maps. *Studies in Linguistics, Occasional Papers*, no. 5. Buffalo: University of Buffalo.

VANSTONE, JAMES W.

1955   Archaeological excavations at Kotzebue, Alaska. *APUA*, v. 3, 75–155.

1962   *Point Hope: An Eskimo Village in Transition*. Seattle: University of Washington Press.

ms. 1   An ethnographic history of the Nushagak River region, Alaska.

ms. 2   Tikchik village: A nineteenth century riverine community in southwestern Alaska.

VON WRANGELL, F.

1839   *Statistische und Ethnographische Nachrichten über die Rus-
sischen Besitzungen an der Nordwestküste von Amerika.* St.
Petersburg: Académie Impériale des Sciences.

WALTERS, VLADIMIR

1955   Fishes of western arctic America and eastern arctic Siberia.
American Museum of Natural History, Bulletin, v. 106, article 5.

WASKEY, FRANK

ms.   Tribal divisions of the Eskimo of western Alaska. At University of Alaska, Department of Anthropology and Geography.

WEATHER SUMMARY ALASKA AREA

1944   United States Navy Department, Hydrographic Office.

WELLS, ROGER

1890   English-Eskimo and Eskimo-English vocabularies. *Bureau of
Education Circular of Information No. 2, 1890.*

WHITTEN, NORMAN E.

1964   Towards a classification of west Alaskan social structure.
APUA, v. 12, 79–91.

WILIMOVSKY, NORMAN J.

1954   List of the fishes of Alaska. *Stanford Ichthyological Bulletin,*
v. 4, 279–94.

1958   *Provisional Keys to the Fishes of Alaska.* Juneau, Alaska: Fisheries Research Laboratory, U.S. Fish & Wildlife Service.

ZAGOSKIN, LAVRENTIY A.

1967   Lieutenant Zagoskin's travels in Russian America, 1842–1844.
*Arctic Institute of North America, Anthropology of the
North: Translations from Russian Sources,* no. 7, edited by Henry N.
Michael.

Index

(See color illustration section for entries identified by *color*. Italic page numbers indicate illustrations.)